THE COMMANDOS

THE ELITE
The World's Crack Fighting Men

THE COMMANDOS

Ashley Brown, Editor
Jonathan Reed, Editor

Editorial Board

Brigadier-General James L. Collins, Jr. (Retd.)
Former Chief of Military History, US Department of the Army

Ian V. Hogg
Authority on smallarms and modern weapons systems

Dr. John Pimlott
Senior Lecturer in the Department of War Studies,
Royal Military Academy, Sandhurst, England

Brigadier-General Edwin H. Simmons (Retd.)
US Marine Corps

Lisa Mullins, Managing Editor, NHS edition

A Publication of
THE NATIONAL HISTORICAL SOCIETY

Published in Great Britain in 1986 by Orbis Publishing

Library of Congress Cataloging-in-Publication Data
The Commandos.
  (The Elite: the world's crack fighting men; v. 2)
  1. Commando troops—History—20th century. I. Brown,
Ashley. II. Reed, Jonathan. III. Series: Elite (Har-
risburg, Pa.); v. 2.
U262.C655 1989   356′.167′0904   88-33089
ISBN 0-918678-40-4

CONTENTS

INTRODUCTION

Parachutes, ghostly white in the dark, drifting silently to earth . . .
inflatable rubber boots landing softly on moonlit sandy beaches . . .
gliders filled with men swooping quietly down out of the clouds . . . a
single file of mute, camouflaged soldiers trekking silently through the
underbrush to a target . . . this is how the scenes of their actions look
just before they strike. These are THE COMMANDOS, the men specially trained to risk their lives in ways not expected of most ordinary
soldiers. But that is because they are not ordinary soldiers . . . they
are THE ELITE.

Daring men have performed such tasks as long as warfare itself
has existed, but the organized operations of specially selected and
trained commandos really began in the first days of the British involvement in World War II. The concept behind the first ten commando units was to find men to volunteer for "special service of a
hazardous nature," train them, and then send them behind enemy
lines, cutting communications, interrupting supply, diverting enemy
attention, and more. Fifty years later, though their methods have
evolved, their goals remain the same.

Throughout the Second World War, on to Korea, the African up-
heavals in the Congo and Rhodesia, and into the Viet Nam conflict,
the commandos glided swiftly and silently through the night. They
came in all varieties and with a host of names—Air Commandos,
Mountain Lions, X-Troop, Eagle Commandos, and more. Britain would
always lead the rest in number and experience, but France, Germany, the United States, and several other nations would see the
value of such special units and put them in the field.

They prepared the way for the Normandy invasion in 1944. They
opened the 1973 Yom Kippur War across the Suez Canal. They met
the rebel tribesmen in Aden in 1967. They battled the FLN in Algeria,
the Argentinians in the Falklands, the North Koreans at Chosin, and
rescued Mussolini from an Italian prison. Training, precision, and
courage were their weapons.

Here in THE COMMANDOS, the stories of twenty-six of these special units pay tribute to the universality of uncommon bravery and
daring, without regard to nationality or cause. There are no "good" or
"bad" sides here, only the brotherhood of the brave. In war as well as
in peace, so long as a resort to arms is necessary to settle disputes,
keep the peace, protect the defenseless, or subdue the tyrannical,
then there will always be a need for men like these who will dare to
be THE ELITE.

LIEUTENANT-COLONEL JOHN DURNFORD-SLATER

Lieutenant-Colonel John Durnford-Slater, commanding officer of 3 Commando at its formation in 1940, was to epitomise the qualities expected from the new force.

Commissioned into the Royal Artillery in 1929, he served for six years in India, enthusiastically participating in the rugby, riding and pig-sticking. But the period 1935 to 1939 found him serving at home with raw recruits and regiments below strength. Worse, when war came he found himself in a backwater, as adjutant of a newly-formed anti-aircraft regiment. When the War Office called for volunteers for 'special service' he jumped at the chance. He became the very first commando soldier to be selected and was immediately promoted from captain to lieutenant-colonel.

A stocky, balding, endlessly energetic man in his early thirties, Durnford-Slater soon earned the unstinting loyalty of his command. His training methods were unorthodox, demanding rigorously high standards in the field, yet allowing complete relaxation when the pressure was off. He held the old-fashioned belief that in any raid he must be the first man ashore and the last away, and his great personal courage in the heat of battle was an example to all who served with him. He was awarded the DSO for his role at Vaagso in 1941, and a bar in Sicily in 1943, a rare accomplishment.

BLOODING THE
COMMANDOS

Operation Archery, a hazardous amphibious assault on the port of Vaagso in Nazi-occupied Norway, was the first chance for Britain's new elite force to prove that it could hit back hard at the Germans

'MY APPOINTMENT,' wrote Lieutenant-Colonel John Durnford-Slater, 'had come through on 28 June [1940]. By July No.3 Commando was in existence. It formed at Plymouth with a strength of 35 officers and 500 men, all of whom had volunteered for "special service of a hazardous nature".'

Of his first troop commanders' meeting Durnford-Slater recorded: 'I sat behind a bare table. The troop commanders formed a semicircle around me. They looked good, they were young, keen and fit, and they leaned forward eagerly to listen.'

'"We're going to operate months before anyone else," I said, "it's up to us to make ourselves the greatest unit of all time."'

'I meant it. Why not? Every man and officer in the unit had been hand-picked and had the true volunteer spirit.'

Durnford-Slater had been appointed commanding officer of one of a total of 10 Commandos that came into being in 1940. Their creation grew from the original thinking of two men in particular, Lieutenant-Colonel J.C.F. Holland, Royal Engineers, and Major (later Major-General, Sir) Collin Gubbins, Royal Artillery, who had joined the War Office's small research department in the late 1930s.

Unlike much of the army establishment in Britain at this time, these men had grasped that small units trained in guerrilla tactics could be extremely useful to the war effort if their activities were co-ordinated with movements of the main forces. At the crucial moment of a major offensive the units could perform devastating raids behind enemy lines, providing invaluable diversion of enemy attention and manpower away from main-force activity.

The characteristics of such units were to be high mobility, thorough training in the use of arms and instruments of sabotage, and peak physical fitness. The Boer War had seen well-organised units of horsemen, the Boer commandos, inflict serious damage on the British forces, and in World War I Germany had formed elite units of 'shock' troops (*stosstruppen*) to attack heavily defended positions on the Western Front. There were clearly great opportunities for similar methods at the outbreak of World War II.

In 1940 the War Office approved the formation of 10 'Independent Companies', in concept the forerunners of the Commandos, recruited mainly from army volunteer reservists. The units underwent rigorous training in preparation for the abortive Expeditionary Force to Finland (Finland concluded a treaty with the Soviet Union in March 1940). Training continued, however, near Fort William in Scotland, where the units practised amphibious landings and field-craft in the most rugged conditions.

In June 1940, as the Dunkirk evacuation was nearing completion, Winston Churchill called for

Above: Part of Vaagso's Nazi-held fish-processing complex, a warehouse containing fish oil, is totally destroyed by the commandos. The wiping out of a source of vitamins earmarked for the German Army at the Eastern Front was one objective of the raid but, more important, the attack persuaded Hitler to redeploy forces away from his defences on the French coast. Below right: Apprehension on the faces of men about to transfer to a landing-craft in the Vaagsfjord. For much of the force this was to be the first taste of armed combat.

Operation Archery
Commando landings

North Vaagso

Kapelnoes Point

②

South Vaagso

Hollevik

Halnoesvik

①

Mortenes

MAALOY ISLAND

VAAGSO ISLAND

ULVESUND

VAAGSFJORD

HUSEVAAGO

Rugsundo 5km

Trondheim
Vaagso
Herdla
NORWAY
Oslo
Stavanger
SWEDEN
NORTH SEA
DENMARK

Key
- ✈ Luftwaffe airfields
- ⚓ German battery
- ➤ Royal Navy task force
- ➤ Commandos

The main commando assault was directed at targets near the entrance to Ulvesund — in South Vaagso, Mortenes and Maaloy Island. Steeply rising cliffs all along the coast protected the invading force, and any German reinforcements would have to advance down the coastal road. In a classic pincer movement, two commando groups secured the flanks of the main assault. The first landed near Halnoesvik①, where a German gun had been reported. A second group landed close to Kapelnoes Point② and mined the road leading from North Vaagso.

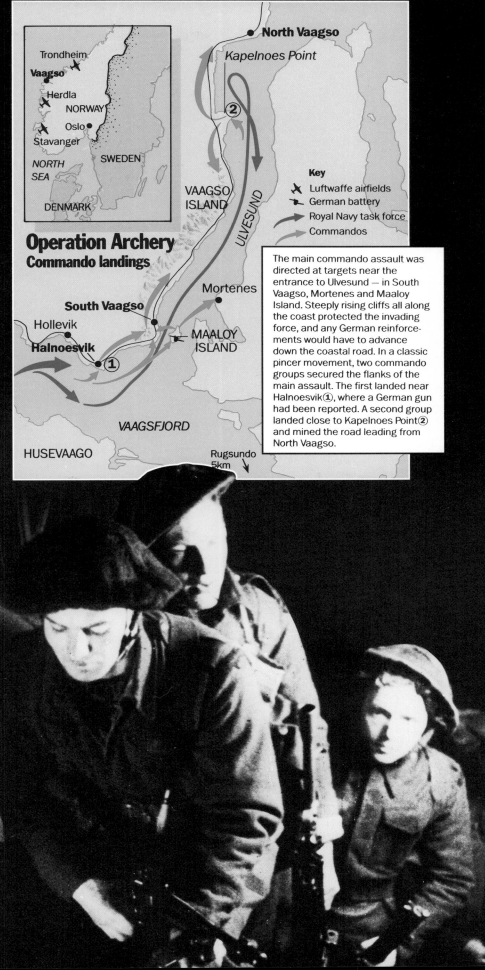

raiding parties on the German-occupied coasts of Europe. One of his staff officers, Lieutenant-Colonel Dudley Clarke, proposed the formation of special-ised units of elite light infantry that could operate from landing-craft. Such a force actually already existed in the form of four battalions of the Royal Marines, and in the Independent Companies. However, Churchill approved the proposal and the War Office set about raising what became a Special Service Brigade of over 5000 all ranks, the 'Comman-dos'. Officers volunteering for 'special service' were to raise their troops from their own divisions.

Only a few had previously been under fire, but they didn't expect to be beaten

The Commandos had been formed to develop a reign of terror down the enemy coasts, and they wanted action. But while the veteran admiral Sir Roger Keyes, the hero of Zeebrugge (1918), was Director of Combined Operations they got very little. Then, on 27 October 1941, Keyes was suc-ceeded by Lord Louis Mountbatten, whose bound-less energy produced results from the moment he took over. Of the operations he mounted, the raid on the Norwegian port of Vaagso was the first and in many ways the most remarkable, for it was that rarest of military operations, one that actually went accord-ing to plan.

No.3 Commando, reinforced by about 100 men of No. 2, formed the raiding force. Most of 6 Troop of No. 3 Commando had been at Dunkirk but only a few of the rest had been previously under fire. Still, they didn't expect to be beaten.

Major 'Mad Jack' Churchill, MC, who commanded Group 3 (5 and 6 Troops) was an officer with unorthodox views, and a real fire-eater. It is believed that he is the only officer to have transfixed a German with an arrow – in the Dunkirk campaign in which he won the Military Cross. Jack Churchill waged war in the spirit of Bayard and Montrose.

The oldest soldier in the unit was the administrative officer, Captain J.E. Martin, who had served with the 9th Lancers on the Western Front (1915-1918) and was to be among the first to land on D-Day in 1944.

The German garrison at Vaagso comprised about 150 infantry with a single tank, and 100 men of the German Labour Corps. The anchorage was protected by two coastal defence batteries. The little islet of Maaloy had a battery of four guns, which turned out to be Belgian 75s taken in 1940. Rugsundo Island had another battery of two heavy guns, thought to be Russian. The northern entrance to Ulvesund was defended by a mobile battery of 105mm guns at Halsor. German convoys in the area were usually escorted by armed trawlers, but no other warships were thought to be in the vicinity. There were airfields at Herdla, Stavanger and Trondheim, from which an estimated 37 Messerschmitt Bf109s could reach Vaagso.

The British force comprised the light cruiser HMS *Kenya*, the destroyers HMS *Chiddingfold, Offa, Onslow* and *Oribi*, the submarine HMS *Tuna*, and the infantry assault ships HMS *Prince Charles* and *Prince Leopold*. Joint force commanders were Rear-Admiral H.M. Burrough, CB, a gunnery expert, and Brigadier J.C. Haydon, DSO, OBE, the commander of the 1st Special Service Brigade, who both took passage in *Kenya*. The RAF based at Wick and Sumburgh in the Shetlands gave some fighter cover, and bombers of Coastal Command were to support the raid.

The force assembled in Scapa Flow, where the final exercises took place. With maps and models the men were briefed until everyone thoroughly understood the plan. On Christmas Eve, the force sailed for

Below: Where the Bren light machine gun really came into its own at Vaagso was in setting up a hail of covering fire while commandos raced for their objectives. An experienced gunner could maintain rapid bursts of fire with dextrous manipulation of the 30-round top-loading magazines. In the course of an assault the top carrying-handle allowed the gun to be quickly moved up into a new position without the gunner needing to come into contact with the hot steel barrel.

The Battle of South Vaagso

0858 Group 2 lands near South Vaagso and m stiff resistance from the German garrison.
1000 Elements of Group 2 reach the north end South Vaagso but fighting continues.
1020 Group 4, the floating reserve, is committ north of South Vaagso.
1035 Captain Peter Young and his men fight th way along the steamship wharf.
1230 Resistance in South Vaagso is virtually o and the demolition of key installations is in pre
1250 The order to re-embark is given.

VAAGS

Halnoesvik

①

VAAGSO ISLAND

South Vaagso

VAAGSFJORD

aid on Vaagso
agso Island, 27 December 1941

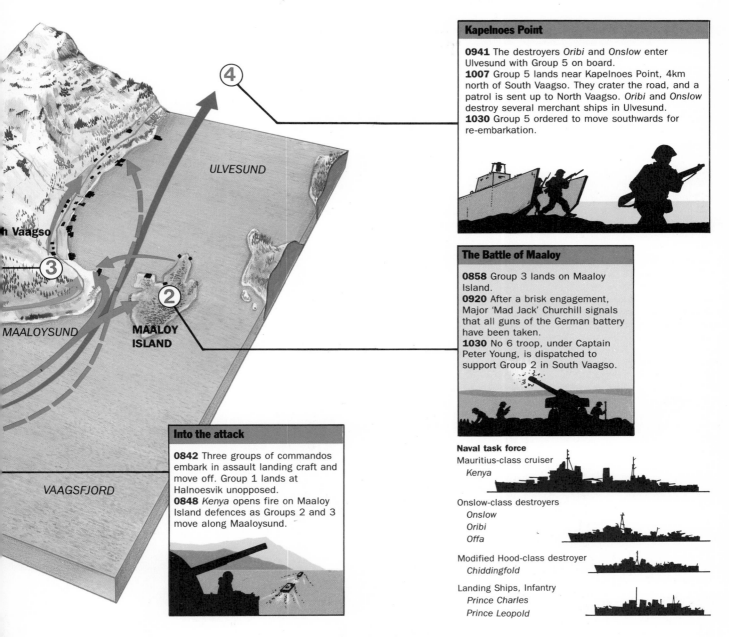

key

Naval task force
Onslow and *Oribi*
Group 1
Groups 2 and 3
Group 4

Kapelnoes Point

0941 The destroyers *Oribi* and *Onslow* enter Ulvesund with Group 5 on board.
1007 Group 5 lands near Kapelnoes Point, 4km north of South Vaagso. They crater the road, and a patrol is sent up to North Vaagso. *Oribi* and *Onslow* destroy several merchant ships in Ulvesund.
1030 Group 5 ordered to move southwards for re-embarkation.

The Battle of Maaloy

0858 Group 3 lands on Maaloy Island.
0920 After a brisk engagement, Major 'Mad Jack' Churchill signals that all guns of the German battery have been taken.
1030 No 6 troop, under Captain Peter Young, is dispatched to support Group 2 in South Vaagso.

Into the attack

0842 Three groups of commandos embark in assault landing craft and move off. Group 1 lands at Halnoesvik unopposed.
0848 *Kenya* opens fire on Maaloy Island defences as Groups 2 and 3 move along Maaloysund.

Naval task force
Mauritius-class cruiser
  Kenya

Onslow-class destroyers
  Onslow
  Oribi
  Offa

Modified Hood-class destroyer
  Chiddingfold

Landing Ships, Infantry
  Prince Charles
  Prince Leopold

ULVESUND

h Vaagso

MAALOYSUND

MAALOY ISLAND

VAAGSFJORD

Sollum Voe in the Shetlands. There was a westerly gale, force eight, coming in from the Atlantic and the assault ships, with their top hamper of landing-craft, rolled in the most astonishing fashion. The admiral was compelled to postpone the raid for 24 hours in order to repair the damage sustained.

At 1600 hours on 26 December the force sailed from Sollum Voe on the last 480km of its voyage. The westerly gale was dying away. The Arctic night passed without incident and the asdic on *Kenya* picked up *Tuna*'s signal, enabling her to make a perfect landfall. By this time the men were assembled at their boat stations. It was bitterly cold.

Major Robert Henriques, the well-known author, who was Haydon's brigade major wrote:

'As we entered the fjord the naval commander gave the order, "Hoist the battle ensign". Now the landing-craft were lowered and those assigned to 3 Commando began to creep toward their three beaches. It was 0842 hours. Hampdens came out of the dark to strike the Rugsundo battery. Tracer climbed slowly upwards into the dawn.'

The arrival of the flotilla had not gone unnoticed; the lookout on Husevaago island was evidently efficient. He tried to get through to the battery on Maaloy. But the battery commander's servant was polishing the officer's boots, and did not even pick up the instrument. The lookout then tried the harbour-master's office in South Vaagso. This time he was able to get through, telling a clerk that he had seen seven blacked-out destroyers entering the fjord. The clerk suggested that he was drunk.

Undeterred by this slur, the lookout signalled by lamp to the signal station on Maaloy, sending: 'Un-identified warships entering fjord.' This was acknowledged by a sailor named Van Soest who, without a word to anyone, jumped into a dinghy and rowed across to South Vaagso to give this information to the harbour-master, Leutnant zur See (Sub-Lieutenant) Sebelin at the Hagen Hotel.

The Maaloy battery disappeared in a cloud of smoke, high explosive, rocks and shattered huts

By this time Group 1 had already dealt with the small German post near Hollevik, Groups 2 and 3 were in sight of Maaloy, and at 0848 Admiral Burrough gave the order: 'Open the line of fire!' And even as Sebelin was contemplating Van Soest's stupidity in not notifying the battery, *Kenya*'s first salvo crashed into the town. Correcting her aim, during the next nine minutes she put approximately 450 6in shells into the Maaloy battery, which disappeared in a cloud of smoke, high explosive, rocks and shattered huts. To soldiers engaged in a sort of maritime Charge of the Light Brigade it was a charming sight. The excitement rose and the men kept their heads down with the greatest reluctance.

Onslow and *Oribi* added their fire to the fury of *Kenya*'s bombardment. It was an impressive volume of covering fire, but even so the landing-craft, moving at no more than 6 knots, were exposed for about 10 minutes to any defensive fire the Germans could produce. Somewhere above Group 2's landing place a machine gun began to chatter. Then at 0857 Durnford-Slater began to fire the 10 red Verey lights that brought in the Hampdens to drop smoke bombs on the landing places of his two main groups.

The action that followed during the next four hours was broadly speaking a street fight made up of a score of minor actions, involving rushing from house to house, from wall to wall, and from gun-site to barracks hut. The men had to solve the tactical problems of a fleeting moment as best they could with rifle, grenade or Tommy-gun at point-blank range. It is a type of fighting in which the casualties fall heavily on the leaders, both officers and NCOs, and especially those on the attacking side. The snow seemed to halve the speed of a charge.

The men of Groups 2 and 3 landed more or less simultaneously. On Maaloy, 5 and 6 Troops stepped ashore without a shot fired. Durnford-Slater, who had just landed with Group 2 stated that he:

'could see everything that took place on Maaloy. Nos. 5 and 6 Troops, only fifty yards from the beach when the naval barrage lifted, were up the slopes of the island like a flash. I saw them advancing through the smoke in perfect extended order. Jack Churchill, who had played them in with his bagpipes, was leading them with considerable dash. On landing, Peter Young saw a German running back to man his gun position. "I was able to shoot him," Peter told me later. Ten minutes after this, Young reached the company [battery] office on Maaloy. One of the company clerks made the literally fatal mistake of trying to wrest Peter's rifle from him.'

Six Troop had found a gap in the wire, conveniently made by a shell from *Kenya*, and occupied three empty gun-sites. The absence of any opposition was a deep mystery. The various groups sent up white

Peter Young, seen here in the uniform of Colonel, the rank he held when he returned from commanding No.3 Commando in the Allied invasion of Europe in 1944. For his part in the raid on Vaagso Captain (Acting Major) Peter Young was awarded the Military Cross.

THE RED WAREHOUSE

When the Maaloy battery had been knocked out, Captain Peter Young, in command of 6 Troop, was sent to assist in the attack on Vaagso where, along with some of 2 Troop, he recalls taking the fight to the enemy:

'The Red Warehouse lay about 60 yards ahead. As we rushed forward through the snow, a German suddenly appeared in the doorway and shied grenades at us. The first two missed and the third failed to go off. Lance-Sergeants Herbert and Connolly, two of my bravest NCOs, came up and threw at least a dozen grenades into the building. I went in, confident that the occupants must be dead; two shots rang out from an inner room; I left before they could reload. We could find no other way in. What was the answer? I looked at the massive red walls. By God! They were wood! Fire! We must set the place on fire. While I was organising this, O'Flaherty and Sherington, exasperated by the long delay, staged another assault on the front door. I ran in after them and had reached the bottom of the stairs when there were rifle shots; they were both hit. I fired towards the flashes and withdrew, unscathed. O'Flaherty staggered out behind me, his face covered in blood; Sherington had been hit in the leg. I sent them to the rear. A moment later the warehouse was ablaze. The Germans still refused to surrender and so we had to push on, leaving Lance-Corporal Fyson (2 Troop) to besiege the burning remains of the Red Warehouse. When it got stuffy the Germans came out and Fyson shot them. We had given them every chance...'

Above: A commando crouches above the blazing buildings of the gun battery on Maaloy island. Top left: The single 3in mortar deployed by the strike force. Heavy artillery support for the raid was provided by the 6in and 4.7in guns on HMS *Kenya*, *Onslow*, and *Oribi* out in the fjord, and bomb attacks by RAF Hampdens early in the action. Top right: Major Jack Churchill, wearing his Wilkinson fighting knife, with a Belgian 75mm field gun that survived the assault on Maaloy. The gun is mounted on a platform that swings around a central pivot to give a 360° range of fire.

Verey lights to signal progress. Where were the enemy? Six Troop rose up and went to look for them among the barrack huts. Push on! There had to be Germans somewhere. At last the problem was solved; out of the smoke came about 15 unarmed German gunners, followed by their CO, Hauptmann (Captain) Butziger, and escorted by Lance-Sergeant George Herbert, MM, and two of his men, Banger Halls and Dick Hughes.

Churchill and his men had taken Maaloy in eight minutes. Looking across the water to South Vaagso it looked as if the resistance there had been no more determined than on Maaloy. Unfortunately that was not the case.

Ill-luck dogged Group 2 from the first. Just as 4 Troop landed, one of the Hampdens, apparently hit by fire from the armed trawler *Föhn*, dropped a 60lb phosphorus smoke bomb right into one of the landing-craft, burning or killing half the troop.

The rest of Group 2 got ashore under cover of a rocky cliff, and an Australian officer, Lieutenant Bill Lloyd (4 Troop), reached the end of the town in time to bushwhack a section of German infantry which was running to take up its defensive position. Led with great dash, 3 and 4 Troops stormed into the town, clearing the wooden houses and factories as they went. Almost from the outset they met a skilled and determined resistance. Oberleutnant (Lieutenant) Bremer was killed defending his strongpoint, and Stabsfeldwebel (Staff Sergeant) Lebrenz took his place. Leutnant sur Zee Sebelin improvised a strongpoint by manning the Hagen Hotel with his HQ personnel and sailors.

Giles crashed through the front door, hurling Mills bombs into every room

It was perhaps 0915 when Captain John Giles (3 Troop) was held up by German infantry ensconced in a large house. In the teeth of short-range fire from the windows, his men worked their way forward, covering each advance with short bursts from Bren and Tommy-gun. Nearing the building Giles, who had the build and spirit of an ancient Norseman, led a desperate charge, crashed through the front door, and stormed through the house hurling Mills bombs into every room until the last German had fled out at

The end of the raid. Left: German prisoners under armed guard aboard a navy transport ship. A total of 89 of the defenders were captured, and about 120 killed. Below: A wounded commando being helped to a Landing Craft Assault (LCA). The Combined Operations attack force lost 22 men, eight aircraft, and suffered about eight wounded.

the back. Then as he stood in the doorway weighing up his next move, a German concealed nearby shot him. With his death and the loss of Lieutenant Mike Hall, whose left elbow was shattered by a bullet, the assault of 3 Troop came to a halt.

Meanwhile Captain Algy Forrester, another real fire-eater, was still moving forward with the remains of 4 Troop. Durnford-Slater described the scene:

'Algy waded in, shouting and cheering his men, throwing grenades into each house as they came to it and firing from the hip with his Tommy-gun. He looked wild and dangerous. I shouldn't have liked to have been a German in his path. He had absolutely no fear. He led an assault against the German headquarters, in the Ulvesund Hotel, and was about to toss a grenade in when one of the enemy, firing through the front door, shot him. As he fell he landed on his own grenade, which exploded a second later.'

Seeing that his initial attack had run out of steam, Durnford-Slater sent for reinforcements. These were deployed along the waterfront, flushing out the enemy and firing the warehouses. The Germans resisted the commando advance with renewed determination, and casualties were suffered by both sides during the fierce exchanges of fire. Captain Young's group, edging forward in a ditch, was covering Durnford-Slater when there was an explosion and the men saw the colonel hurtle through the air and disappear. A German sailor concealed in a side-street had thrown a grenade at him and badly wounded one of his orderlies. This done, he had put up his hands: Sergeant Mills, rifle in hand, walked purposefully towards him: 'Nein, nein!' cried the German. 'Ja, ja!' said Mills and shot him. 'Yeah, well, Mills, you shouldn't have done that,' said Durnford-Slater, but, of course, if one is about to surrender it is a mistake to go throwing bombs about. The colonel now gave orders for a timed withdrawal and by 1445 all the demolition tasks were completed and the troops had all re-embarked.

Under new management, Combined Ops really meant business

Vaagso was a hard fight. The garrison of Maaloy was captured or killed. The men of the Rugsundo battery scored a hit on *Kenya*, but suffered nine casualties.

In Vaagso town the defenders lost 11 killed, seven wounded and 16 missing, presumably POW. They had fought with courage and tenacity. The commandos lost 20 killed and 57 wounded. The RAF lost eight aircraft, with their crews. About 16,000 tonnes of enemy shipping were sunk, and 77 Norwegian volunteers sailed away with the raiding force.

The raiders returned to base feeling that they had not done too badly. For the first time since Dunkirk the Germans had been given a bloody nose in Northern Europe. They had brought back more prisoners than the British Expeditionary Force had taken in the Dunkirk campaign. A sprinkling of 'gongs' descended upon the surviving participants and the impression spread abroad that, under new management, Combined Ops really meant business.

THE AUTHOR Brigadier Peter Young, DSO, MC joined the Commandos as a Lieutenant in 1941. He served in Europe, the Mediterranean and the Far East, ending the war as Brigadier of No. 3 Commando.

Commando, Vaagso Raid, December 1941

Although raised as an elite fighting force, the commandos were kitted out in standard British Army fashion. This soldier is no exception, wearing khaki battledress over which is a leather jerkin and 1937-pattern web equipment that includes a pouch for Bren gun magazines and a holster for a .38in revolver. As Vaagso was an amphibious operation inflatable lifebelts were worn; the nozzle of this man's lifebelt juts out from the jerkin front, while above it is a spare Bren magazine. The steel helmet is covered in khaki sacking, a common practice during the raid. Mobile firepower was an important factor in the commandos' success and an ideal support weapon is carried here, the .303in Bren light machine gun.

No.3 Commando, from its formation in July 1940 to its eventual disbanding in 1946, saw action regularly throughout the north European and Mediterranean theatres of World War II. The unit's first major test came in December 1941 in a daring raid against German installations at Vaagso on the Norwegian coast. At Dieppe in August 1942, No.3 Commando was assigned the task of silencing the guns of the Berneval battery; although only a few men were able to get ashore after running into a German naval force on the way in, the commandos successfully scaled the cliffs and disrupted the battery's fire. No.3 Commando was then shipped to the Mediterranean where it was

Nº 3 COMMANDO

UNITED WE CONQUER

involved in the Cassibile and Malati bridge landings in Sicily and further actions at San Venere and Termoli in Italy in 1943. From the Mediterranean the commandos returned for training in Scotland where they prepared for the D-Day landings. Once ashore in France, they operated in Normandy until September 1944. The following March they crossed the Rhine, clearing the area to the north of Wesel, and then launched a night attack on Osnabruck and a raid on a V-2 rocket factory near Leese in early April. No.3 Commando's final action of the war was on 29 April 1945 when they were involved in clearing operations at Lauenburg.

On D-Day, 6 June 1944, No.3 Commando had the critical task of preparing the way for the British forces that landed in Normandy

NO.3 COMMANDO'S assault on the Normandy beaches was an eventful one; on the way in three of its five landing craft were hit by shellfire, but, disregarding the storm of German smallarms fire that raked across the beaches, the commandos raced across the open sand towards their first objective. No.3 Commando, with Nos.4, 6 and 45 Royal Marine (RM) Commando, made up the 1st Special Service Brigade, under the command of Lord Lovat, whose first main task was to seize and make secure the coastal strip on the eastern flank of the Allied landings. They were then to push quickly inland, seizing the bridges over the Orne river, and link up with 6th Airborne Division which had been landed to the northeast of Caen in the early hours of D-Day. By securing the east bank of the Orne as far as Caen, the Brigade would establish a defensive barrier against any German counter-attacks into the Allies' vulnerable eastern flank.

With a strength of around 280 soldiers, No.3 Commando had returned from operations in the

SPEARHEAD OF INVASIO

Mediterranean in January 1944, and, with the arrival of 165 reinforcements, preparations for D-Day began in earnest. The Commando had moved to the Combined Training Centre at Dorlin on the west coast of Scotland and there the newcomers were absorbed into the existing unit. Shooting, training exercises and working with landing craft formed the core of the Commando's activities.

In addition to preparing the men, much attention was also paid to increasing the firepower of the Commando. Normally, a Commando troop was allotted five Bren light machine guns, while an infantry company – about twice the size of a troop – had nine. Colonel Peter Young decided that the way to increased firepower lay in raising the Bren allotment to eight guns per troop so that at a pinch a troop would be able to do much the same job as an infantry company. Also, in unit headquarters, every fourth man carried a Bren, which meant that on the day the Commando's six troops would be, in effect, supplemented by a seventh.

At the end of May the troops of No.3 Commando were moved into barbed-wire 'concentration camps' near Southampton. With the men sealed off from the outside world, last-minute preparations and briefings for the invasion took up the first few days of June. Models and aerial photographs were pored over, and the whole operation was gone through time and time again, so that every man knew by heart what he had to do. Confusion was to be expected; all sorts of details might go wrong but as long as the main aim was kept firmly in view the commandos would succeed. With their preparations complete, on the afternoon of 5 June the troops of No.3 Commando embarked from their camp at Southampton for the Normandy coast.

Once across the landing beaches, on the 6th, Colonel Young re-formed the unit at 1000 hours and assessed the immediate situation: 'We were in touch with 45 Commando in the brigade forming-up place, but progress was delayed by minefields, confining the brigade to one track. No.6 Commando was ahead but the advance was still maddeningly slow. I pushed on to the Bénouville bridge to find out what was going on.'

Taking a small group of commandos with him, Young advanced inland until he met up with some of the men of 6th Airborne Division, who were clearly

Left: Commandos of 1st Special Service Brigade storm ashore on D-Day. Left above: Commandos on their way to embarkation points for D-Day, with the bicycles that proved so useful at the Bénouville bridge.

STORMING THE BEACHES

'D-Day, H+90: the flotilla is steaming ahead, 45 Commando to starboard, 3 Commando to port, the craft leaping about like young lambs. Ahead big guns are flashing, but as yet not a sound comes back to us from them. Gradually the dawn brightens and the mist begins to clear; ahead big ships are silhouetted against a gloomy sky. Now we are moving among the great warships roaring out their broadsides, cruisers first, then the battleship *Ramillies* belching forth 15in shells – a sight to remember. We put on more speed, the soldiers forget to be seasick, and then, suddenly, with almost magical precision, the columns of craft form into line abreast.

Land ahead now – a hundred yards away a column of water shoots into the air, while to port a tank landing-craft burns fiercely, ammunition exploding as the crew go over the side. Ashore is a line of battered houses whose silhouette looks familiar from the photographs; they must surely mark our landing-place. Ouistreham is not much more than a thousand yards to port now. Somewhere on the front are the guns that are shelling us; the flashes are visible every few seconds.

The beach at last! The ramps are pushed out and hang for a moment above the water. My weight on the starboard gangway submerges it and I find myself in five feet of water splashing ashore. Ahead the sand is marked by the track of one of our swimming tanks which has safely crossed the beach, enough to explode any mines that may have been there.'

Lieutenant-Colonel Peter Young – commanding officer, No.3 Commando – describing the landings in Normandy on 6 June 1944.

pleased to have some company at last. The bridge over the Orne at Bénouville was intact but was coming under rifle fire from a château on the west bank of the nearby Caen canal. A number of dead Germans lay sprawled around an abandoned glider. Young saw half-a-dozen commandos of 3 Troop who had dismounted from their bicycles and were taking cover under a low bank to the left of the road leading to the bridge. Calling over to them he shouted:

'What are you waiting for?'

'They're sniping the bridge, Sir.'

'Well, get on your bikes and go flat out; you'll probably get away with it!'

They leapt to their feet; one man fell, shot clean through the head, the rest reached the other side. They were immediately followed by Young and his group who ran across the bridge as fast as their feet would take them.

The commandos then swept through the village, killing six or eight of the enemy and capturing more than 20

Operations like this were the hallmark of the commandos. As leaders of a spearhead force, their commanders were encouraged to take the initiative and to capitalise on any tactical advantage open to them in the heat of the moment. Decisions were made fast and movements were decisive. Commando training emphasised speed and dash and, as with all elite offensive units, risks were taken when the opportunity for success presented itself. By mid-afternoon most of No.3 Commando was over the bridge and had taken up defensive positions, ready to repel the expected German counter-attack.

In order to strengthen the Allied defence along the Orne it became clear that the village of Amfréville would have to be taken. Amfréville stood on a low ridge east of the Orne overlooking a large part of the Allied lodgement area; if it was not secured, the German artillery would set up observation posts there and be able to direct heavy shell-fire down on the Allied beach-head around Ouistreham. As 3 Troop was in the vanguard of the advance they were hastily ordered by Lord Lovat to take the village without delay.

The two surviving officers of 3 Troop, Roy Westley and Keith Ponsford, led the men forward to be met by a hail of fire from the entrenched Germans which brought them to a temporary standstill. Westley was hit in the arm and, while he was having his wound dressed, Ponsford took over command. He immediately ordered his sergeant-major to reorganise the troop while he made a swift reconnaissance around the right flank, finding a covered approach from which to launch a new assault. After clearing the

Below: Commandos (in berets) meet up with men of the 6th Airborne Division, who had been landed earlier in the day. Below right: Royal Marine commandos of 1st Special Service Brigade fighting in the Normandy hedgerows. Bottom: The move inland off the beaches on D-Day. Heavily laden commandos move forward, to secure vital bridges.

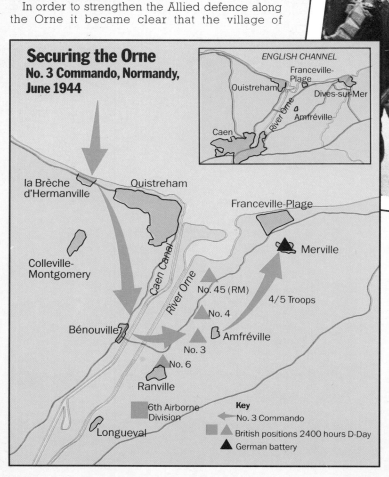

Securing the Orne
No. 3 Commando, Normandy, June 1944

ENGLISH CHANNEL

Ouistreham
Franceville-Plage
Dives-sur-Mer
Amfréville
Caen
River Orne

la Brèche d'Hermanville
Quistreham
Franceville-Plage
Colleville-Montgomery
Caen Canal
River Orne
Merville
No. 45 (RM)
4/5 Troops
No. 4
Bénouville
No. 3
Amfréville
No. 6
Ranville
6th Airborne Division
Longueval

Key
No. 3 Commando
British positions 2400 hours D-Day
German battery

houses which overlooked the village square, Ponsford put one of his sections in position to give covering fire. Here the 2in mortar proved invaluable as its high-explosive bombs – fired at a low angle – did much to demoralise the German garrison.

When he considered that his men had the advantage in the firefight with the Germans, Ponsford and his troop charged across open ground to capture the village school building, the main centre of resistance. Seizing this the commandos then swept through the village, killing six or eight of the enemy and capturing more than 20 others. In this dashing assault the troop suffered no casualties. They then took up a position in the hedges east of the village, where Westley, his wound bandaged, rejoined them.

Confronted by a minefield, Pooley led his men straight through it; a cold-blooded decision that paid off

While No.3 Commando consolidated its position during the evening of D-Day, reinforcements began to arrive. Hundreds of gliders of 6th Airlanding Brigade came down in the open fields between Ranville and Amfréville and, although they ran into a considerable barrage of ack-ack fire, casualties were very light. The morning of D-Day+1 passed peacefully but at 1300 hours two troops from No.3 Commando were ordered to support No.45(RM) Commando's attack on Franceville-Plage by clearing the battery at Merville to the south-east. Under the command of Major John Pooley, 4 and 5 Troops were chosen for the assault.

While 4 Troop gave covering fire, Pooley led 5 Troop into the attack. Confronted by a minefield he led his men straight through it, a cold-blooded decision, but one that paid off in the event as they got through with only three

men wounded. Although there were only a few Germans in the battery, they were very resolute and held out for some time. Once in the heavily-concreted gun emplacements, the commandos quickly dealt with the defenders, although one lone German, armed with an MG42 machine gun, gunned down Pooley at close range.

Meanwhile, under the direct command of Colonel Young, 4 Troop had come forward to the battery, and helped with mopping-up operations. With the battery in their possession, the two troops then reorganised. Stuck as they were, far away from the main Allied lines, it would only be a matter of time before the Germans launched a counter-attack that would cut off the commandos, putting them in an impossible position with little hope for resupply and replenishment of ammunition. However, by the time a withdrawal had been cleared with brigade headquarters, German reinforcements were closing in on 4 and 5 Troops and a fighting withdrawal had to be instigated.

The Germans had now brought up two self-propelled guns, and supported by these they counter-attacked. Firing at short range, these guns caused many casualties among the now vulnerable commandos, and before long the ditch by the road where the two troops lay was full of wounded. The men of the medical section did a magnificent job, but most of the injured were to fall into the hands of the enemy. To add to the commandos' problems, some of the troops ran into a deep minefield where many

The standard sniper rifle used by the British Army during World War II was the Lee Enfield No. 4 Mark 1, designated the Mark 1 (T) to signify that it was fitted with the No. 32 telescope, and had a cheek rest screwed to the butt.

During the fighting in the small fields and narrow lanes of the Normandy 'bocage', sniping came into its own, and the men of No. 3 Commando soon proved themselves expert at it. 'It was on 15th June that we inaugurated the sniping season. We had selected and trained snipers when we were in England. The men chosen were the best shots, but this, oddly enough, did not work at all, for we soon found many of the best marksmen had not the temperament for the lonely work of a sniper.

Many of the men who enjoyed sniping were by no means remarkable shots, but they would creep up so close to the enemy that they could not miss! In fact in this game stalking is as important as shooting. An enterprising character in 1 Troop, Trooper Fahy, made himself a camouflage suit from denim overall, hessian strips and odd pieces of material that came to hand. Then nothing would do but he must go off and try his luck. He and Trooper Leedham, a cool, resolute Irish Guardsman, similarly attired, showed me their suits and persuaded me to let them loose. I sent them down to the Longuemare crossroads and they were back within half an hour, having shot two Germans. The sniping went very well; indeed our bag gradually increased to quite respectable proportions, and that without loss to ourselves.

Snipers from 3 Troop accounted for five Germans in one day; after this the enemy became so careful that it was hard to find targets.'

Peter Young

were badly wounded, while all the time the main body was shelled and mortared as it retreated. When they at last reached Allied lines, both troops were down to half strength; one section of 4 Troop had gone into action with 23 men and come out with only eight. Not since the Dieppe raid of 1942 had No. 3 Commando suffered such misfortune.

While the exhausted 4 and 5 Troops rested in reserve, the remainder of No. 3 Commando was positioned around Amfréville, where its defences were strengthened. The expected counter-attack materialised on D+2 when a German battalion began to close on No. 3 Commando's positions.

Lieutenant Herbert charged forward armed with a Bren, firing bursts from the hip at the enemy ahead

The leading German company was spotted by 6 Troop – only 40 men strong – and rather than wait passively for the Germans to launch their assault, 6 Troop's commander, Captain John Alderson, decided to mount a spoiling attack.

Dodging in and out of the hedgerows, 6 Troop caught the Germans by surprise and many of their leading soldiers began to surrender as the commandos opened fire. Alderson ordered one section of men to move into an orchard to the right of the road of advance. They doubled up a ditch past several cottages but when they reached the orchard, they came under fire immediately from the next hedge. The fire was returned, silencing the enemy who could be seen running along the hedge to the road

where they fell into the hands of Alderson and were disarmed. The commandos were in their element, carrying out a classic raid consisting of rapid advances, alternating with short pauses to put down a withering fire – including that of a 2in mortar used pointblank with its base plate rested against a tree.

Another section under Lieutenant George Herbert met stiff resistance but, realising that the attack must not get bogged down, he charged forward courageously, armed with a Bren, firing bursts from the hip at the enemy in a ditch ahead. His men immediately followed his example and the Germans fell back under the brunt of the assault. Then, while pausing to change magazines, Herbert was himself shot by a German; the bullet cut the ribbon of his DCM and he fell forward on his face, killed instantly. The loss of their CO only served to reinforce the determination of the troop and they launched in to finish off the assault with renewed vigour.

The whole enemy attack had now been brought to a standstill and the German prisoners – numbering at least 45 men – were brought back to commando lines. In this brisk firefight the Germans lost 30 killed and at least as many wounded while 6 Troop's losses were one officer killed and one wounded, and two sergeants and five privates wounded.

Over the next few days the Germans mounted a number of assaults which were all beaten back by the commandos; while they were not being attacked the troops of No. 3 Commando were shelled and mortared. By 13 June, however, the worst was over, and the Germans gave up the initiative and dug in 1000m east of No. 3 Commando's positions. It became a war of sniping and patrolling. Throughout the rest of June No. 3 Commando maintained its positions, sending out patrols to harass the enemy, until the great retreat began and the German forces fell back towards Falaise.

THE AUTHOR Brigadier Peter Young, DSO, MC joined the Commandos as a Lieutenant in 1941. He served in Europe, the Mediterranean and the Far East, ending the war as Brigadier of No. 3 Commando.

Far left: Weary commandos snatch a moment's rest along a country lane in Normandy. For a week after the D-Day landings, the men of No.3 Commando were engaged in heavy fighting, spearheading the Allied assault and reacting to German counter-attacks. Left: Success for these commandos who have just achieved one of their objectives. The man in the centre is armed with a Thompson sub-machine gun. Above: The author, Brigadier (then Lieutenant-Colonel) Peter Young, commander of No.3 Commando, being presented to King George VI.

Between 1940 and 1945, the Commandos achieved an impressive array of 38 battle honours awarded for actions fought in all the main theatres of World War II. Some of the honours were awarded for lengthy campaigns while others were earned in lightning raids against key points in the enemy's defences. Many actions, like the audacious raid on the dry-dock facility at St Nazaire in France on 28 March 1942, which put the dock out of action for the remainder of the war, were a complete success, while others, like the Dieppe raid of 19 August 1942, were marred by the loss of many commando lives. But battle honours are awarded for courage and determination taken to the limit, and not for easily won battles.

The first of the Commandos was raised in June 1940 to operate as a unit of storm troops, or, as Winston Churchill dubbed them, 'leopards'. Conventional military thinking in the British Army at the outbreak of war in 1939 was opposed to the formation of such elite offensive units, but it did not take long for the Commandos to prove their immense value. One of the keys to the Commandos' success was that they were relatively small, tightly-organised units with a great deal of operational flexibility, verve and imagination. When the first units were raised each Commando consisted of 10 Troops of 50 men, but this soon proved unwieldy and in early 1941 the contingent number of Troops was reduced to six, each fielding 65 men. Close comradeship and a fierce loyalty to their officers combined with a rigorous and often unconventional training made them, in General Dempsey's words, 'the finest body of soldiers I have ever seen anywhere'.

COMMANDO BATTLE HONOURS

Commandos maintained a high level of discipline and cohesion in battle, but on many occasions individual soldiers performed acts of extreme heroism and the long list of decorations awarded to the officers and men of the Commandos bears witness to their prowess. During World War II, a total of eight Victoria Crosses was awarded, six posthumously. Two were awarded to Lieutenant-Colonel A. Newman and Sergeant T. Durrant for the raid on St Nazaire, and a further two went to Corporal T. Hunter and Major A. Lassen, a Danish commando, for action at Lake Comacchio in Italy in April 1945. Major Lassen was the first foreigner ever to receive the award. During the celebrated raid to 'get' Rommel at his HQ in North Africa on 18 November 1941, Lieutenant-Colonel Geoffrey Keyes led the assault by No. 11 Commando and was awarded a VC for his courage while another was awarded to Major P. Porteous of No. 4 Commando for his part in the assault on the coastal battery and its garrison at Varengeville during the Dieppe raid. At Kangaw in Burma in February 1945 a massive Japanese assault was held by men of No. 1 Commando during which a further VC was awarded to Lieutenant G. Knowland for conspicuous gallantry during the bitter engagement. The eighth VC was awarded to Lance-Corporal H. Harden for his part in the fighting along the Maas river in Holland in January 1945.

In addition to the Victoria Crosses, 37 Distinguished Service Orders (plus nine bars), 162 Military Crosses (plus 13 bars), 32 Distinguished Conduct Medals and 218 Military Medals were bestowed upon the commandos.

MALAYAN EMERGENCY

Trained to operate on sea or land, the Royal Marines were adept at fighting in the tropical forests of Malaya during the Emergency

THE EVENING of 23 March was warmer than usual and the commander of Z Troop, 45 Commando, RM, Lieutenant Nigel Mitchell, had just taken his customary shower after yet another day's fruitless patrolling in the squatter areas of his 'patch' around the town of Kampar. It had been a day of friendly frustration, in which neither the local Chinese, nor the reticent Malays had been inclined to give away any information about the Chinese communist 'bandits' of the MRLA (Malayan Races Liberation Army). Only two days before the MRLA had raided a local village, burning the odd basha (hut), stealing identity cards and demanding rice and other seasonable commodities, before disappearing once more into their jungle haven.

In 1951 45 Commando was based in the foothills around Tapah on the main north-south road through Malaya, and its five troops were spread over some 2000 square miles, from the swampy coastal plains around Telok Anson to the mountainous Cameron Highlands. The troops operated with a measure of independence, but worked closely alongside the Malayan Police Force, which had mostly British officers, and the colonial District Officers.

Such was the daily pattern of life, constant patrolling, with results hard to come by, and with a never-ending battle to win over the 'hearts and minds' of the Malays – an aphorism coined by the Director of Operations, Lieutenant-General Sir Harold Briggs. Incidents in the area were frequent, and the terrorist strategy of hitting hard and then melting back into the jungle, leaving scarcely a trace, made the gathering of intelligence of paramount importance.

Mitchell's MOA (Marine Officer's Attendant) brought him a Tiger beer from the cool-box and the captain poured it into a long glass before settling comfortably under the fan continually rotating above his head. He looked through the glassless window of his hut at the troop flag which hung limply in the evening stillness. He counted the red stars, embroidered upon it by the local Chinese tailor, each representing a bandit killed by Z Troop.

Suddenly the telephone rang. Mitchell lifted the receiver casually and heard the excited voice of his friend, Paddy, the local British officer of the Malay Police. Apparently, a bandit had surrendered to one of his outlying police posts only half-an-hour before and had said that he was prepared to lead a military patrol back to his old camp. They arranged a rendezvous (RV) for 15 minutes time. Months of careful preparation and procedures were put into action; the stand-by patrol of one section, on this occasion strengthened by some cooks and the troop clerk, was given just 10 minutes to draw weapons, check ammunition and kit, and get ready to move to the RV.

The duty section had had a 48-hour standoff from the daily grind of incessant patrolling, but was at instant readiness and the men took the emergency in their stride. Although such alerts had happened before, each of the marines felt a surge of adrenalin as he quickly packed his kit. Not knowing how long the operation would take, each man collected two days' rations, and made last-minute personal prepa-

MALAYAN EMERGENCY

The focus of resistance to the Japanese occupation of Malaya in World War II centred on the Malayan People's Anti-Japanese Army (MPAJA), a guerrilla force organised and led by the Malayan Communist Party (MCP). At the close of the war the British returned to Malaya and reimposed old-style colonial rule, and the MCP began to work for political and trade union reform. In July 1948 the MCP initiated a guerrilla war against the British and the old MPAJA was reformed as the Malayan Races Liberation Army (MRLA). Organised in bands of up to 200 men, the MRLA, made up of ethnic Chinese, drew its greatest support from the Chinese squatters living along the jungle fringes.

The MRLA waged a campaign of terror against local officials, attacked economic targets and attempted to set up 'liberated' areas. The MRLA's most striking success during the Emergency was the murder of Sir Henry Gurney, the British High Commissioner, in October 1951.

The British responded to MRLA insurgency with a thoughtful strategy most effectively practised by General Sir Gerald Templer, who arrived in Malaya in early 1952. Templer continued the 'new village' programme, a plan devised by General Sir Harold Briggs, to move the squatters into protected areas and deny the MRLA secure bases and food. Templer also improved the links between the police and military, placing particular emphasis on the collection of intelligence concerning the MCP. The general also instituted a system by which guerrillas were encouraged to surrender in return for money.

Under Templer's imaginative regime, the MRLA began to suffer heavy losses, and by July 1960 when the Emergency was lifted, almost 7000 guerrillas had been killed.

rations before collecting his weapons and priming the patrol's grenades.

Only one marine, who had gone back to his hut to drop off the keys and change in his pocket – items which might create unwanted and dangerous noise while moving through the jungle – was temporarily adrift, but all were ready as the armoured 3-tonner, known colloquially as 'The Coffin', drew up. In a few words, Mitchell outlined the object of the patrol and, within the prescribed quarter-of-an-hour, they had embussed and were on their way. The troop's second-in-command was left at the base to detail another section as that night's standby.

The brief tropical twilight, which falls in a matter of minutes, came and went during the five-minute trip to the rendezvous. During the journey, NCOs checked their maps, orientated their minds to the area which they already knew so well, and satisfied themselves that their men were fully prepared for any contingency that might lie ahead. The men knew that the whole operation might prove, as they had so often in the past, to be what the marines called a 'busted flush'. The NCOs also knew that their men's preparedness and eagerness might once more end in frustration; it had all happened before – and not just once. Informers were notoriously unreliable in betraying their own jungle-bound comrades unless there was sufficient incentive. Perhaps this time the police had provided such an incentive.

The marines knew that the rubber trees could easily hide a waiting terrorist

At the appointed RV, the British police officer, along with a Malay inspector, met the marines with the thoroughly frightened bandit. The convoy quickly reformed and sped by tree-lined rubber plantations to the remote police post where the bandit had surrendered. The eeriness of the encircling gloom made the rubber trees stand out like rows of soldiers on parade, but the marines knew that their apparent slimness could easily hide a waiting terrorist.

The SEP (surrendered enemy personnel) led them beyond the police post along a wide track through another rubber estate. This time, one that was waning and overgrown, a perfect position from which to stage an ambush. The estate gave way to open 'lalang', a thick, high grass, impossible to see through and often difficult to penetrate, which finally opened out into a Chinese squatter area. The column was halted by a small bridge that was too narrow for the truck to cross; the marines debussed quietly and took up carefully rehearsed positions. By the flickering light of a dozen Tilley pressure lamps, they could see shadowy figures moving among the rough squatter bashas of attap and corrugated iron.

Mitchell and the police officer crossed the bridge, and gave the all-clear. The patrol slowly moved into the waiting jungle along a well-worn track with the SEP, closely guarded up front, leading the way. His manner was hesitant at times, but he made no attempt to run away, even if it had been possible. The commander was always mindful of the pre-arranged ambush into which his patrol might be led, but while he had the SEP in a prominent position at the van, he considered it safe to follow. It was now about 1930 hours and the Malayan night had engulfed them all. However, Mitchell remembered that there had been a full moon the night before and that its bright rays had occasionally penetrated the jungle canopy 200ft above their heads.

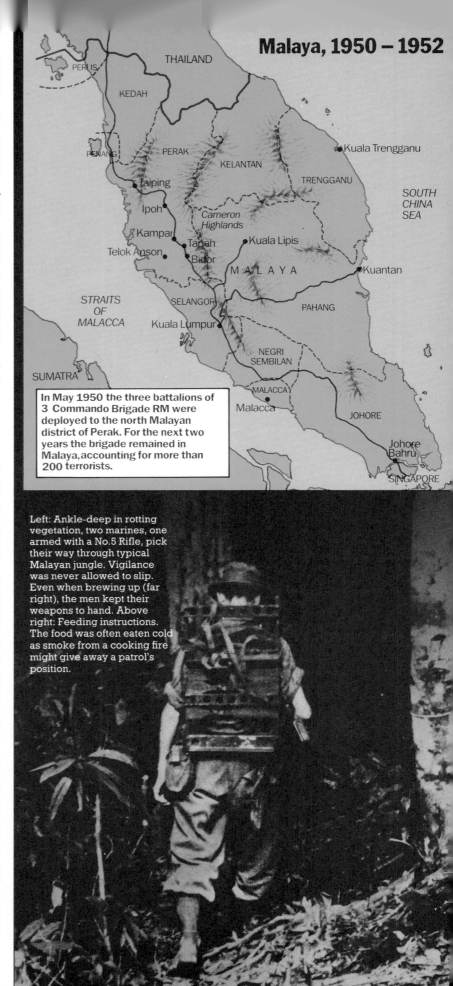

Malaya, 1950 – 1952

THAILAND
PERLIS
KEDAH
PENANG
PERAK
Taiping
Ipoh
Kampar
Telok Anson
Tapah
Bidor
KELANTAN
Cameron Highlands
Kuala Lipis
MALAYA
SELANGOR
Kuala Lumpur
Kuala Trengganu
TRENGGANU
SOUTH CHINA SEA
Kuantan
PAHANG
STRAITS OF MALACCA
SUMATRA
NEGRI SEMBILAN
MALACCA
Malacca
JOHORE
Johore Bahru
SINGAPORE

In May 1950 the three battalions of 3 Commando Brigade RM were deployed to the north Malayan district of Perak. For the next two years the brigade remained in Malaya, accounting for more than 200 terrorists.

Left: Ankle-deep in rotting vegetation, two marines, one armed with a No.5 Rifle, pick their way through typical Malayan jungle. Vigilance was never allowed to slip. Even when brewing up (far right), the men kept their weapons to hand. Above right: Feeding instructions. The food was often eaten cold as smoke from a cooking fire might give away a patrol's position.

24

As the path wound through the jungle edges, the marines passed small pineapple plantations – signs of cultivation that meant that the locals inhabited the area regularly. The jungle was far from silent; the constant hiss and buzz of animals and insects made the marines well aware of the dangers that might befall them, freezing in their tracks more than once. They were wholly dependent on the eyes and ears of the leading scouts who had considerable jungle experience and were highly trained in detecting the unusual. When a scout raised a hand, the men behind froze. The occasional bark of a pi-dog rent the air.

Gradually, as the patrol pushed into the jungle, dwelling places and signs of habitation were left behind, and after moving a further two miles down the track, the marines arrived at a river's edge. The captured bandit pointed to a large sampan hidden among the mangrove roots. With no more than a sibilant whisper of command by Mitchell, the patrol embarked in the craft, just as they might have done in a landing craft in more conventional surroundings.

The leading scouts took up their position in the bows, once more the eyes and ears of the patrol. Other marines took up the crude paddles and poles. Slowly, the sampan emerged from the shadows of the bank and then moved gingerly upstream. The marines felt unduly naked and exposed as the bright moonlight picked them out in mid-stream. For an hour the journey continued, the gently flowing river

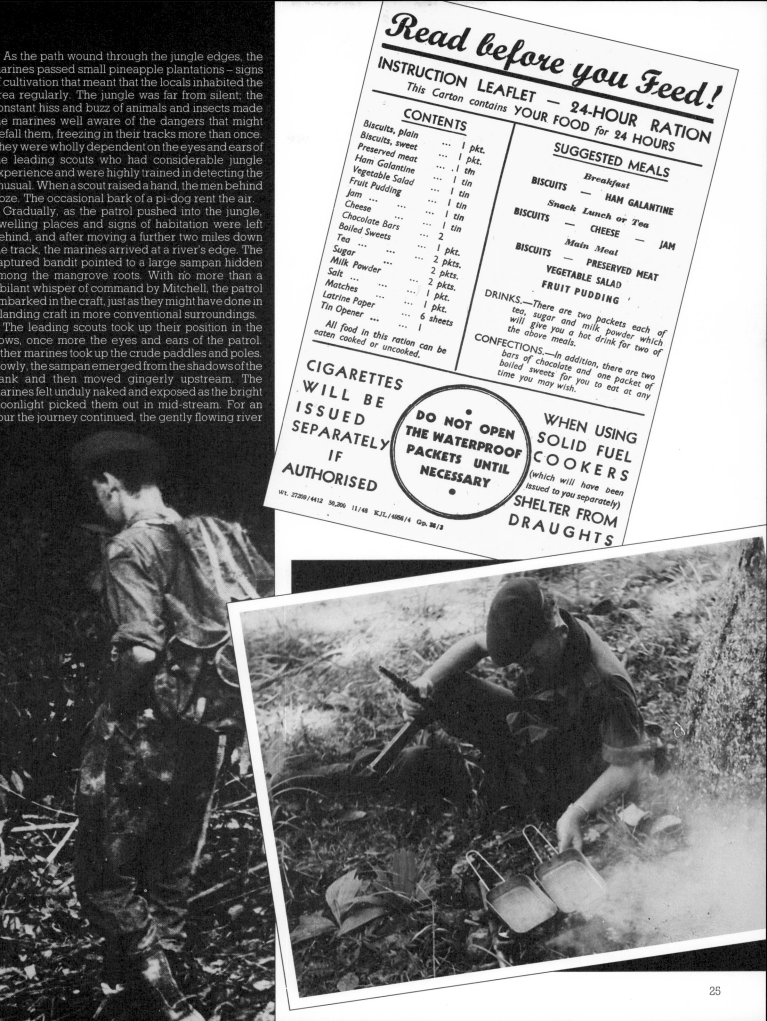

Read before you Feed!

INSTRUCTION LEAFLET — 24-HOUR RATION

This Carton contains YOUR FOOD for 24 HOURS

CONTENTS

Biscuits, plain	... 1 pkt.
Biscuits, sweet	... 1 pkt.
Preserved meat	... 1 tin
Ham Galantine	... 1 tin
Vegetable Salad	... 1 tin
Fruit Pudding	... 1 tin
Jam	... 1 tin
Cheese	... 1 tin
Chocolate Bars	... 2
Boiled Sweets	... 1 pkt.
Tea	... 2 pkts.
Sugar	... 2 pkts.
Milk Powder	... 2 pkts.
Salt	... 1 pkt.
Matches	... 1 pkt.
Latrine Paper	... 6 sheets
Tin Opener	... 1

All food in this ration can be eaten cooked or uncooked.

SUGGESTED MEALS

Breakfast
BISCUITS — HAM GALANTINE

Snack Lunch or Tea
BISCUITS — CHEESE — JAM

Main Meal
BISCUITS — PRESERVED MEAT
VEGETABLE SALAD
FRUIT PUDDING

DRINKS.—There are two packets each of tea, sugar and milk powder which will give you a hot drink for two of the above meals.

CONFECTIONS.—In addition, there are two bars of chocolate and one packet of boiled sweets for you to eat at any time you may wish.

CIGARETTES WILL BE ISSUED SEPARATELY IF AUTHORISED

Wt. 27209/4412 50,200 11/48 KJL/4856/4 Gp. 38/3

DO NOT OPEN THE WATERPROOF PACKETS UNTIL NECESSARY

WHEN USING SOLID FUEL COOKERS (which will have been issued to you separately)

SHELTER FROM DRAUGHTS

JUNGLE FIGHTING

During the early stages of the Malayan Emergency the security forces recognised that there would be no easy victory against the elusive MRLA, and that ultimate success would depend on perseverance and aggressive patrolling. Jungle fighting has always been a daunting prospect, requiring iron discipline, alertness, cunning and a wide range of specialised combat skills. It is also invariably unrewarding, with a great deal of time and effort expended for little tangible gain.

Yet, for all these difficulties, the servicemen fighting in Malaya quickly learnt to 'read' the jungle and adapt to the appalling conditions. Although most men went through a three-week familiarisation course before arriving, much of their subsequent expertise was gained on the job, in the routine sweeps against suspected MRLA bases. On occasions, the security forces mounted large-scale sweeps involving thousands of men, but mostly the campaign was a battle of wits fought between small groups of men.

The two most effective methods of containing MRLA activity were patrols and ambushes. Trailing guerrilla bands depended on good, up-to-date information, supplied either by local contacts or by the Special Branch. However, contact often relied on the good judgement of patrol leaders who usually developed an instinctive 'feel' for their own operational area.

Every successful engagement had a value beyond the destruction of an encampment or the death of a handful of guerrillas; patrols always took the greatest care to recover weapons, destroy foodstuffs and collect documents. In this way, the authorities were able to disrupt future guerrilla activities and build up an accurate overview of MRLA strategy, a process that ultimately led to the defeat of the insurgents.

sometimes narrowing to a stream, and the sampan brushing the roots and rushes on the banks. The marines saw movement at every turn; the huge mangrove roots looking like monstrous arms stretching out to engulf them; and the twinkling lights of the fireflies measured their slow progress towards their goal.

Once, a large water buffalo loomed up alarmingly on one bank and gazed inquisitively at the dark and silent intruders. As the stream narrowed, the overhanging leaves hid the watery moon, giving the patrol a feeling of greater security.

Then, suddenly, the SEP pointed at a rough landing stage, alongside which a waterlogged sampan nestled lazily in the shadow of the bank. The patrol's sampan nosed alongside and the marines quietly disembarked. A tiny path led from this point into the interior, and the well-trained marines silently melted into the jungle-covered sides of the track to await further orders from Lieutenant Mitchell. The captive rebel muttered that the bandit camp lay about a mile up the track and that it should contain three males and one female. With but a waft of the hand as a signal, the patrol took up their well-practised formation. The leading scouts, cradling their Australian Owen guns – more reliable than their issued Stens and with bolts which were less liable to catch in the thick undergrowth – moved silently forward. The rest of the marines carried the No.5 Rifle – shorter, lighter and more practical in the close-range battles likely to be fought in the jungle.

The SEP was reluctant to take up his position so near the front, but his ever-alert guard nudged him along with his rifle. Mitchell followed with his two Bren-gunners close behind, to ensure that the maximum firepower would be available to counter an enemy ambush.

Progress was slow: each snapping twig reverberating like a shot and each movement of a jungle animal causing the patrol to freeze in the blackness. For half-an-hour the section moved, not a word passing between them, but every man knowing that he could depend fully on his fellow marines in any emergency. A silent signal was now passed forward for the patrol to halt. The police officer, interpreting for the bandit, told Mitchell that the camp was now only 100yds ahead on the left side of the track. Mitchell looked at his Service Rolex, glowing mistily in the dark. The time was 2250, more than three hours since they had set out.

Once again the patrol crept forward, the men edging their way through the dense undergrowth, every noise sounding loud enough to waken the dead. A signal from the front brought Mitchell up to study a small lean-to basha underneath some saplings. The scout had done his work well. A second lean-to could be seen a few yards away, and then Mitchell detected the faint smell of dying wood smoke which confirmed that the bashas were occu-

Royal Marine, Malaya 1952

This marine is wearing the light, loose-fitting dress that was ideally suited to the rigours of patrolling through Malaya's dense, humid jungle: olive green shirt and hat with jungle green trousers. The veil around the neck is worn as a scarf, but was often tied over the face to protect the wearer from insects. Footwear consists of canvas and rubber jungle boots. An ammunition pouch and water bottle hang from the 44-pattern web belt. Armament consists of a 9mm Owen sub-machine gun. Despite its weight, the Owen was an effective weapon in close quarters combat.

pied. As he signalled for the rest of the patrol to come forward slowly, a startled wild pig scuttled away into the night, the echo being enveloped in the darkness. A voice from the hut called out in Chinese. The marines stopped dead in their tracks, hearts beating fast, safety catches forward and fingers on the trigger. Each man's eyes opened a little wider, his ears straining to pick up the slightest sound. Suddenly, the marines spotted a shadow of movement in the saplings and the silhouette of a man, black against the penumbra of the moonbeams, became visible. A sentry was climbing onto a platform in the trees.

A burst of carbine fire signalled the patrol to open up, the sudden noise of Bren and Owen guns shattering the stillness of the night. Jungle creatures screeched and scuttled from their night hides in a cacophony of sound and movement, adding to the strange unreality of the scene. The sentry tumbled from his perch and fell like a stone as the first burst of withering fire swept the camp site with a hail of lead.

The patrol, still wary of any unexpected development, moved into the camp

After a few seconds, the patrol commander ordered the cease-fire and only a distant echo of the sudden noise could be heard disappearing into the impenetrable jungle. The patrol, still wary of any unexpected development, moved slowly into the camp area. The body of the sentry was soon found, in his hand the pin of a 36 grenade which had failed to explode. Another male body was found in the basha. Further searching revealed no-one, but faint, recently-used tracks were found leading away from the far side of the camp. Half the patrol followed these tracks, painfully aware that the enemy were quite capable of laying an ambush for the unwary. However, the track came to an end in a swamp and the follow-up was abandoned.

The remaining marines and the police officer searched the camp area with the aid of shaded torches, collecting any papers and documents that could be found. Stolen identity cards, propaganda leaflets, and carefully kept diaries were recovered along with a newly-made uniform and other items of clothing. Two weapons, one of which was later identified as having been taken from a marine who had been killed some months previously, were also discovered. One of the guns was in such a neglected state that it would have been more dangerous to the firer than any attacker.

The captured bandit then revealed a supply dump containing several sealed tins of rice and these were systematically destroyed. The well used for drinking water was contaminated, and the cooking and eating utensils were thrown in it, along with the 'gash' (food).

Meanwhile, the two dead bandits were lashed to carrying poles for their final journey back for identification by the police. Before the patrol moved back along the path with the two bodies and 'booty', a match was put to the bashas. They burned rapidly and created a ruddy glow, lighting the faces of the patrol and accentuating the marines' grim but triumphant expressions. Their silent burdens, however, swung haplessly in deeper shadow. Later, another two stars were added to the troop flag.

THE AUTHOR Captain Derek Oakley served with 45 Commando, Royal Marines during the Malayan Emergency. He is currently the editor of the Royal Marines' journal *The Globe and Laurel*.

Left: Z Troop's flag flutters over the Royal Marine base near Kampar; each star represents a successful hunt and another bloody nose for the communist insurgents. Top and background: Native bashas go up in flames. By denying the enemy safe havens, the security forces gradually broke their will to resist. Although sweeps against guerrilla hide-outs were conducted on the basis of intelligence provided by informers, local knowledge, learnt from hard experience in the field, greatly contributed to final victory. Above and centre: To many, the jungle was a harsh, unforgiving foe, but most soldiers, like these young marines, quickly adapted to their strange surroundings. The photograph above shows the author (second from right) with a group of fellow marines, immediately after a patrol.

CROSS-CHANNEL OPERATIONS

The parties selected for lightning raids on the northern French coast varied in size from one or two officers and eight to 10 other ranks, down to just one officer and one NCO. Normally the teams were transported to their objectives by Motor Torpedo Boats (MTBs), or sometimes Motor Gun Boats (MGBs), which had been adapted to carry a dory. Originally developed in 1941 at the famous yacht-builders' yard of Camper and Nicholsons at Southampton, the dory was a very light, seaworthy craft which varied in length from 18 to 22ft. Several types were in use by the end of the war, some propelled by long, tapered oars, some by engines.

On operations, the MTB was anchored within about half a mile of the shore and the dory was launched. If there was surf, an Intruder rubber dinghy was used to take the party to the beach, leaving the dory at anchor just beyond the breaking waves. The coxswain and a radio operator, who also doubled as the motor mechanic, always remained with the dory. Radio contact was kept between the landing party and the dory, and between the dory and the MTB. Additionally, the MTB and the dory had the link of an S-phone, a primitive homing device that helped the dory to return to the mother ship. On the passage to the target area the MTB was usually escorted by MGBs, while a fighter escort took over for the return trip.
Below: An MTB begins a mission.

With Normandy selected for the D-day landings, small raids were mounted to convince Germany that the Allies would beach near Calais.

BY SPRING 1943, Allied plans for the invasion of Occupied France were well advanced. It was critical during this period that German Intelligence should not learn that Normandy had been chosen for the landings, and a number of different types of deception operation were mounted to convince Hitler that the heavily defended Pas-de-Calais, the area surrounding and lying southeast of Calais port, had been selected as the Allied route into Europe.

Among these deception operations was a programme of cross-Channel raids which, in addition to gaining valuable information on defences, was designed to create the impression that the Pas-de-Calais was now of paramount importance to the Allies. A series of raids in the summer of 1943 was followed by another in November and December, while a third series was launched in May 1944, this time with the purpose of discovering how to trigger the underwater explosives in the German beach defences.

Of all the cross-Channel raiding that took place between 1940 and 1944, this programme of deception is the least known. Yet the objectives were vital ones and the men employed on them were the pick of the Commando organisation. Their coolness and courage is well documented in the citations for the numerous decorations that they received.

Most of the men used in the summer raids, codenamed Forfar, came from No.12 Commando and were under the command of Major F. W. Fynn, MC, a veteran of several hit-and-run Norwegian raids. But they also included elements of No.2 Special Boat Squadron (2 SBS) and No.10 (Inter-Allied) Commando, and totalled 14 officers and about 115 men, though only a fraction of these were ever used operationally. When No.12 Commando was disbanded in November 1943, operational responsibility for the next series of raids, codenamed Hardtack, devolved mainly on the two French Troops of No.10 (Inter-Allied) Commando, though the most experienced men from No.12 Commando were retained by the Holding Operational Commando for further cross-Channel raiding. One or two members of 2 SBS and the Inter-Allied Commando's X Troop – which consisted mainly of anti-Nazi Germans and Austrians – were also used, and the combined group was codenamed Layforce II after its commander, Major Peter Laycock. In the last series of raids, codenamed Tarbrush, volunteers for hazardous duty from the Royal Engineers were used as the landing parties

and they were taken to the shore mainly by officers and NCOs who had gained experience in the earlier operations.

The Forfar raids were codenamed from Able to Pound, each codename being allotted to a certain area to be raided. If a raid had to be aborted, or if it was decided to remount it, it took place under the same codename. Out of the 14 or so that were planned, 11 were mounted, and seven landed, and they took place during the three dark, moonless periods between July and September 1943. Deception being what it is, the raid commanders were not told the true nature of the operations, but were simply told to reconnoitre the landing areas and try and snatch a prisoner.

A good deal of ingenuity was employed in finding new ways to climb the perpendicular chalk cliffs

The Hardtack raids, which were numbered Hardtack 4 to 37, began during the dark period in November 1943. As can be seen, a large number were envisaged, but because of adverse weather conditions and the intervention of COSSAC (Chief of Staff to the Allied Supreme Commander), who was increasingly nervous about any kind of raiding as D-day approached, only seven were carried out.

The most intensive of the three series of cross-Channel raids were the Tarbrush ones. A number of these were aborted, but enough landed to give SHAEF (Supreme Headquarters Allied Expeditionary Force), which had ordered the raids, the information it required.

During the summer months of 1943, a programme of intensive training was carried out on the Isle of Wight: the commandos were instructed in the use of pitons and ropes for climbing cliffs and abseiling down them, and Freshwater Bay was used as a testing ground for the handling of dories. A good deal of ingenuity was employed in finding new ways to climb the perpendicular chalk cliffs in the middle of the night without waking the sleeping seagulls. Much amusement was caused by two naval men who had invented a rocket-propelled grapnel which shot 300ft in the air but wakened the dead in the process.

The men taking part in all three series of operations were equipped not only with the very latest equipment – lightweight American automatic rifles,

Top: French members of No. 10 (Inter-Allied) Commando practise an amphibious landing with dories. Above left: Commandos prepare their abseiling gear on an Isle of Wight cliff top, while (left) men rehearse a cliff assault with full equipment.

CROSS-CHANNEL RAIDERS

Formed in January 1942, No.10 (Inter-Allied) Commando contained volunteers from several nations who were pledged to join the Allied fight against Hitler, and it provided many of the men who participated in the cross-Channel raids. Above: The Commando's principal officers were as follows: standing, left to right; Captain Lutyens, Captain Clarke, Lieutenant-Colonel Lister (commanding officer), Major Laycock (second-in-command), Captain Hilton-Jones (X Troop), and Captain Hodges. Seated, from left to right, are: Lieutenant Woloszowski (Polish Troop), Captain Mulders (Dutch Troop), Captain Danloy (Belgian Troop), Captain Hauge (Norwegian Troop) and Captain Kieffer (French Troops). Far right: With the aid of this postcard, a French fisherman was able to pinpoint the positions of German installations for commandos on the operation named Forfar Beer. Inset, far right: In a photograph taken during Forfar Beer, commandos using ladders attempt to scale cliffs near St Pierre-en-Port.

walkie-talkie sets, silenced Sten guns and silent 'de Lisle' carbines – but were given escape kits that included foreign currency, compasses, and maps on silk that showed the best escape routes to Spain. During one Hardtack raid these proved vital additions to the raiders' equipment.

The first raid, Forfar Easy, was launched under the command of Lieutenant Hollins on the night of 3/4 July 1943, when his party landed on the French coast near Onival. Other raids followed in quick succession during this dark period and those that followed. One, Forfar Love, was undertaken by four members of the SBS, when they attempted to reconnoitre Dunkirk pier in two canoes, while in another, Forfar Item, the team was parachuted inland of St Valéry-en-Caux on the night of 2/3 September and was then picked up by dory.

But perhaps the most audacious of the Forfar raids was Forfar Beer, led by their overall commander, Major Fynn. The night before Forfar Item took place, Fynn relaunched this operation for the fourth time. On two occasions he had been unable to land but on the third attempt he got ashore and lay under the cliffs until the following evening; but he still had no luck in capturing a prisoner. However, this experience convinced Fynn that if information was to be gained of an area, and if a prisoner was to be taken, it was essential to be ashore for more than a few hours. He therefore persuaded Combined Operations Headquarters to put him ashore for a second time, and to allow him, if he did not immediately capture a prisoner, to lie up for several nights between attempts to take one. His party included such experienced raiders as Lieutenant I.D.C. Smith, Lieutenant McGonigal, Company Sergeant-Major Brodison, and Corporals Barry and Nash, as well as a French member of No.10 (Inter-Allied) Commando.

The party landed between Eletot and St Pierre-en-Port just after midnight on 1/2 September, and after sending out two reconnaissance parties, Fynn and his men laid up for the day under some cliffs. When day broke, fishermen appeared on the beach. In the afternoon Fynn decided to risk interrogating one of them, and the French commando whistled one over. The fisherman was informative and that evening Brodison and Smith reconnoitred in the direction of the path he had told them would take them up the

cliffs. However, they were spotted and fired upon, forcing them to return.

This setback did not deter Fynn. Knowing now that a way up the cliffs could be found once the wire at the end of the beach had been negotiated, he decided to delay the return of the dory by sending a message via two carrier pigeons that they had brought with them. Unfortunately, the birds were noticed by some peregrine falcons, which quickly swooped on them, destroying the only means of communication Fynn had with his base.

By now the Germans had been fully alerted and the next morning two aircraft began to search the area. However, the raiders were well concealed and when the fisherman returned he gave the reassuring news that the Germans believed the raiders had now returned to England. The fisherman had brought a number of postcards and was able to indicate on these the positions of the German strongpoints.

Another abortive attempt was made to climb the cliffs and then, after night had fallen, Fynn and Brodison tried to make some headway through the wire at the end of the beach. They managed to crawl some distance through the wire but it eventually proved impenetrable. Time was now running out, so Fynn exploded a bangalore torpedo and then fired a silenced Sten at the sentry-box, in the hope that he would be able to lure the Germans out and take a prisoner. When this failed to produce any reaction, the two raiders were forced to return along the beach where the dory was waiting to take the party back to the MTB.

The commander tried to swim back to the MTB but was drowned, as was the dory coxswain

There was now a lull in cross-Channel raids until the dark period in November, when a preliminary Hardtack operation was mounted. During the following month several more were launched, as the Forfar ones had been, from the coastal forces' bases of Dover, Newhaven, and Dartmouth.

The first Hardtack raid ended in disaster. A party of one French warrant officer and five members of No.1 French Troop, No.10 (Inter-Allied) Commando, landed on the beach near Gravelines, situated between Calais and Dunkirk. On this occasion, the dory took the party onto the beach but was overturned in the surf after landing it. The force commander tried to swim back to the MTB but was drowned, as was the dory coxswain. The five stranded Frenchmen escaped inland but the two remaining crew of the dory stayed behind and were captured.

Casualties were also incurred during two raids on the Channel Islands, when Lieutenant McGonigal raided Sark and Captain Ayton of the SBS landed on Jersey. Both parties encountered minefields and Ayton and two of McGonigal's party were killed. A chance of revenge had to be passed over during a following raid, which took place on the coastline between Dieppe and Le Treport, when a patrol of 15 Germans was seen to be advancing towards the cliff top where two of the raiders were hiding. Lance-Corporal Howells was all for ambushing them with his Thompson sub-machine gun and had to be ordered back down the cliff face by Corporal Nash, who realised that discretion on this occasion was the better part of valour.

All of these raids on the north coast of France were launched to confuse the Germans of the Allies' intentions, but several others were planned in order

Cross-Channel raids
1943-1944

In the summer of 1943, as the Allies prepared for the invasion of German-occupied Europe, a small band of commandos launched a series of cross-Channel raids designed to gather information on German coastal defences while conveying the misleading impression that the planned invasion beaches lay in the Pas-de-Calais area somewhere northeast of le Havre. The 'Forfar' raids of July — September were followed by 'Hardtack' raids in November and December.

In May 1944, with the 'Overlord' invasion less than a month away, a new series of commando reconnaissance and deception missions, designated 'Tarbrush', was launched in the Pas-de-Calais area.

The final Tarbrush operations took place on Walcheren in the Netherlands in October 1944.

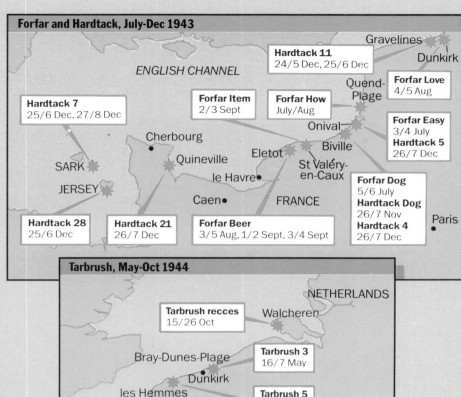

Forfar and Hardtack, July-Dec 1943

ENGLISH CHANNEL

Hardtack 11
24/5 Dec, 25/6 Dec

Gravelines
Dunkirk

Quend-Plage

Forfar Love
4/5 Aug

Hardtack 7
25/6 Dec, 27/8 Dec

Forfar Item
2/3 Sept

Forfar How
July/Aug

Onival

Forfar Easy
3/4 July
Hardtack 5
26/7 Dec

Cherbourg

Quineville

Eletot

Biville

Forfar Dog
5/6 July
Hardtack Dog
26/7 Nov
Hardtack 4
26/7 Dec

SARK

le Havre

St Valéry-en-Caux

JERSEY

Caen

FRANCE

Paris

Hardtack 28
25/6 Dec

Hardtack 21
26/7 Dec

Forfar Beer
3/5 Aug, 1/2 Sept, 3/4 Sept

Tarbrush, May-Oct 1944

NETHERLANDS

Tarbrush recces
15/26 Oct

Walcheren

Bray-Dunes-Plage

Tarbrush 3
16/7 May

Dunkirk

les Hemmes

Tarbrush 5
15/6 May

PAS-DE-CALAIS

BELGIUM

Quend-Plage

Tarbrush 8
15/6 May

Onival

Tarbrush 10
17/8 May

Key
Cross-Channel raids

FRANCE

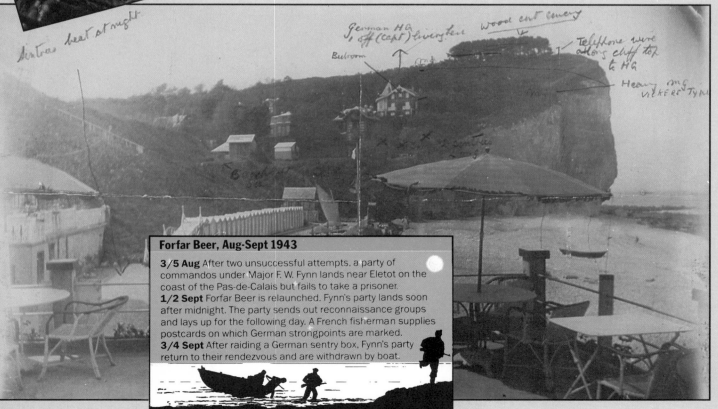

German HQ *I, off (capt) livinghere* *Wood cut away*
Bedroom
Telephone wire along cliff top to HQ
Heavy MG Vickers type
entres boat at night

Forfar Beer, Aug-Sept 1943

3/5 Aug After two unsuccessful attempts, a party of commandos under Major F. W. Fynn lands near Eletot on the coast of the Pas-de-Calais but fails to take a prisoner.
1/2 Sept Forfar Beer is relaunched. Fynn's party lands soon after midnight. The party sends out reconnaissance groups and lays up for the following day. A French fisherman supplies postcards on which German strongpoints are marked.
3/4 Sept After raiding a German sentry box, Fynn's party return to their rendezvous and are withdrawn by boat.

RAIDER EXTRAORDINARY

Sam Brodison joined the Royal Irish Fusiliers in 1934 and gained his first taste of warfare in Palestine in 1936. Following the declaration of World War II, he was wounded during the fighting in Belgium in 1940, and was then posted back to Ulster. Bored by routine training, he became one of the first volunteers for the newly formed Army Commandos, joining A Troop, No.12 Commando.

The first cross-Channel raid in which Brodison, a tough, burly Irishman, participated was at Ambleteuse in July 1941, where he was again wounded when a stray piece of shrapnel from a German E-boat shell hit him in the face. Brodison went on to take part in no less than 18 raids during the war years. In the early ones, such as the raid on the Lofoten Islands off Norway in December 1941, he was a member of a large contingent from No.12 Commando, but during the later Forfar, Hardtack and Tarbrush operations he worked with a small team of officers and NCOs who, like himself, had become highly experienced in cross-Channel raiding. This group proved to be the backbone of the deception raids, and Brodison's exemplary bravery and coolness was recognised by a Mention in Despatches and the award of the Military Medal. Following the completion of the last Tarbrush raid, Brodison was parachuted into Yugoslavia to work with the partisans on various sabotage missions.
Below: Sam Brodison climbs a wall during a training exercise.

to examine the defences at the invasion beaches in Normandy. Two were vetoed at the last moment by COSSAC, but a third, Hardtack 21, was mounted from Newhaven on the night of 26/27 December. Commanded by Lieutenant Francis Vourch, a party of five Frenchmen reconnoitred the beach at Quineville, which on D-day was to become part of the US 4th Division's 'Utah Beach'. Vourch's orders were to reconnoitre a stretch of coastline 500yds in length and to record the beach obstacles there, as well as any inundations which might hinder progress inland.

Vourch landed at 2350 hours, and after a 15-minute walk came to a marsh into which he and his party sank up to their knees. However, they eventually managed to reach hard ground. Then, halfway between a small bank of sand and a flooded inland area, they came across an anti-tank obstacle that COSSAC badly needed to know about. It had been detected in aerial photographs and had been labelled Element C, but up to that time no-one knew its exact dimensions. Now Vourch was able to supply the information needed, and for that achievement he was awarded the Military Cross.

A bomb had caused a chain of explosions all along the foreshore, just beneath the water

All the raids planned for the dark period of January 1944 were cancelled. A further series of 10 Hardtack raids planned for February was also cancelled when a total ban was put on all raids on the French and Belgian coasts by the Allied High Command. Then, ironically, it urgently requested a further series to be carried out in May.

The reason for this about-turn was that a British bomber had dropped a bomb short during an attack on a coastal battery, and this had caused a chain of explosions all along the foreshore, just beneath the water. Photographs were taken and the matter reported, and Professor J.D. Bernal, a mine expert then working at Combined Operations Headquarters, suspected a new type of mine.

The fact that the Germans might well have manufactured some new sophisticated device to defend the beaches greatly concerned the D-day planners. A request was urgently made for a new raiding force to be established immediately, and Captain Bryan Hilton-Jones, commander of X Troop, No.10 (Inter-Allied) Commando, was given the task of forming it. Four areas were chosen for reconnaissance; Bray Dunes, Les Hemmes, Quend-Plage, and Onival. The raids, codenamed Tarbrush 3, 5, 8 and 10, were planned for the next dark period, 14-19 May. The force was codenamed Hiltforce, and each raiding party consisted of one commando officer and two commando other ranks as dory crew, with one commando other rank as dinghy crew and signaller. One officer of the Royal Engineers and one NCO were to carry out the beach reconnaissance and bring back a mine.

In total, eight Tarbrush raids were launched during three nights between 15 and 18 May. On the first night only Tarbrush 8 was able to land. The two sappers made a detailed reconnaissance of the beach defences and then tried to remove a sample of mines they found attached to wooden stakes. While attempting this the officer, Lieutenant Stone, slipped and accidentally hung on to the mine to save himself from falling. 'As nothing happened,' commented a report which was rushed to Winston Churchill after the raids, 'it did not appear very sensitive.' Stone was

Left: An overgrown wall is used for training with grapnels. Below left: A much-decorated commando squad which survived 14 raids on France, and three more on Norway. Front row: CSM Brodison, MM, Captain Smith, MC, and Lance-Corporal Howells (Mentioned in Despatches); back row: Corporal Nash, MM, Captain Magonigal, MC, and Rifleman Coleman (Mentioned in Despatches). Bottom: Blacked up commandos hide up during a Forfar raid.

unable to remove the device but he reported back that it was an ordinary Tellermine 42 waterproofed with grease.

The information acquired on this first reconnaissance was reassuring, but by no means conclusive, and the other three raids were remounted the following night. Tarbrush 10 again failed to land because of the weather, but the other two got ashore. One clashed with a German patrol and after both parties opened fire, the raiders were obliged to withdraw before finding any mines.

Tarbrush 5, however, did provide the confirmation SHAEF required. Despite the fact that a torch was seen flashing on the beach, two sappers went in to land, only to encounter a German sitting smoking a cigarette about 150yds from them. Undeterred, they proceeded up the beach and, right under the nose of the German sentry, investigated some mined stakes. Later on they were able to confirm that these too were ordinary waterproofed Tellermines.

They hid among the beach defences, and then in the water, and eventually the patrol moved on

By now SHAEF had almost conclusive evidence that the sympathetic explosions which had been photographed from the bomber had been caused by inadequately waterproofed Tellermines whose firing pins had been corroded by sea water. Nevertheless, it was decided to remount the last raid, Tarbrush 10, just in case any extra information could be gathered.

Up to then the Tarbrush raiders' luck had held, but now it ran out. It was raining hard at Onival when the two sappers were landed from the rubber dinghy. The coxswain was the raid's military commander, Lieutenant George Lane of X Troop. No mines could be found, so Lane and the sapper officer left to find some of the anti-tank obstacles codenamed Element C, which they had been ordered to photograph with an infra-red camera. After the two officers had left, the sapper NCO and Lane's radio operator were seen by a German patrol and fired upon. They hid among the beach defences and then in the water, and eventually the patrol moved on. The officers did not return, and after the time designated for them to leave the beach had passed, the two NCOs left the dinghy out of the water for the use of the officers and swam back to the dory.

When the dory returned to the mother ship without the officers, Hilton-Jones, who was on the MTB, took personal command and returned to the shore. He could find no trace of either of them, and it transpired that they were both made prisoners of war.

The casualties sustained during all three series of operations had been considerable. But the raiders' achievements, that the Germans remained baffled as to the Allies' intentions, and that the D-day planners could launch the Normandy landings without fear of an unknown German beach device, went some way to compensate for the sacrifices made. Those who had died had not done so in vain.

THE AUTHOR Ian Dear served as a regular officer in the Royal Marines, 1953-56. He is now a professional writer on military and maritime subjects and is author of *Ten Commando*, a book on No.10 (Inter-Allied) Commando which is to be published in 1987 by Leo Cooper Ltd.

NO SURRENDER

Hitting hard and fast, a small group of Australian commandos exacted a heavy toll of Japanese forces on the island of Timor

DURING WORLD WAR II, eight units of Australian commandos were trained in New South Wales by British Captains Michael Calvert and F. Spencer Chapman, army officers from the 104 Military Mission. Known as 'Independent Companies', these units were originally intended for operations in North Africa. In late 1941, however, with Japanese forces poised to sweep south, it was decided to deploy the newly formed commando companies to the Pacific islands. Fighting against overwhelming numbers of seasoned Japanese troops, most of the Australian commandos were either killed or captured – with the exception of one remarkable unit. For 10 months, by reconnoitring and raiding enemy positions on Timor, a small force of Australian commandos managed to convince the Japanese that they were up against a unit of battalion strength.

A mountainous island 300 miles long and 60 miles wide, Timor had a population of some 900,000 people. In the west was Dutch Timor, part of the Dutch East Indies, and in the east was a Portuguese colony that insisted on maintaining its neutrality. The Dutch administrative capital was Kupang, while that of the Portuguese colony was Dili. Since both towns possessed an airfield and harbour, it was feared that Japanese forces would attempt to use Timor as a forward base from which to threaten Darwin, less than 400 miles away in Australia's Northern Territory.

Commanded by Major Spense, the 327 officers and men of the Australian 2/2nd (Independent) Company arrived at Kupang, on the southern tip of Timor, on 12 December 1941. The Japanese attack on Pearl Harbor had taken place four days earlier, and Spense's three platoons had been deployed to Timor to join 'Sparrow Force', under the command of Lieutenant-Colonel W.W. Leggatt. The island's defences now amounted to some 2000 men, comprising the Australian 2/40th Infantry Battalion, 2/2nd Company, and 500 troops from the Royal Netherlands East Indian Army (RNEIA), commanded by Lieutenant-Colonel L. van Straaten.

On 17 December a combined force of RNEIA troops and commandos sailed along Timor's northern coast and landed at Dili, experiencing no resistance from the Portuguese colonial administration. While the Dutch soldiers occupied the township, 2/2nd Company deployed a section under the command of Lieutenant McKenzie to secure the airfield. The company then established platoon bases in the hills to the south of Dili, a move that enabled the commandos to familiarise themselves with the terrain that was to become their hunting ground. Fostering friendships with the local Timorese villagers, the men of 2/2nd Company mapped the area and carefully worked out tactics that would be employed in the event of a Japanese attack.

Dysentery and malaria soon began to exact their toll – claiming 70 severe cases at any one time – but the men had been trained to fend for themselves under the most severe conditions. Accordingly, they

A total of 60 officers and NCO's were originally recruited in Western Australia on the understanding that they would form an entirely Western Australian unit. They were given very little information as to their likely role, only that they would be required for 'Special Service'.

On arrival at the training camp at Wilson's Promontory, at the southern tip of New South Wales, the officers and NCOs were divided into separate groups during a six-week intensive training schedule that concentrated on demolition, booby traps, field craft, weapons handling and radio signalling. At the end of the course, the officers and NCOs of 2/2nd (Independent) Company were selected. These men then took on responsibility for creating the company from the other ranks, also Western Australians, who arrived shortly after. Specialist troops, including sappers and signallers, were also brought into the unit.

Once the company had been formed, the recruits continued a training schedule that assigned physical fitness, sound discipline and high morale as the top priorities. Training in wild and remote terrain, the company conducted exercises alongside specialist units from New Zealand.

The men were also instructed on the value of creating and maintaining a network of contacts with the local population. Since the company would be fighting without regular supplies, in an area where the attitude of the local and colonial population was an unknown factor, the establishment of such a network was seen as crucial to the company's ability to carry out its tasks.

Top left, left to right: Lieutenant-Colonel Spense, Lieutenant Smyth, Major Callinan and Captain Boyland. Acting on information from one of the many commando OPs (above left), Sergeant Smith leads a patrol through the hills of Timor (left).

The Battle for Timor
2/2nd Independent Company, 1942-43

WETAR STRAIT

Dili

Salazar Plateau

Lautem Plateau

PORTUGUESE TIMOR

OMBAI STRAIT

Ermera

Let-Fote

Maubisse

Atsabe

Bobonaro

Quicros

Mape

Betano

PORTUGUESE
TIMOR

Occusi

Suai

DUTCH TIMOR

Kupang

T I M O R   S E A

Borneo

Pacific Ocean

Celebes

New Guinea

Java

Timor

Timor Sea

Darwin

Indian
Ocean

Australia

Key
Japanese landings

adopted the procedure of resting during a malaria attack, usually one hour each day, and ignoring it for the remainder of the day.

On 19 February 1942, Japanese aircraft devastated Darwin. That same night, the Imperial Navy's warships bombarded Dili prior to the landing of troops along the beaches of Portuguese Timor. Enemy troops headed straight for the airfield, where McKenzie's section had completed the installation of demolition charges. Bren-gun teams and commandos with Thompson sub-machine guns halted their advance temporarily, but the radio was down and the section cut-off. After scribbling down a message from McKenzie, Lance-Corporal Doyle mounted an old Dutch bicycle and rode out through the airfield gates – where the Japanese were massing for another attack. The enemy soldiers were so amazed by Doyle's audacity that not a single shot was fired. Doyle continued riding to Dili, where he contacted Captain Bernard Callinan, the company's second-in-command, and informed him of the situation.

Back at the airfield, McKenzie's defensive perimeter was holding firm. Corporal Curran killed four enemy soldiers with his bayonet as they tried to cross a ditch on the edge of the airfield, and Privates

Poynton and Thomas poured a hail of fire into their adversaries – earning themselves distinguished reputations as close-quarters Tommy-gunners. When dawn revealed the true size of McKenzie's force, the Japanese soldiers began massing for a final attack. The section commander decided to pre-empt them by blowing the airfield and fighting a withdrawing action. An attack by three commandos with sub-machine guns surprised the Japanese sufficiently to allow the rest of the section to slip away after detonating the demolition charges. By the time the last commando had left, the bodies of 200 Japanese soldiers lay strewn around the airfield.

Over 1000 enemy troops had landed in the first wave, and three more waves followed closely behind. The RNEIA force made an attempt to withdraw back to Dutch Timor, but disintegrated in the face of Japanese attack. The 2/2nd Company maintained patrols to the west and southwest of Dili until forced to retire. So far, its casualties were small; two killed and one captured. However, when 16 commandos were captured driving into Dili, all but one were executed on the spot. Communications between the three platoons – dispersed between Dili and Atsabe 30 miles to the south – were tenuous. The last message received from Darwin was that the town was under attack. The commandos wondered whether Australia was being invaded, but their radio link to Darwin was down and they had no way of knowing for sure. They decided to continue fighting the kind of war for which they had been trained. In the words of Callinan, 'It was to be a case of defence by offence.'

The commandos increased their own mobility by each employing a Timorese 'creado' and pack pony to help with the carriage of ammunition and equipment (left). When the action started, the porter would issue the commando with his weapons and then disappear into the bush. Far left: The officers of 2/2nd Independent Company. In the foreground are Captain Rolf Baldwin, Major Bernard Callinan (reading magazine) and Captain E. Hennesey. Captain G.R. Dunkley and Major G.C. Laidlaw can be seen in the left of this picture. Above: The enemy proved unable to dampen the commandos' team spirit.

A patrol was despatched to Dutch Timor, but only confirmed the company's worst suspicions regarding the fate of Sparrow Force. Supported by light tanks, a force of 5000 Japanese troops had come ashore on the beaches near Kupang. A further 18,000 soldiers had landed during the next two days. After four days and nights of continuous fighting, without food or water and low on ammunition, Leggatt's force had surrendered. Many of the Australian and Dutch soldiers, however, had escaped from the clutches of the Japanese and made for the hills – towards Portuguese Timor and the Independent Company.

The commandos sent Ross back to the enemy commander in Dili with their message – no surrender

The Australian Consul at Dili, David Ross, was escorted into the hills by Japanese soldiers and turned loose. He had been instructed to locate the commandos, inform them that all fighting on Timor had ceased, and request their surrender. Ross delivered the message – but he also gave the company all the information he had on Japanese strength and deployment. Countering the Japanese demands with a military myth that they were part of a special unit that had not surrendered, the commandos sent Ross back to the enemy commander in Dili with their message – no surrender.

Company headquarters were established at Atsabe, an area of rough country 30 miles south of Dili, and the three platoon commanders – Captains Rolf Baldwin, G. Laidlaw and G. Boyland – designated their sections to hold a series of villages and areas stretching 100km from the Portuguese-Dutch border in the west, to a high ridge overlooking Dili in the east.

A reconnaissance patrol in the southwest of Portuguese Timor located Brigadier Veale, a senior officer who had arrived at Kupang to take command of Sparrow Force shortly before the Japanese invasion. Veale had escaped from Dutch Timor and crossed the border, and was accompanied by some 200 Australian soldiers from the 2/40th Infantry Battalion. In addition, 150 RNEIA troops had been drawn together under Colonel van Straaten. In conference between van Straaten, Veale and Spense, it was decided that the Dutch and Australian infantry would guard the border against attack from the west, while the commandos concentrated their efforts on the Japanese in Portuguese Timor.

The enemy gradually began moving out of Dili, occupying villages, townships and Portuguese administrative posts. Leaving a garrison of 500 at Ermera, 25 miles southwest of Dili, the Japanese continued the search for their quarry, pressing on towards the township of Lete-Foho – where a force of commandos lay in wait. With company headquarters and platoon bases under threat, the commandos hacked at the sides and rear of the enemy column. One sniper, Private Wheatly, took out eight Japanese in one day. By the end of April, the Japanese had moved back to Ermera.

By the beginning of May, with the Japanese showing little inclination to move out of Dili and Ermera, the company moved in closer. They formed a 60-mile long defensive arc around the area and manned it with 300 fighting troops. This force comprised the commandos, and the fittest of the Australian and Dutch troops – trained in jungle warfare at an ad-hoc training camp under one of the Independent Company's best corporals. This training, supplemented by the ministrations of Captain Dunkley, the company medical officer, had resulted in the formation of a fourth platoon.

Unable to answer him in Japanese, Laidlaw shot him from a range of three yards

Taking the fight to the Japanese, the commandos co-ordinated hit-and-run raids on roads and bridges, attacking convoys and shooting up relief and reinforcement parties. On one occasion, three commandos hid within 100yds of an enemy observation post for two days while they monitored the routine. They struck at breakfast time on the third day, killing 12 Japanese soldiers before disappearing into the scrub. Although most of these raids were small-scale, mounting Japanese casualties soon began to have an adverse effect on enemy morale. Rewards were placed on the heads of the commandos, and the Japanese brought in an anti-guerrilla expert from Malaya. Dubbed the 'Singapore Tiger' by the commandos, the Japanese major did not live long. Only weeks after his arrival on Timor, he fell into a commando ambush and perished along with 25 enemy soldiers.

On 15 May, Captain Laidlaw and 20 commandos slipped into Dili under cover of darkness. As they were passing a machine-gun post, one of the Japanese soldiers tried to strike up a conversation with Laidlaw. Unable to answer him in Japanese, Laidlaw shot him from a range of three yards. Taking their cue, the commandos took out the post and opened fire on the ranks of the Japanese as they poured out of buildings from all sides. Before the enemy could get organised, the commandos slipped quietly into the darkness.

At the end of May, a Catalina flying boat came in from Darwin bringing much-needed supplies – food, boots, coinage to pay natives, quinine to fight malaria, and ammunition. It left carrying some of the sick and wounded, together with Brigadier Veale and Colonel van Straaten. Major Spense was therefore promoted to lieutenant-colonel and given command of all Australian and RNEIA troops, and the newly

promoted Major Callinan was given command of the Independent Company. In the words of Major Callinan, the war now became 'highly organised', with radio communication firmly established between the company's four platoons – and the enemy being hit wherever possible.

In June, however, signs began to appear of increased Japanese activity. David Ross was again despatched to find the commandos, under instructions to offer them proper treatment as prisoners-of-war if they surrendered. The Japanese commander had informed Ross that, based on his readings of the Boer War and combat experience in Manchuria, he believed a minimum of 10 regular troops were required to kill one guerrilla. If the commandos refused to surrender, he threatened to use whatever force necessary to destroy them. Ross delivered the message, but Lieutenant-Colonel Spense was not interested and invited Ross to stay. Ross accepted the offer and was later evacuated to Australia. All through July 1942, Spense's headquarters at Mape, 10 miles south of Atsabe, received reports of Japanese reinforcements arriving at Dili and Kupang. A series of small raids failed to entice the enemy out of Dili, and it became increasingly obvious that the Japanese commander was building up his forces and preparing to carry out his threat. A storm was brewing.

In early August Japanese bombers and Zero fighters commenced bombing and strafing missions over the villages and townships south of Dili. Both Mape and Bobonaro, the headquarters of 2/2nd (Independent) Company, were hit. A few days later, two 500-strong columns moved out of Dili. A further two columns were reported to be advancing east from Dutch Timor. The Japanese were intending to box the commandos in. In the western sector, the Japanese employed Timorese natives from Dutch Timor to screen their advance. Moving through the villages, these natives incited their counterparts in the Portuguese colony to side with the Japanese. Gradually, the enemy encirclement tightened. Rather than retreat into the difficult terrain to the east, Spense decided to launch a counter-attack. Plans were rapidly drawn up, but when a green flare illuminated the night sky 12 hours before going into action, the men braced themselves for what they expected to be a full-scale enemy offensive. Remarkably, reconnaissance patrols reported no signs of an impending attack. When dawn came, it was realised that the Japanese were withdrawing. Scarcely believing their good fortune, the commandos followed the enemy columns all the way back to Dili, harassing them as much as possible.

In September, the Japanese 48th Division, comprising veterans from the Philippine and Java campaigns, arrived in Dutch Timor and quickly des-

The underlying theme of the commandos' training had been living off the land and launching long-range raids behind enemy lines. In the rugged terrain of Timor, the training was put to the test. Radio communications (right), at first hampered by a lack of equipment, were firmly established by the end of April 1942 after a team of commandos, assisted by a Portuguese official, obtained an intact transmitter from the Qantas Empire Airways office in Dili. Above: Commandos from the 2/2nd Company liaise with the tribal elders of a village in Portuguese Timor. Such villages invariably proved the safest hiding place for the commandos' ammunition and supplies. Below: A group of Timorese 'irregulars' pose for the camera.

patched a force to Portuguese Timor. By 21 September, a force of 400 enemy soldiers had occupied the township of Maubisse, five miles northeast of Atsabe, and was attempting to penetrate inland. Foiled at first by ambushes, a 350-strong column eventually began to make inroads, forcing the commandos to withdraw. Two days later, Captain Dexter and his men were resting up at a Portuguese administrative post when the phone rang. It was the local Japanese commander, informing Dexter that he was coming to destroy him. Dexter politely thanked his adversary for being so informative, and promptly executed a decisive ambush that drove the Japanese back to Maubisse. Meanwhile, the 2/4th Independent Company had been put ashore at Betano, on the southern coast of Portuguese Timor, and proceeded to join up with Callinan's unit. However, the Japanese had spotted the landing and reacted quickly in order to counter the new threat.

The company's combat losses had been remarkably small – totalling only 26

On 27 September, 2000 seasoned enemy troops moved out from Dili and advanced towards Betano. Ambushes made their advance extremely costly, but they could not be stopped. By attacking the villages in which commandos were known to operate, the enemy incited large numbers of the Timorese against the Australians. Inexplicably, however, the Japanese withdrew back to Maubisse.

By the end of November, with the food supply rapidly diminishing and malaria endemic, the 2/2nd Company was approaching the limit of its endurance. The men had been in continuous action for nine months, under conditions of great physical and mental hardship. Lieutenant-Colonel Spense therefore recommended to Northern Force Headquarters, Darwin, that the company be evacuated. Finally, between 11 and 19 December 1942, the 2/2nd Company and its attachments were withdrawn.

The tenacity of 2/2nd Company during 1942 had forced the Japanese to divert a division of troops to Timor, at a time when the fighting for New Guinea and Guadalcanal was at its height. The company's combat losses had been remarkably small – totalling

only 26 – while those of the Japanese amounted to over 1000. Following the evacuation, Lieutenant-General Thomas Blamey, commander of the Allied land forces in the Southwest Pacific and Commander-in-Chief of the Australian Army, conveyed the following message to the commanders of the Timor 'irregulars':

'Please accept on behalf of yourself and the men under your command my congratulations and appreciation of the magnificent manner in which your task in Timor has been accomplished. Your deeds have earned you the gratitude and admiration of all Australians.'

THE AUTHOR John Brown is an Australian freelance writer who has contributed a number of articles to military publications. He has spent many years researching Australia's contribution to the Pacific campaign of World War II.

A LINK WITH AUSTRALIA

The resilience of the 2/2nd Independent Company on Timor was complemented by the commandos' unrivalled ingenuity. Cut off from home, the men were determined to re-establish radio contact with Australia. Signalman Loveless, together with the help of other commandos and a Portuguese official, managed to scavenge enough spare parts to build a rudimentary radio transmitter. Working tirelessly until their task was completed, the men constructed the device at company headquarters – the finished product filled a space 10ft square. Connected by wires stolen from cars and Japanese vehicles, the parts were spread around the floor of the hut and on a host of makeshift benches. The batteries of the transmitter were charged by a generator, which in turn was driven by a rope around a series of wheels. One of these wheels had a handle, enabling it to be turned by up to four Timorese helpers. On 20 April the primitive transmitter sent out a weak signal that was picked up in Darwin. However, the batteries ran out before any detailed message could be relayed. Signalman Loveless tried again the following night, using a priority reserved for commanders-in-chief of the services. Loveless and his colleagues were elated to hear all stations close down while their message was concentrated upon. Eventually, their call sign was accepted. Australia at last knew that the company was alive and fighting on Timor. Notices from the War Office reading 'Missing, presumed killed or captured' could now be revised. Before signing off, the commandos requested medical supplies and new batteries for the radio. These were air-dropped to Portuguese Timor some days later.

It was to one of her most famous soldiers, Saad el Din Shazli, that Egypt owed the creation of her commando units. Shazli began forming paratroop forces in the aftermath of the 1956 War with Israel, and by 1959 the first such unit was operational.

In 1960 Shazli himself commanded an Egyptian paratroop battalion serving with the UN forces in the Congo and paratroop and commando units subsequently saw service during Nasser's intervention in the Yemen Civil War, on the side of the Republicans. During the build up to the Six-Day War, in the first days of June, 1967, the 33rd and 53rd Commando battalions were air-lifted to Amman, with the intention of taking out Israeli airbases in the event of war; but they suffered in the general disaster that befell the Jordanian Army.

During the 'War of Attrition', in the late 1960s, these special forces were able to gain experience in small-scale raiding and reconnaissance. In February 1970 the expertise of the Egyptian commandos was shown quite clearly: during that month they successfully ambushed an Israeli patrol on the East Bank of the Suez Canal and a naval auxiliary vessel within the Israeli port of Elat was blown up by frogmen.

In his preparations for the Yom Kippur War, Shazli expanded the special forces. By October 1973, he could dispose of the 140th and 182nd Parachute Brigades, two heli-borne air assault brigades, and seven commando groups, of which three (the 127th, 129th and 133rd) were attached to operational commands, while the rest remained at the disposal of GHQ.

CROSSING THE CANAL

Egyptian special forces spearheaded the surprise attack across the Suez Canal that opened the Yom Kippur War in October 1973

AT 1415 HOURS on 6 October 1973, Egyptian commando squads sprinted for the water's edge on the west bank of the Suez Canal, dropped into their rubber assault craft and began paddling furiously across the 200yd-wide waterway. As jets screamed overhead on their way east, the commandos could see the Israeli defences of the Bar-Lev Line slowly vanish in an inferno of bursting shells and drifting dust clouds, but here and there the water of the Canal was titched by return automatic weapons fire or fountained upwards under the impact of mortar shells, eaving assault boats drifting in mid-stream with imp, bloodied bundles aboard. The Yom Kippur War had begun.

In 1967, the forces of Egypt, Syria and Jordan had undergone a grievous defeat at the hands of the Israeli Defence Forces (IDF). The Egyptians had suffered large losses in territory, and the whole of the Sinai peninsula up to the Suez Canal had been occupied by the Israelis. The Egyptian armed forces were desperate to regain some of the prestige lost during the crushing defeat of 1967; and so the forces that took part in the surprise attack on the Israelis in 1973 were motivated to perform their tasks to the best possible effect. They were prepared to take high losses to achieve their objective – the recapture of the east bank of the Suez Canal – and had prepared for months, and in some cases years, to deal with resistance that they knew would be tough. There were two problems that the Egyptians faced: first of all, how to breach the defences of the Bar-Lev Line, the fortifications along the Suez Canal (based around 30 strongpoints, the *moazim*); and, second, how to deal with the Israeli armoured forces that would rush to the aid of the Bar-Lev Line garrisons. In both these areas, the Egyptian commandos were asked to play a key role.

The Egyptian Army's Chief of Staff, Major-General Saad el Din Shazli, who had masterminded the plans for crossing the Canal and overseen the detailed training for the operation, had, in fact, been one of the officers who had developed the idea of special forces within the Egyptian Army, and he had supervised the expansion of such units in the 1970-73 period. By October 1973, there were two paratroop brigades, 28 battalions of commandos and a marine brigade ready for action.

Shazli saw these elite units as fitting into his offensive in three ways. First, they would carry out

Left: The barrel of an Egyptian tank points menacingly towards Israeli defences on the Bar-lev Line, as Commandos survey the terrain.

Crossing the Bar-Lev Line
Egyptian commandos, October 1973

On the afternoon of Yom Kippur, 6 October 1973, the troops manning the Bar-Lev defensive line along the Suez Canal in Israeli-occupied Sinai were the victims of a surprise assault spearheaded by crack squads of Egyptian commandos. By the following day most of the Bar-Lev Line was in Egyptian hands.

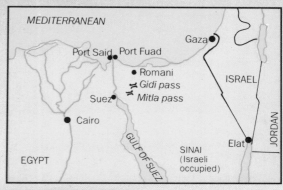

Sinai bridgehead

As the Egyptian 2nd and 3rd armies cross the canal to consolidate the bridgehead, further commando insertions are made near the Mitla and Gidi passes.
7 Oct Despite further commando landings on the coast, the Budapest stronghold remains in Israeli hands.

Key
→ Egyptian forces
→ Israeli forces
■ Israeli strongholds
□ Israeli command posts

Hitting the strongpoints

6 Oct 1400 As the Egyptian bombardment of the Bar-Lev Line begins, commando squads cross the Suez Canal. Spearheading the Egyptian attempt to regain Sinai, the commandos take out most of the strongpoints. At the Quay and Budapest, Israeli garrisons put up stiff resistance.

THE BAR-LEV LINE

The Bar-Lev Line was conceived during Egypt's War of Attrition against the Israeli forces occupying Sinai, and was named after the then Chief of Staff of the Israeli Defence Force, General Chaim Bar Lev. It was intended as a chain of 30 fortified observation posts called *moazim*, strung out along the eastern bank of the Suez Canal from the Mediterranean to the Gulf of Suez, a distance of approximately 100 miles.

The aim was to provide early warning of Egyptian attempts to cross the Canal. Each of these strongpoints consisted of a central command and accommodation bunker connected by sandbagged trenches to four bunkered fire-positions. The bunkers were constructed from concrete approximately 5ft thick, their roofs being reinforced with rails lifted from the old trans-Sinai railway and covered with a deep overhead layer of sand. The outer perimeter consisted of a bulldozed embankment and ditch with barbed wire obstacles, surrounded by minefields. Some strongpoints were equipped to release fuel into the Canal, which would then be ignited in the event of attack, but these installations do not seem to have been used, and when the Egyptians examined them many of the nozzles were found to have silted up. The *moazim* were held in platoon strength but were not equipped with anything heavier than machine guns and mortars, although firing ramps for tanks were constructed inside most of their perimeters. Behind the chain of *moazim* lay two parallel roads, the Artillery Road, 6 miles from the Canal, along which lay the Israelis' artillery response and the strongpoints' reinforcement armour, and the Lateral Road, 20 miles from the Canal, along which lay the armoured counter-attack reserves.

the detailed preliminary reconnaissance of the Canal's east bank defences. Second, they would act as the spearhead of the Canal crossing itself, neutralising the strongpoints of the Bar-Lev Line and setting up anti-tank ambushes that would deal with the Israeli armoured response. And third, they would be inserted by helicopter deeper into Sinai where they would disrupt communications, attack senior officers' command posts and ambush reinforcements trying to reach the front.

In the sectors of Major-General Abd al Muneim Wassel's Third Army in the south, and of Major-General Saad Mamoun's Second Army in the north, the crossing points for the commandos lay between the Bar-Lev Line *moazim*. Once the boats had touched the opposite bank, their crews scrambled ashore, dragging flexible assault ladders up the towering sand ramparts for use by the follow-up infantry units, tank-hunter teams and artillery

Above: Egyptian soldiers race into action past a knocked-out Israeli M-48 Patton. Left: Egyptian infantry and equipment reach the east bank by means of a pontoon bridge across the Suez Canal and a passageway blasted out of its steep sandbank ramparts by the innovative use of high-pressure hoses. Below: One of the 30 Israeli *moazim*, along the Bar-Lev Line.

observation parties. The commandos then closed in on the strongpoints with quick bursts of fire, moving rapidly, the attacks terminating in tossed grenades and the rattle of Kalashnikovs. To their surprise, the Egyptians found that only 16 of the Bar-Lev positions were manned and the resistance that was offered by these differed widely according to whether their garrisons had manned their weapon pits, or were still sheltering from the bombardment in their bunkers.

At the southern end of the line, for example, the post known as the Quay gallantly held out for a week until its commander was authorised to negotiate surrender through the Red Cross. This position was built on the breakwater of Port Tewfik harbour, and since this was only 6yds wide the commandos experienced the greatest difficulty in getting close enough to launch an assault. One particularly determined group, using man-pack flamethrowers, actually broke into the defences, although none survived this daring assault.

Elsewhere, the commando attacks on the *moazim* were more uniformly successful. In some cases the garrisons accepted their fate philosophically and became prisoners of war when it was apparent that they were not going to be relieved. In others they fought on until most of their men were dead or wounded. In a very few, those that were still able and very lucky somehow managed to fight their way out and back to their own lines.

It is indicative of the thoroughness with which the Egyptians had prepared their offensive that they were able to make use of an Israeli tradition and turn it to their own advantage. Never since its formation had the Israeli Army allowed its members, and especially those who were wounded, to fall into enemy hands if rescue was humanly possible. It was a point of honour that any call for help should be answered promptly, even if it involved heavy loss.

As the Israeli tank commanders pressed on to try to relieve the Bar-Lev Line defences, they were hammered by artillery and mortar fire from the west bank of the Canal; more fell victim to the mines that the commandos had laid. But, most important of all, certainly from the point of view of the effect that they had on Israeli morale, were the commando ambushes.

The Egyptians had specialised weapons to take on tanks: some were conventional man-portable rocket launchers such as the RPG-7, but others were more unusual. The Sagger AT-3 Anti-Tank Guided Weapon

(ATGW) for example, was a wire-guided rocket that its operator aimed, and then guided to its target with a joystick. The whole assembly packed down into a suitcase and was easily carried by its two-man team. The Sagger needed a skilled operator, and one who would not panic at the sight of approaching enemy armour. Egyptian tank-hunter teams, secure in the knowledge of how effective their weaponry could be, were prepared to wait until the range was right before they engaged their targets.

On the marshy northern sector, Israeli tank crews had to operate with restricted visibility because the hail of fire from Egyptian smallarms forced them to keep all hatches closed; some ploughed off the hard approach roads and bogged down, making them even easier meat for the tank-hunting teams. Many Israeli tank crews hardly saw their opponents before the missiles hit their vehicle. Within 24 hours, Major-General Mandler's armoured division, the IDF's only regular counter-strike formation in Sinai, had lost 170 tanks.

Elsewhere, the success of the Egyptian commandos was less even, and Shazli's intention to insert them deep into Sinai caused heavy losses. Thirty-man troops were inserted singly or in pairs by Mil Mi-8 'Hip' transport helicopters close to their objectives deeper into Sinai, the extent of their operations ranging as far as Sharm-el-Sheikh at the southern tip of the peninsula. In the majority of cases, the local Israeli response was more effective than it had been along the Bar-Lev Line and the damage was contained. The largest insertion was made in battalion strength but the helicopters were spotted by Israeli Air Force Phantoms while over-flying Ras Suda in the Gulf of Suez and fourteen of them were shot down; the majority of the 250 men who formed this raiding force died in this incident or were captured afterwards.

Another use of commando troops was in an operation involving the 130th Marine Brigade, equipped with amphibious PT-76 light tanks and BTR-50 armoured personnel carriers, crossing the Great Bitter Lake while para-frogmen raided Israeli positions on the eastern shore. The intention was that, once ashore, the marines would break through the

Israelis' forward defences in the area and reinforce those commando units which had been inserted by helicopter near the strategically important Mitla and Gidi passes; but the IDF, aware of the danger, had both routes covered by an armoured brigade and the attempt was abandoned after casualties began to mount among the thin-skinned vehicles.

It was, in fact, in the northern sector that the commandos made their presence most keenly felt, and nowhere more so than in the epic struggle for Strongpoint Budapest, around which fierce fighting raged for much of the war. Budapest did not form part of the main chain of Bar-Lev fortifications but lay on a sandbank approximately 7 miles to the east of Port Fuad with a broad belt of swampland to the south. It was manned by an 18-strong infantry garrison, which had been reinforced with a troop of tanks when it became clear that the Egyptians intended crossing the Canal in strength. On the afternoon of 6 October an Egyptian task force, consisting of 16 tanks, the same number of armoured personnel carriers, jeep-mounted recoilless rifles and lorry-borne infantry, launched an attack along the coast road from Port Fuad with air and artillery support. This was re-pulsed with the loss of seven tanks and eight APCs, but under cover of the fighting a commando unit was put ashore a mile east of Budapest, isolating the strongpoint.

The Israelis were aware that Budapest had come under heavy attack, but not that it had been cut off, and, at about midnight, made an attempt to reinforce the garrison with eight tanks from Ma-jor-General Adan's newly arrived armoured di-vision. The commandos, however, had mined the only approach and when one tank was damaged they put up parachute illuminating flares which shed their harsh light on the scene. Several Sagger ATGWs were launched and two more tanks were hit. The remainder with-drew, their commander believing angrily that he had been engaged by the Israeli tanks within the strongpoint.

At first light the Israelis resumed their advance but halted when it was seen that the commandos had laid a belt of mines stretch-

Below left: Commandos raise the Egyptian flag on the Bar-Lev Line, to celebrate their successes in the first stages of the Yom Kippur War. The Egyptians took the Israelis by surprise by launching the assault on Yom Kippur Day, the Jewish Day of Atonement, when Israeli TV and radio stations, which carried the reservist call-up codes, would be off the air.
Below: Although defeated, Egyptian military pride remains intact as evidenced by a show of military strength at a march-past in Cairo after the Yom Kippur War.

ing across the entire width of the sandbank. From a range of only 500yds, a volley of Saggers roared out towards the tanks, disabling a further vehicle. Again the Israelis withdrew, now fully aware of the situa-tion. The attack was renewed later in the morning, the tanks having been reinforced with a 120mm mortar battery and an infantry company borrowed from a reconnaissance unit. The commandos, invisi-ble to the tanks crews, held their fire until the Israeli infantry were clearly outlined against the shallow contours of the sandbank and then opened up with their automatic weapons, killing 15 and wounding 30.

During the night of 6/7 October a large commando group was similarly inserted at Romani, some 20 miles to the east of Budapest. This group actually attacked one of Adan's armoured brigades while it was reversing off its transporters, knocking out two tanks and a half-track. A tank battalion was detailed to deal with the commandos, who promptly went to ground among the dunes but returned to the attack at the first opportunity and destroyed yet more vehi-cles. Colonel Nir, the Israeli brigade commander, asked Adan for infantry with which to deal with the Egyptians and an *ad hoc* unit was formed from reconnaissance units. Adan later recorded in his book *On The Banks of the Suez* that Nir 'de-scribed at length the fierce-ness with which the Egyp-tians had fought. We had taken more casualties in the fighting, but 100 Egyptian commandos had been killed and we now held their com-manding officer captive.... I was happy with the results but frustrated that it had taken a full three hours to overcome the Egyptians. By my evaluation, the commandos' fighting had been impressive.'

Having formed units from the reconnaissance troops to hunt down the commandos, however, Adan's command was unable to receive all the intelligence that was necessary to make an effective attack on 8 October. In fact, Adan lost 70 tanks during this unsuccessful attack, and the Israeli high command was plunged into gloom as there seemed no way of making an impres-sion on the Egyptian forces.

The commandos, then, had contri-buted significantly to the success of the Egyptian Army in crossing the Suez Canal. They had spearheaded the cros-sing, led attacks on Israeli armour, and, even though losses had been heavy, inhibited the Israeli ability to make a successful armoured counter by their activities deeper in Sinai. The later turn of events, when the Egyptians advanced still further into Sinai and met a decisive check, cannot obscure the achievements of the commandos in those early days of the Yom Kippur War. Indeed, the end of the war saw them acting as bravely as ever. At Ismailiya the 182nd Paratroop Brigade fought Israeli paratroops to a standstill – salvaging honour in defeat.

THE AUTHOR Bryan Perrett served in the Royal Armoured Corps. He contributes to military jour-nals and his books include *A history of Blitzkrieg*.

TALKING
LOGISTICS

COMMANDO LOGISTIC REGIMENT

3 Commando Brigade, Royal Marines, has its own fully integrated logistic unit that provides for its needs. In 1982, no other British land formation possessed such a facility; a failing that now, in the aftermath of the Falklands War, has been rectified.

Based in Plymouth, the Commando Logistic Regiment comprises five squadrons: Transport, Workshops, Ordnance, Medical and Headquarters.

In addition, the 3 Commando Brigade Air Squadron, Royal Marines, sometimes comes under the regiment's command for administrative purposes.

Workshop Squadron is responsible for the repair of vehicles, electronic equipment and weapons, while Ordnance Squadron handles the hundreds of different items that are needed as spares and daily supplies. Medical Squadron is responsible for running two second line Dressing Stations that can be upgraded by the addition of Field Surgical Teams. Headquarters Squadron, together with the Signal Troop, is responsible for controlling logistical operations.

The men who make up the regiment are mainly Royal Marines, supplemented by commando-trained personnel from the Royal Army Ordnance Corps (RAOC), Royal Mechanical and Electrical Engineers (REME) and the Royal Corps of Transport (RCT), in addition to Royal Navy surgeons and medical assistants.

During the Falklands campaign, the unsung heroes of the Commando Logistic Regiment supplied the needs of two entire brigades

ARMIES DO NOT MARCH on their stomachs alone, and no military operation can even be considered until the logisticians have judged it feasible. Theirs is the science of making the improbable possible, and they are crucial to the success of all military operations. On 14 June 1982, after a conflict that had lasted over two months, Argentinian forces on the Falkland Islands finally surrendered. During the height of the campaign, one unit had worked relentlessly in an attempt to ensure the re-supply of 3 Commando Brigade, Royal Marines, commanded by Brigadier Julian Thompson. In the latter part of the campaign, the regiment also supplied 5 Infantry Brigade. Under the command of Lieutenant-Colonel Ivar Hellberg, the Commando Logistic Regiment was responsible for delivering enormous quantities of food, ammunition and fuel to the front line – regardless of weather and battle conditions.

In the early hours of 1 April 1982, the Commando Logistic Regiment, Royal Marines, was recalled to Plymouth, most of its personnel having recently returned from a winter of arctic training in Norway. By 0630, most hands were back in barracks. Contingency plans had already been discussed, but, up until this point, they had involved sending only a company or battalion-size group to the South Atlantic. Captain Paddy George, the adjutant of the regiment, was taken aback at the scale of Operation Corporate: 'It was a shock to hear suddenly that the entire brigade was now sailing. It was a frantic weekend.' The regiment had to place 14,000 tons of stores into 27 ships in less than 72 hours. As if this herculean task was not enough, the men had to know the exact location of every box and package.

Throughout the south of England, depots checked their War Maintenance Reserve (WMR) and made sure that every item was carefully labelled. A massive fleet of Royal Corps of Transport trucks and requisitioned civilian heavy goods vehicles then began to transport the stores to the docksides. Remarkably, the vast majority of the stocks had been packed, labelled and loaded onto the Royal Fleet Auxiliary (RFA) and Landing Ship Logistics (LSL) vessels by noon on 5 April. However, it was a very slimmed-down unit that sailed out of Plymouth harbour on 5 April. Only half the regiment was embarked, mostly on LSLs *Sir Galahad*, *Sir Lancelot* and *Sir Percivale*.

At Ascension Island, the work began in earnest – the haste with which the Task Force had sailed made necessary a complete restow. This was a massive

operation, working flat out day and night with mexe floats and helicopters. Everything had to be put back into the ships in the reverse order for the assault – the plan for which was now taking shape. Lieutenant-Colonel Hellberg knew the size of the task that lay ahead:

'Initially I departed with just over half the regiment. I knew it was not enough, so pressed Brigadier Julian Thompson and General Jeremy Moore for the balance of the regiment, which eventually joined me in the South Atlantic on HMS *Intrepid*. The regiment was complete (less a small detachment on Ascension Island and a rear party back at home), on landing at San Carlos on 21 May.'

From Ascension, the Task Force sailed south. On *Sir Galahad*, a few days before the landings at San Carlos, Hellberg issued his orders. The regiment would set up a Beach Support Area (BSA) at Ajax Bay,

Left: At Wideawake Airfield on Ascension Island, the British and American flags fly side by side in the midst of an ammunition and supply dump. Far left: During the Ascension restow, a Wessex helicopter transfers stores onto the LSL *Sir Percivale*. At this stage of the operation, it was imperative that the logisticians loaded stores in the reverse order to that in which they would have to emerge when the assault force landed on the Falklands.

Page 45: Under the shadow of a folded-up Sea King helicopter, men of the Commando Logistic Regiment unload a consignment of high-explosive squash-head ammunition destined for one of the FV 101 Scorpion CVRTs. This photograph was taken onboard HMS *Fearless*, during the restow operation at Ascension. Below: A Sea King helicopter moves SAS troops from HMS *Hermes* to HMS *Intrepid* during the voyage down to the Falkland Islands. Below left, inset: Re-supply at sea (RAZZ), in the rough waters of the South Atlantic.

under the command of Captain Eddie Birch, the officer commanding Transport Troop. The BSA would be kept topped up with supplies from the LSLs, and the remainder of the staff would remain afloat in order to handle the business of re-supply.

Under the cover of darkness, the landing force entered San Carlos Water in line ahead. As the vessels passed the flashes of shells and red lines of tracer from the battle on Fanning Head, everyone went on deck to watch. Captain George later recalled the scene:

'Initially it was like a show – even the first Argentinian air attack a bit later on, which everyone watched out of curiosity. After this first attack though, the attitudes changed and there was a very fast shift into reality.'

On 24 May, three days after the landings, both *Sir Galahad* and *Sir Lancelot* were damaged by an Argentinian air raid. One bomb lodged in *Sir Galahad* without detonating, forcing the vessel to be evacuated.

The air raids, combined with the sinking of the *Atlantic Conveyor* on 25 May, provoked a radical change of plan. The balance of the Commando Logistic Regiment, together with its Headquarters Squadron, went into Ajax Bay. The regiment was soon reinforced by a defence company raised from the permanent staff of the Commando Training Centre at Lympstone, and a Blowpipe Troop. The defensive capability of the BSA was further augmented by 0.5in Browning machine guns, loaded with one-in-one tracer, and General Purpose Machine Guns on anti-aircraft mountings. Now that the majority of the regiment was ashore, the defence of the BSA was organised by the regimental second-in-command, Major Terry Knott, using Defence Company and all those in Workshop Squadron not actually engaged in the repair of equipment. The Medical Squadron, under the command of Surgeon Commander Rick Jolly, had set up a field hospital in a derelict meat-packing factory. To emphasise that the hospital was a joint red and green-beret facility, a large sign was painted over the door – 'The Red and Green Life Machine.' However, the Beach Support Area was now a prime target for the Argentinian Air Force. On 27 May, three enemy Skyhawks made their first deliberate attack on ground troops.

The aircraft concentrated their first bombing run on Blue Beach, near San Carlos Settlement. The second pass was directed at Ajax Bay itself. Using 1000lb parachute-retarded bombs, the Skyhawks scored two direct hits on the field hospital. Surgical teams dived for cover, only to emerge seconds later and continue working. A third bomb hit open ground 100yds in front of a small shell scrape in which Lieutenant-Colonel Hellberg, Major Jerry Wells-Coles (DQ of 3 Commando Brigade), and Regimental Sergeant-Major Graham George had squeezed for shelter. Two unexploded bombs were left suspended in the structure of the dressing station and were later cleared by Lieutenant Bernie Bruin, RN, affectionately known as 'Bernie the Bomb'.

That night, the weather was filthy. Massive piles of ammunition had been off-loaded onto the Beach Support Area in preparation for the forthcoming attack on Darwin and Goose Green, and one of these

SUPPLY ON DEMAND

The word logistics is derived for the Greek *logistikos*, meaning 'skilled in calculating', and attention to the provision, movement and supply of armed forces has become inextricably linked with the success, or failure, of strategic planning. This has always been known, and what Field Marshal Archibald Wavell referred to as the 'crux of generalship' has a long history.

One of the finest early examples of logistical planning was provided by the Duke of Marlborough, prior to the Battle of Blenheim in 1704. In the space of five weeks, Marlborough marched his 20,000-strong army from Cologne to the Danube to confront the French Army. It was as a direct result of Marlborough's careful attention to detail that his force covered the necessary 250 miles and arrived at Launsheim fit and ready to fight. The Duke had even taken the precaution of sending messengers ahead to Heidelberg, arranging the stockpiling of fresh shoes and saddlery for his army. Since these very early days, Marlborough's remarkable achievements have been adapted to the changing face of modern warfare. The logistical operations during World War II provide ample proof of this development.

In Burma, the Chindits received invaluable supplies via air-drops, enabling them to wreak havoc on Japanese lines of communication. Similarly, the Allies mounted an enormous re-supply operation to support the Chinese armies of General Chiang Kai-shek.

Logistics also played a crucial part in the Allied invasion of Normandy in June 1944. In particular, the 'Mulberry' harbours guaranteed the off-loading of supplies and men, making the Allies independent of port facilities.

Although the science of logisitics has long been practised, the example set by the Commando Logistic Regiment during the Falklands campaign of 1982 created new precedents for future military operations.

had exploded and was burning as a result of the air attack. This set off sympathetic explosions of 105mm artillery shells in widely separated dumps. The explosions continued to go off sporadically until 0500 hours the next morning. Captain George later described this ordeal:

'We felt very vulnerable surrounded by the huge piles of ammo. The work and the situation was very draining. We got twitched about any aircraft – even if only Argie photo-recce runs. We were a sitting target, but thankfully we were never hit again.'

Although the Browning machine guns had proved extremely effective in putting the Argentinian pilots off their aim, not all the threats came from the enemy. One rogue Blowpipe missile chased Padre David Leighton down a hill!

The regiment had been very lucky. In spite of heavy and accurate bombing – twelve 1000lb bombs had been dropped – only two men had been killed and five badly wounded. 45 Commando rear echelon was not as fortunate; six men were killed outright and many wounded when the command post suffered a direct hit.

While 3 Para and 45 Commando awaited the order to advance, the regiment worked hard. Due to the high intensity of the Argentinian air raids, most of the work had to be done at night. These raids, combined with the naval battle out to sea, had caused havoc with the logistical plan. Before land operations could even start, a reserve of daily combat supply rates (DCSRs) – enough to sustain the units for five days – had to be unloaded.

There were simply not enough jerry cans to get fuel to the Rapier missile sites

Colonel Hellberg, known as 'Chief Pudding' throughout 3 Commando Brigade, always attended Brigadier Julian Thompson's Orders ('O') Groups. Together with the artillery CO, Lieutenant-Colonel Mike Holroyd-Smith, he stood at the Brigadier's elbow:

'3 Commando Brigade's COs knew each other very well and could do business realistically. I always felt like the village spoil-sport at the Brigadier's 'O' Group. I had to frustrate many of the operational plans that were proposed throughout the war, as the supplies necessary to carry them out could not always be made available in the right place at the right time.'

Most nights, at around midnight, Hellberg boarded a Rigid Raider and went out to HMS *Fearless* as she returned to San Carlos Water from the safety of the open sea. These nocturnal meetings with Commodore Michael Clapp, the Commodore Amphibious Warfare, were held in order to determine which supply-carrying ships would return to San Carlos the next night for four hours' unloading of vital supplies.

Medical Squadron was set up and working at Ajax Bay, having been moved off the ships early. Casualties were already being casevaced in from the Unit Regimental Aid Posts. These were treated before being flown to the hospital ship *Uganda*. From here, the RFAs *Hydra*, *Hekla* and *Herald* ferried the wounded to Montevideo, Uruguay, where VC10s of the RAF's No.10 Squadron flew them to the United Kingdom.

Fuel soon became a serious problem. The helicopters used it up rapidly, and once the Harriers started operating from Port San Carlos, 50,000 gal-

lons were needed every 24 hours. There were simply not enough jerry cans to get fuel to the Rapier missile sites (whose generators drank it remorselessly), nor out to the units on the battlefield. Bulk handling had proved to be too vulnerable and inflexible – more jerry cans were needed. On Red Beach, Private Potter, Royal Army Ordnance Corps, ran the entire petroleum, oils and lubricants (POL) supply depot singlehandedly. Until the arrival of 81 Ordnance Company with 5 Infantry Brigade on 1/2 June, Potter was unrelieved for eight days. During this time, he worked tirelessly around the clock, occasionally asking his mates for help when he was really pushed – even then, only Potter knew how to operate the equipment. One of Potter's biggest problems was coping with the huge Air Portable Fuel Containers (APFCs) when the landing site was being used for casualties. The helicopters would occasionally deposit the APFCs onto the sides of a spur next to the POL depot, and then cast off. The massive, spongy black globes would roll ponderously

3 Commando Brigade Logistic Regiment
Falklands 1982

Key
- ▲ Beach Support Area
- ■ Forward Brigade Maintenance Areas
- ● Distribution Points
- --- Tracks

FALKLAND SOUND

EAST FALKLAND

Douglas

Port San Carlos

Fanning Head

Ajax Bay
San Carlos
Big Mt
Teal Inlet
Mt Simon
San Carlos Water
Mt Usborne
Estancia House
Mt Estancia
Wireless Ridge
Mt Kent
Two Sisters
Stanley
Wickham Heights
Bluff Cove
Mt Harriet
Fitzroy
Darwin
Goose Green
SOUTH ATLANTIC

LAFONIA
CHOISEUL SOUND

Far left: Onboard *Sir Lancelot* and heading towards battle, the men of the Commando Logistic Regiment and 45 Commando strike a confident victory pose for the camera. Lieutenant-Colonel Ivar Hellberg, the commanding officer of the regiment, is seen here in the bottom right of picture. On arrival at San Carlos Settlement (top left), the 'loggies' form a human chain to unload stores from two offshore LCMs. Below: Having collected ammunition from the Beach Support Area, two Wessex helicopters deliver their precious cargo to front-line artillery positions.

down the spur, gathering momentum and speed as Potter chased after them.

The battle for Darwin and Goose Green made even greater demands on the logistical system. Ammunition expenditure was very much higher than expected, particularly with regard to the artillery and mortar units. At this point, however, the helicopters came into their own. Flying casualties into Ajax Bay, they would land right next to the ammo dumps, thus enabling them to collect their return cargo of supplies with the minimum of delay.

At Ajax Bay, casualties took priority over everything. Captain George later recalled the waves of helicopters that arrived at the Medical Dressing Station (MDS) following the Bluff Cove tragedy on 8 June: 'It was like *MASH*. At the first sound of the helicopters, everyone drifted towards the MDS to help bring in these terribly wounded people.' As casualties were rushed from the heli pad, those without intravenous needles had them shoved into their arms in an effort to get vital fluid back into their system. White Flamazine cream – similar in consistency to shaving foam – was applied to seal, cool and sterilise the wounds. Once resuscitation and primary surgery had been administered at Ajax Bay, the casualties were flown out to the British hospital ship *Uganda* as soon as possible.

During the period immediately following Bluff Cove, enormous strains were placed on the Medical Squadron. However, Leading Technician Stewart McKinley had brought 300 units of blood with him from *Canberra*. It was blood that had been given by the British troops one week before landing, and for which investment some received an excellent return. McKinley was also responsible for the complicated and hazardous process of blood matching. He had no well-equipped laboratory – only a six-foot table on which he had to perform miracles. In spite of this, there were no mismatches. This would have

PRISONERS OF WAR

Following the battle at Goose Green, the Commando Logistic Regiment was informed that 1200 Argentinian prisoners were on their way to Ajax Bay. Captain Paddy George was convinced he had misheard. Nevertheless, the regiment built a concertina-wire cage, organised shelter at night inside the meat packing factory and gave the PWs compo rations. Captain George later described the scenes following an International Red Cross visit:

'They were not very satisfied, but they realised that the conditions of the PWs were significantly better than those of the regiment, who lived outside in slit trenches. They also asked the CO for a taxi and for directions to the nearest hotel!

'I was struck and heartened by the reactions of the soldiers and marines to the PWs. When Argentinian planes were shot down during raids, the men cheered and then threw nutty (confectionery) over the wire to the PWs.

'The Argies had apparently been told that Green Berets took no prisoners, so when they arrived they expected to be killed. Once they had been given hot food, warm shelter and nutty, they soon cheered up.'

Below right: After emergency treatment has been administered on the battlefield, stretcher bearers rush the wounded for casevacing to the 'Red and Green Life Machine' (inset right). After the tragedy at Bluff Cove, Flamazine cream was applied to seal the wounds (inset far right), and burned hands were placed in plastic bags to allow for the swelling. Top, far right: Surgeon Commander Rick Jolly was uncompromising in his insistence that Argentinian wounded should receive the same treatment as British troops. Centre top: Assembled in Fox Bay, Argentinian prisoners of war await their orders. Centre below: Using a field set provided by the Commando Logistic Regiment, the POWs are able to cook British Army compo rations. Left: A stockpile of Argentinian ammunition captured during the battle for Goose Green.

been an excellent record even under ideal conditions. The Medical Squadron's surgical teams never lost anyone who made it alive onto the tables at Ajax Bay. Out of 1025 men treated (one third of whom were Argentinians) including 310 major surgical operations, only three men subsequently died.

The arrival of 5 Infantry Brigade at San Carlos Water on 1/2 June had caused a huge problem, since the brigade came ashore with no cohesive logistic support. Nor did the unit have any transport – all the Chinooks, save one, had gone down with the *Atlantic Conveyor*. The Commando Logistic Regiment was therefore ordered to take on the re-supply of both brigades. In the space of one day, the 'loggies' went from looking after 4700 soldiers, to just over 9000.

When 3 Commando Brigade had moved forward into the area around Mount Kent, a Forward Brigade Maintenance Area (FBMA) had been set up at Teal Inlet, some 27 miles east of San Carlos Settlement. From here, a detachment from the Logistic Regiment would re-supply 3 Commando Brigade during its attack on Stanley. A Distribution Point (DP) was set up further forward, at Estancia House. Each night, the LSLs sailed around the north coast of East Falkland from San Carlos to Teal, bringing much-needed supplies and equipment. A second FBMA was moved southeast to Fitzroy in support of 5 Infantry Brigade, and a further DP was set up at Bluff Cove.

During the final battle for Stanley, vast amounts of material had to be brought up – artillery ammunition in particular. The daily supplies for both brigades

weighed 150,000kg, and a further 46,000kg of mortar and other ammunition also had to be shifted to the front line. Artillery batteries were capable of using five day's worth of ammunition in as many hours. After the success of the initial night attacks, ammunition stocks were therefore running very low. Waves of helicopters were forced to resort to daylight flying direct to the artillery gun-lines in order to keep the shells thumping into Argentinian positions.

Following the ceasefire on 14 June, the pressure on the regiment began to ease – for a short time at least. Embarked in the *Elk* ferry, the regiment sailed round to Stanley and set up camp in the offices of the Falkland Islands Company. The FBMAs were withdrawn, but the regiment continued to supply the troops around Stanley. Captain George later described the scene: 'It was like a film set, thousands of PWs and mounds and mounds of rifles and discarded equipment.' With over 11,000 Argentinian prisoners and 800 inhabitants to contend with, the regiment worked as hard as ever before.

Embarked on *Canberra*, 3 Commando Brigade pulled out first. The Commando Logistic Regiment was the last to leave, having become heavily involved in the cleaning up of Stanley. Tired and quiet, relieved and peaceful, the majority of the regiment boarded LSL *Sir Percivale* and sailed towards the airstrips of Ascension Island.

Operation Corporate had proved, beyond all doubt, the value of an integrated logistic unit, and the regiment's training schedule had passed the most exacting examination – that of battle. Captain Paddy George has his own conclusions:

'Don't quote me on this, but logistics is theoretically very easy – getting something from A to B. The problems are simple to solve but difficult to execute. The scale and quantity produces tremendous pressure … There are huge and spreading implications to everything.'

Where warfare is concerned, while the amateurs are discussing tactics, the real professionals are talking logistics.

THE AUTHOR Major Hugh McManners, as a captain, was one of the Naval Gunfire Forward Observers of 148 Commando Forward Observation Battery during the Falklands campaign of 1982. He is the author of *Falklands Commando*, recently published in paperback. Both author and publisher would like to thank Brigadier Ian Baxter, Colonel Ivar Hellberg, Surgeon Commander Rick Jolly and Major Paddy George for their invaluable help in the preparation of this article.

VALOUR AT ST NAZAIRE

52

HMS CAMPBELTOWN

With the success of the St Nazaire raid hinging on the destruction of the outer caisson of the *Normandie* dock, Combined Operations had to ensure that a sufficient explosive charge would be delivered right on target in a heavily defended area. The solution of ramming it home in the bow of a ship large enough to withstand the guns of the coastal defences was proposed by Captain J. Hughes-Hallett, the chief naval planner, and despite strong opposition to the idea he rightly insisted, 'No destroyer, no operation'.

The Royal Navy was unwilling to sacrifice a valuable ship, but eventually they supplied HMS *Campbeltown*, one of 50 old destroyers exchanged by the US for rights in the Caribbean. Since the approach to St Nazaire was to be over shallow water, the ship was stripped of heavy weapons and fittings, aiming for a draught of 10½ft. For protection against the coastal guns the bridge and deck were lightly armoured, and eight quick-firing cannon were installed. Her profile was altered so that, with a German ensign at her stern, she could gain valuable time on the run up to the port by posing as a German vessel.

Located in a concrete-encased steel tank in the bow was a time-bomb of 24 powerful depth-charges, containing four-and-a-quarter tons of high explosive, linked by a Cordtex fuze to an eight-hour-delay pencil fuze. It was calculated that the bow would crumple on impact up to the forward turret pillar, and the explosive was set behind it to blast directly against the dock caisson.

In late March 1942 a small task force of British Army commandos launched a surprise attack on the dry-dock at St Nazaire. Lieutenant-Colonel Stuart Chant-Sempill, who led a demolition team, recounts the story of one of the most daring and successful raids of the war

OPERATION CHARIOT, a daring assault on St Nazaire, has been described as 'the greatest raid of all', and the famous commando Lord Lovat, DSO, MC, wrote, 'It was the most spectacular seaborne raid carried out in World War II.' Some 619 officers and men of the Royal Navy, and British Army Commandos, went up France's Loire river on the morning of 28 March 1942 to smash the port's harbour complex. The mission was successful, but 159 were killed, 200 were wounded and captured, and of those who returned to England many were wounded.

By early 1942 the Allies had suffered very serious losses at sea: the US Pacific Fleet had been crippled at Pearl Harbor a few months before, the Royal Navy had lost the battle-cruisers HMS *Hood* off Iceland, and HMS *Repulse* and the new HMS *Prince of Wales* in the China Sea; German U-boats were sinking hundreds of thousands of tons of Allied shipping every month. The autumn before, the Royal Navy had only just managed to sink the *Bismarck*, a 56,000-ton monster ship, after a desperate chase and fight in the Atlantic. However, another huge ship, the *Tirpitz*, was lurking in Norwegian waters with the *Scheer* and *Lützow* pocket-battleships, waiting to attack Britain's weakened lifeline, then stretched to breaking point across the Atlantic.

If the *Tirpitz* and other powerful ships like the *Scharnhorst* and *Gneisenau* could break out into the Atlantic, the Allies were in danger of losing that battle, and with it the war. The Germans' main problem in the naval sphere was to reach the haven of St Nazaire, the port on the Atlantic coast of France that had the largest dry-dock in the world and was able to accommodate these large ships. St Nazaire was also far enough beyond the range of the RAF's bombers, such as Wellingtons, to be comparatively safe from air attack.

Lord Louis Mountbatten, then head of Combined Operations in Richmond Terrace, off Whitehall, was ordered to prepare an attack on the port from the sea. His planners, led by Captain John Hughes-Hallett RN, had to make do with limited forces: an old destroyer, HMS *Campbeltown*, two flotillas of Coastal Forces, equipped with 16 MLs (motor launches), a single motor gun boat, *MGB314*, and a fast motor torpedo boat, *MTB74*. The MLs were each armed with 20mm Oerlikon cannon, plus heavy machine guns, and four had torpedo tubes mounted on their bows. *Campbeltown* deserves special mention as it was destined to play an illustrious part in the operation. She was rearmed for the raid with eight 20mm Oerlikon quick-firing cannon, placed abaft the bridge structure on 'bandstands'. Her old torpedo tubes, situated aft, were removed to lighten her, and a quick-firing, high-angle 12-pounder gun was fitted on the foredeck of the ship. Two of her four funnels were removed, and the tops of the two remaining stacks were cut back and at a slant to make her look like a German Möwe-class destroyer.

Troops from the other Commandos were trained in the demolition of dockside installations

Of the Commando assault force, some of us had already seen action in France and Belgium, or Norway. In 1940, I had been evacuated from Bray Dunes, just north of Dunkirk, on 30 May. We were all original volunteers, drawn from every regiment and corps of the army, including guardsmen, highlanders, soldiers from several county regiments, sappers and cavalrymen, who had been training and on 'alerts' since the Commandos had been formed in 1940. The main assault force comprised some 200 officers and men from No. 2 Commando, and special demolition teams from No. 1, 2, 3, 4, 5, 6, 9 and 12 Commandos numbered another 90 volunteers, with a high proportion of 16 officers. The assault force was led by Lieutenant-Colonel Augustus Charles Newman. All of these men had been training especially hard since January 1942, but didn't know for what. The men of No. 2 Commando were trained in street-fighting at night, and the troops from the other Commandos were trained in the specialist demolition of dockside installations, caissons, bridges, cranes and pumphouses. Any casual snooper seeing groups of soldiers running about the docks of Burnt-island in Scotland, the Barry Docks at Cardiff, and then at Southampton must have wondered about the small brown-paper parcels that we carried about the docks, all of which had long lengths of string connecting the parcels one to the other. In fact, the packages were filled with sand to simulate special packs of

Left: British commandos in training for the St Nazaire raid of March 1942. Supported by fast motor boats (right), the assault teams had to destroy the gates of the port's *Normandie* basin (above right), the largest dry-dock in France.

Just two days before the small strike force of Operation Chariot sailed from Falmouth, Admiral Karl Dönitz, commander of Germany's U-boat arm, received a War Directive from Adolf Hitler concerning Allied attacks with limited objectives. Although St Nazaire was now the most heavily defended port on the Atlantic coast, he nevertheless subjected the garrison to renewed scrutiny.

Stationed on both sides of the Loire estuary were the 28 70mm, 150mm and 170mm guns of 280 Naval Artillery Battalion, with a battery of powerful 240mm railway-mounted guns at La Baule, seven miles from St Nazaire. These heavy weapons were supplemented by an entire brigade of anti-aircraft artillery. Three battalions were disposed in well-chosen sites in and around the port, and their 43 20mm, 37mm and 40mm guns were positioned to give effective fire against either air or sea attack. Many were fixed on the roofs of concrete blockhouses, making them virtually invulnerable to fire from water level. Lying in the harbour waters were four harbour defence boats, each provided with a range of armament. Also in St Nazaire on the night of the raid were 10 minesweepers, three tankers and nine U-boats, while at sea were the five destroyers of the 5th Torpedo Boat Destroyer Flotilla.

Altogether there were about 6000 German personnel in the area, including a brigade of 333 Infantry Division stationed some miles inland. The Germans were confident that an attack would be suicidal – the force might be able to get in but there was small chance of it ever getting out.

St Nazaire
March 1942

In the early morning of 28 March 1942 HMS *Campbeltown*, accompanied by a small force of motor launches, a gun boat and a torpedo boat, sailed into the Loire estuary towards the German-held port of St Nazaire. Their task was to destroy dock installations that could have made a crucial difference to the war in the Atlantic.

The flotilla rendezvoused with the submarine HMS *Sturgeon* late on 27 March off the French coast near the estuary of the Loire. At 2330 RAF bombers flew over St Nazaire in a decoy raid. The naval force remained unchallenged for some two hours, until German searchlights illuminated the leading vessel at around 0122.

At 0134 *Campbeltown* crashed into the dock gates and her commandos went into action. The 'greatest raid of all' was under way.

① Falmouth to St Nazaire

26 Mar 1400 The Operation Chariot naval force, with the commando assault and demolition teams on board, leaves Falmouth accompanied by the escort destroyers *Athelstone* and *Tynedale* and a lone RAF Hurricane.
27 Mar 0705 The flotilla adopts daylight anti-submarine sweep formation after an uneventful night, and turns eastwards towards the French coast. Soon afterwards, *Tynedale* investigates a vessel on the horizon. The vessel is a U-boat – *Tynedale* attacks and drives the submarine off.
2215 The flotilla reaches the rendezvous with HMS *Sturgeon*.
28 Mar 0122 German searchlights detect the leading vessel. A few minutes later, enemy coastal defences open fire.

The approach

plastic explosive, and the string represented Cordtex simultaneous detonating fuzes.

When we finally gathered together in Falmouth, we were smuggled on board HMS *Princess Josephine Charlotte*, which had just arrived from Scotland and was berthed alongside the docks. The *PJC*, as we called our new home, was a troop-carrier and we lived on the ship for the next few days, before being briefed and transhipped to the fleet of 16 MLs, the MGB, the MTB and *Campbeltown*, all of which had been skilfully distributed and hidden up the River Fal and in Falmouth docks. We sailed at 1400 hours on 26 March. It was calm and the weather was unusually warm, with no wind. We relaxed after the strain of preparations, briefings and discussions, which had taken our minds off what was to come.

At around midnight on 27 March, we met our rendezvous ship, the submarine HMS *Sturgeon*

I was on the *Campbeltown* with all the other men from No. 3, 4, 5, 6, 9 and 12 Commandos and my team from No. 1 Commando: Sergeants Butler, Chamberlain, Dockerill and King – four stout-hearted men from Norfolk and Suffolk. We sailed all that day and night, and into the next day, 27 March. We had reduced our speed from 12 to eight-and-a-half knots to reduce the risk of creating too much wash that might be seen by any German air patrols. There were odd scares, but nothing really to worry us. After 20 hours or so, we were way down into the Bay of Biscay, and at 0705 hours on the 27th, we slowly turned eastward and steamed all day towards the French coast.

Night fell, and we had our last meal, hot stew I seem to remember, and then settled down to wait as the sailors kept station and signalled quietly and

briefly to each other down the two columns of vessels. At 2015, we turned northeast towards the Loire. Lieutenant Tom Boyd in *ML160* and Lieutenant Irwin in *ML270* led the columns of seven MLs each. *MGB314*, the command ship, led the main party, followed by *Campbeltown*. Two more MLs brought up the rear and finally *MTB74*, made her own way to the objective so that her great speed could be handled with a necessary independence to allow her five engines to function in unison. At around midnight on 27 March, we met our rendezvous ship, the submarine HMS *Sturgeon*. We sailed close by her as she lay on the surface, flashing her recognition signal 'M' out to sea. She had been there all day, submerged and checking her bearings. The sea was flat calm, and we were 'spot on' in our reckoning and timing.

By 0100 hours on the 28th we had sailed ever closer to our objective, but were still undetected. Our decoy of some 60 RAF medium bombers had already alerted the German defences, and searchlights were sweeping the sky. There was light cloud, some say it rained a little, but I can't remember – I was too intent on the enemy. Whatever the facts, the RAF crews could not identify their targets and flew away as per their strict orders of the day, which forbade any bombing of targets in France unless they could be seen. However, the bombers had alerted the 90 or

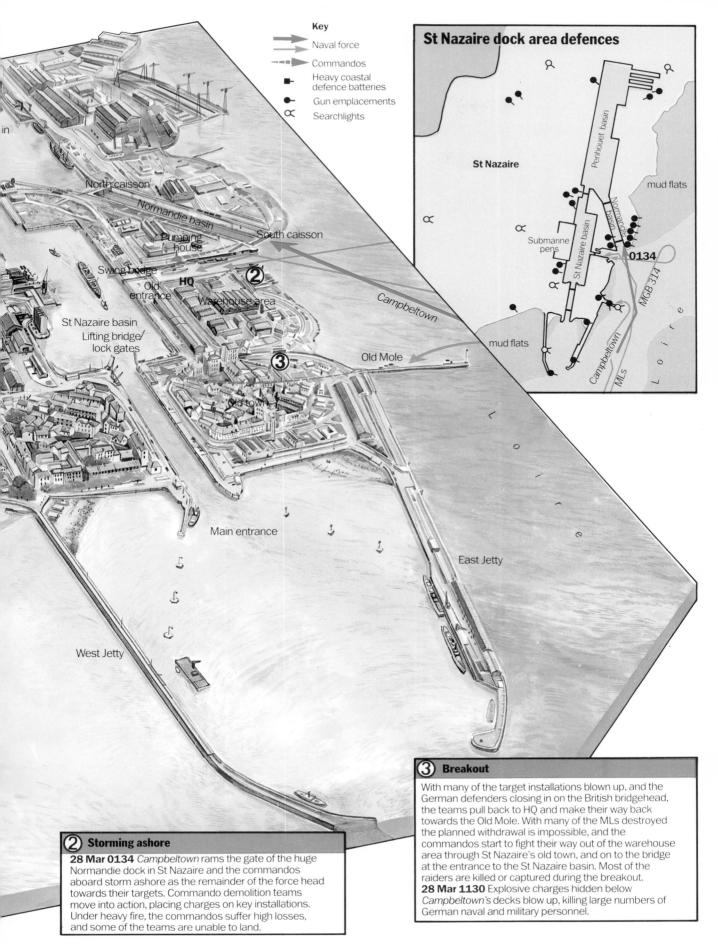

St Nazaire dock area defences

Key
→ Naval force
- - → Commandos
◼ Heavy coastal defence batteries
● Gun emplacements
✗ Searchlights

St Nazaire

Penhouet basin

mud flats

Normandie basin

0134

Submarine pens

St Nazaire basin

Campbeltown

MLs

MGB 314

Loire

mud flats

North caisson

Normandie basin

Pumping house

South caisson

Swing bridge

Old entrance

HQ

Warehouse area

Campbeltown

St Nazaire basin

Lifting bridge/ lock gates

Old Mole

Old town

Main entrance

East Jetty

Loire

West Jetty

② Storming ashore

28 Mar 0134 *Campbeltown* rams the gate of the huge Normandie dock in St Nazaire and the commandos aboard storm ashore as the remainder of the force head towards their targets. Commando demolition teams move into action, placing charges on key installations. Under heavy fire, the commandos suffer high losses, and some of the teams are unable to land.

③ Breakout

With many of the target installations blown up, and the German defenders closing in on the British bridgehead, the teams pull back to HQ and make their way back towards the Old Mole. With many of the MLs destroyed the planned withdrawal is impossible, and the commandos start to fight their way out of the warehouse area through St Nazaire's old town, and on to the bridge at the entrance to the St Nazaire basin. Most of the raiders are killed or captured during the breakout.
28 Mar 1130 Explosive charges hidden below *Campbeltown*'s decks blow up, killing large numbers of German naval and military personnel.

more heavy and medium guns around St Nazaire, the heaviest defences of any port on the Atlantic coast. Searchlights started, somewhat casually it seemed, to probe the dark waters of the Loire estuary and finally latched onto our leading vessel, Lieutenant-Commander Dunstan-Curtis's *MGB314*.

Our German-speaking signaller, F.G. Pike, flashed messages to the German defences that 'we were German vessels returning to port having been attacked by British forces out at sea'. There was a degree of hesitation and their lights were switched off. A few minutes later, however, they switched them on again and then uncertainly fired across our bows. Firing increased to a crescendo as all the guns opened up. Within minutes, the waters of the Loire were ablaze with light and flame. Almost immediately, we replied with a barrage so intense that the enemy fire faltered and almost stopped. We had some 40 Oerlikon 20mm cannon, 12 machine guns of all calibres, a quick-firing gun and a heavy pom-pom. Our reply was unexpected – but not for long.

We 'struck' our German flag, which we had flown ever since leaving Falmouth as a *ruse de guerre*, and replaced it with a very dirty and bedraggled White Ensign. All along the twin lines of MLs racing along astern of us, other White Ensigns fluttered to their mastheads. Battle was joined.

The clash was point-blank and casualties were immediate. In the words of Boyd, 'The weight of fire caught one's breath.' Colonel Newman on board *MGB314*, Commander Robert Ryder's flagship, said of *Campbeltown*, 'Her sides seemed to be alive with bursting shells'. The ship was taking heavy losses: we were on fire forward; one Oerlikon was already out of action and its gun-layer was dead, swinging in his harness. I was almost obliterated by a shell which

Army commando, St Nazaire March 1942

This sergeant, a member of one of the demolition parties, wears khaki battledress, scrubbed anklets and ammunition boots with thick rubber soles. Under his blouse, he wears a naval roll-neck sweater and a lifebelt, of which the inflation tube is just visible. Equipment consists of a rucksack filled with 60lb of explosives; large pouches contain grenades and ammunition for his Browning automatic pistol. Like most men on the operation, this NCO also carries a Fairburn-Sykes commando dagger.

Top: The key element of the action, HMS *Campbeltown*, its bow packed with high explosive, lies embedded in the dry-dock gates. The placing of the charges, a delicate affair, was overseen by a Royal Engineer, Captain Bill Pritchard (above left). Right, top and centre: German troops secure the waterfront; others watch over prisoners (right).

burst alongside me where I lay on the deck. I was only wounded, twice in my right arm, once in my left leg, and peppered with shrapnel splinters all down my legs and in my face. The coxswain on the bridge of the *Campbeltown* was killed at the wheel, and another sailor who took his place was also killed. Then Lieutenant Nigel Tibbets, DSC, RN, our demolition expert, took his place, only to hand over the wheel to Commander Stephen 'Sam' Beattie, VC, RN, who steered his ship to its target.

Despite severe casualties, fire and damage, the *Campbeltown* increased its speed to over 20 knots. The ship crashed into the gate at 0134 hours, four minutes later than planned and some 35 hours after sailing from Falmouth. In the words of Ryder, who covered our approach from *MGB314*, Beattie's role 'shines as a hallmark and principal achievement of the expedition. I can think of no other case where so much depended on the unfaltering seamanship in action of one man'.

Other vessels were not so fortunate. The smaller craft in particular suffered dreadful losses. Only seven survived the sea fight out of the 18 that had sailed from Falmouth. Of others more is to be told, but meanwhile on board the *Campbeltown*, those of us who had survived were struggling to disembark and proceed to our objectives in the dockyard of St Nazaire. Despite the hot reception, the entire demolition element on board the *Campeltown* had survived. Slowly and methodically, we left the ship as it lay embedded in the gate, lying at an angle of some 25 degrees out of the flood tide of the Loire estuary. Many of us were wounded, but somehow we slid down the 18ft ladders that had been dropped over the side of the ship onto the caisson of the dry dock, which was over 160ft wide.

I and my four sergeants made for the pumphouse, each one of us carrying 60lb of explosives

We, in the demolition teams, were preceded by Captain Donald Roy, DSO, (No. 2 Commando) and his assault team, who raced to the pumphouse, climbed to its rooftop, blew up the battery, and killed the crew before racing to other enemy positions to do likewise. Protected by Lieutenant 'Hoppy' Hopwood, MC, (No. 2 Commando), we followed and ran quickly, or hopped in my case, to the two winding stations, the further dry-dock inner caisson and other installations. I and my four sergeants made for the pumphouse, each one of us carrying a rucksack containing 60lb of explosive. However, we ran into an unforeseen obstacle: the large steel doors of the pumphouse were shut tight, unlike those at Southampton which had always been left open in case of air raids. But Captain William 'Bob' Montgomery, MC, a Royal Engineer in the Special Service Brigade and second-in-command of the demolition teams, slapped a magnetic explosive charge on the lock and blew the doors open.

The pumphouse was immense and we had to find our way in the dark, down 40ft into the chamber below where the pumps were standing. Sergeant Chamberlain, who was wounded in the legs, was left to guard our rear at the top of the stairs, and slowly but steadily we climbed down to the huge impeller pumps. There were four of them, plus smaller ones, all connected by long, steel drive-shafts to the electric motors 40ft above, on the ground floor. We worked as quickly as possible in the half light of our waist-torches. I took over the task of laying some 40lb of plastic explosive on the moulded castings of No. 3 pump, while Dockerill, Butler and King laid similar charges on the other three. We also slapped charges on the four smaller ancillary pumps which were all part of the system that could fill or empty the dock in a matter of a few hours.

After 20 minutes, we had prepared the whole for destruction. Joining all the charges to large ring-mains of Cordtex, we were ready to 'blow'. Sending Butler and King up ahead, I waited with Dockerill until the other two shouted that they had got back up to the top of the stairs. Then, counting three, Dockerill and I squeezed the 'pins' of our two detonators and slowly but steadily climbed the stairs. We had 90 seconds or so in which to make the doors leading out into the docks. We took 60 seconds to climb the stairs, the longest minute I can ever remember. We somehow made it and collapsed outside, gasping in the cool night air. Almost immediately there was a shattering explosion, and bricks and dust fell all around us. We had done the trick: when we re-entered the pumphouse, we saw the electric motors lying at grotesque angles, and some of the floor had fallen in. The explosion was greater than we had anticipated and was heard on the Hunt-class destroyers HMS *Atherstone* and HMS *Tynedale* waiting out at sea to cover our withdrawal. The crew of HMS *Sturgeon*, by then withdrawing towards Brest in the north, also heard the noise of the shattering explosion of the pumphouse.

After furious fighting, the area was cleared and the charges were left hanging over the dockside

Meanwhile, the other demolition teams had already achieved varying degrees of success. Lieutenant Christopher 'Chris' Smalley and his party destroyed No. 1 winding station, Lieutenant Corran Purdon likewise destroyed No. 2 winding station, but only after a second attempt, for his first charges did not explode. At the other end of the dry-dock, 400yds away, Lieutenant Robert Burtenshaw and his team ran into a group of enemy soldiers. After furious fighting, the gate area was cleared and the charges were left hanging over the dock side and caisson into the water of the Penhouet basin opposite the U-boat pens. The two teams sustained several casualties during this demolition and at one time had to withdraw back from the caisson. But, finally, Sergeant Frank Carr, DCM, and a sapper of No. 5 Commando, who proved to be a cool, calm character, went back and checked the charges right across the length of the caisson, a distance of 164ft. Carr then pressed his igniter. There was a muffled roar and the water churned, indicating that the charges had been successfully 'blown' below the water.

However, our losses were heavy. Burtenshaw was wounded several times and eventually killed, Lieutenants William Etches and Gerard Brett were both wounded, and more than half of the demolition teams were killed at the far end of the dock. But their combined efforts had rendered the dock totally useless. However, the damage sustained by the MLs was also devastating. The German defences stiffened as the fighting grew fiercer, and their overwhelming firepower at point-blank range smashed the flimsy hulls of the vessels. Many sailors and commandos were killed and, worse, many were drowned in the waters of the Loire, covered as it was by blazing petrol from ruptured fuel tanks. Desperate and courageous efforts were made by the Royal

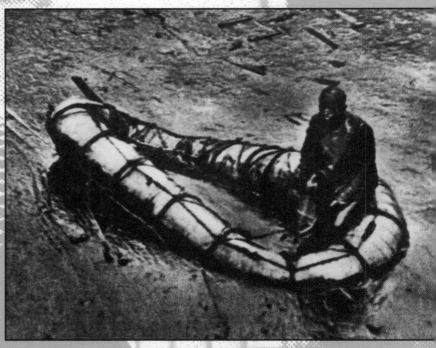

Navy to bring their vessels alongside the docks, particularly alongside the Old Mole jetty which stuck out into the Loire. But even when they actually drew alongside, the MLs were hit, caught fire and blew up.

Lance-Corporal Luis Eric de la Torre (No. 3 Commando) took to a life-raft after his vessel was hit and remembered the tragedy out on the Loire:

'The scene on the river was so confused . . . everywhere you looked there were heads bobbing in the water, and there was burning oil all over the place. We had a wounded officer lying across the raft. Then somebody shouted, "Look out, there's a patch of burning oil ahead", and we all started swimming, trying desperately to push the raft out of the way. Then, a voice suddenly started up, coming out of the darkness. He was singing "Oh God our help in ages past".'

Those few who had survived the terrible fire of the German guns and had made it ashore, joined up with those of us who had landed from the *Campbeltown*, and we made our way to the RV, where Colonel Newman was waiting with his small HQ force. Cheerfully, he told us to collect and wait until everyone had been accounted for. Almost immediately, however, Major W.O. 'Bill' Copeland, DSO, the second-in-command of the Commando forces, said to Newman, 'Good God Charles, look at the river!' It was full of burning MLs.

What were we to do? We were virtually surrounded by the enemy; we could hear them calling to each other and see bursts of smallarms fire as they closed in on our position in the middle of some railway trucks alongside the waters of the river. There was, however, complete calm and an almost cheerful atmosphere as we were told by Copeland, 'This is where we walk home.' We turned our backs on the scene and started to fight our way through the docks towards the town, with the intention of escaping south towards Spain, some 600 miles away. So confident were we that we never thought otherwise! But I was shot in my right knee and fell. Sergeant Butler, MM, (No. 5 Commando) and Private Jimmy Brown, MM, carried me a short distance, but I told them to leave me. I was shortly joined by a young soldier of No. 2 Commando. An hour passed and we lay in the shadow of a large warehouse. Suddenly, three Germans in steel helmets and black uniforms appeared out of the night – it was by then about 0300 hours. They shouted at us and, as the young comman-

Above left: One of the survivors of the gun-boat flotilla, his body covered in oil, waits to be taken captive on the morning after the raid. After trading shot for shot with the port's defences, eight of the force's 18 small support craft were sunk. Onshore, once the Germans had secured the dock area, prisoners were interrogated (left). However, the secret of the *Campbeltown* was never revealed and at 1130 hours on the 28th the ship exploded, smashing the gates of the dry-dock. Above: An aerial photograph taken several weeks after the operation shows the dock sealed off by a massive sand embankment, the twisted wreckage of the gates and the bowless *Campbeltown*.

do beside me stood up, they shot him at a yard's range. After shouting again, they dragged me into a small cafe, and there I was, a prisoner of war. As dawn broke, I was carted off to hospital in La Baule, a few miles north of St Nazaire.

But the raid was not over. At 1130, as the Germans swarmed all over the docks, and particularly the wreck of the *Campbeltown*, she exploded with a tremendous roar. Over four tons of Ammanol blasting powder hidden below her decks exploded and cut through her hull and into the caisson, blowing her off the sill and into the giant dock, which was then holding two large cargo ships. There were reported to be over 60 German officers and 340 soldiers and sailors on her at the time. They were all killed and blown to pieces. The mess was horrible, and small pieces of German bodies hung from the wreck of the pumphouse and the other buildings nearby. No-one lived who was in the wrecked ship, but there were hundreds of others who had been on the *Campbeltown*, but left the ship before the explosion. The German admiral commanding at St Nazaire was one.

Seven MLs and Curtis's *MGB314* escaped from the inferno of the Loire. Of these vessels, three MLs made their way far out to sea and then sailed home on a voyage of non-stop drama, including aerial attacks from the Luftwaffe. They shot down one plane and arrived off the coast of Cornwall with a few gallons of fuel left in their tanks.

The effects of the raid took a long time to assess. At first, the Germans claimed that we had failed and then spread the story all over the world. They also made a great fuss and play with the destruction of the MLs, and displayed photographs of wrecks found drifting in the waters of the Loire. One particular photograph of a kilted Scottish soldier sitting on the ground in the docks, his face swathed in bloody

HEROES OF ST NAZAIRE

From first to last, Operation Chariot was marked by bravery and determination of a high order. Each commando, already a volunteer for special service, had been warned by Lord Mountbatten, Chief of Combined Operations, 'We are writing you off', yet not one responded to the invitation to stand down. In the face of battle they showed great courage, and their effort and sacrifice was recognised by the awarding of a wealth of decorations which in normal circumstances would have been quite disproportionate to such a small force.

No less than five Victoria Crosses were awarded, and the citations were careful to express a debt not only to the individuals who received them, but also to the men alongside whom they fought. The captain of *Campbeltown*, Lieutenant Commander S.H. Beattie (right, top), received the VC in tribute to his seamanship and also to 'a very gallant ship's company'. Sergeant T.F. Durrant (right, centre top), who had been wounded many times and was finally killed while attempting to defend his Motor Launch against the German destroyer *Jaguar*, received a posthumous VC. His award was actually recommended to the force commander, then a prisoner of war, by a German officer who had witnessed his tenacity. The commanders of both the commando and the naval forces, Lieutenant-Colonel C. Newman (right, centre) and Commander R.E.D. Ryder (right, centre below) were awarded the VC in recognition of the perseverence shown by both them and their men under fire. Finally, Able Seaman W. Savage (right, bottom) was awarded a posthumous VC for silencing every gun aboard a harbour defence boat, including its 88mm gun, with the pom-pom mounted on his motor gun boat, before meeting his death later in the battle. His medal was dedicated 'also for the valour shown by many others' of coastal forces. In their great achievement, the named and unnamed heroes of St Nazaire gave new courage to Occupied France.

bandages, was shown to illustrate the heavy casualties we had suffered. He did, in fact, die from his wounds a few days later; he was Private John McCormack of the Cameron Highlanders and No. 2 Commando.

However, aerial photographs taken by the RAF in the months that followed the raid showed that the dry-dock was being purposely silted up to protect and contain the waters of the Penhouet basin and the U-boat pens. Stories of the delayed explosions of the *Campbeltown* and of 'Micky' Wynn's time-fuzed torpedoes filtered through the French Resistance to Whitehall. Finally, when I was repatriated from Germany at the end of 1943 as a *Grand Blessé*, I was the first officer to be released who had actually taken part in the fighting and destruction of the main target, the dry-dock, before being captured.

After the destruction of the dry-dock at St Nazaire, no German capital ship ever ventured into the Atlantic again

Five commandos (four were wounded) walked away from St Nazaire and got to Spain and back home. Later, there were several audacious and great escapes. A sailor, Lieutenant Commander 'Billy' Stevens, DSC, walked out of Colditz with the famous Airey Neave. A party of commandos led by Sergeant 'Dick' Bradley, MM, Sergeant Alf Searson, MM, (both of No. 2 Commando) and Private Jimmy Brown walked out of a camp in Poland and escaped.

To emphasise the importance of the destruction of the dry-dock and the effect it had on the German Kriegsmarine, no German capital ship ever ventured into the Atlantic again. The battleship *Tirpitz* was finally sunk by the RAF. Battle-cruisers, like the *Scharnhorst* and *Gneisenau*, the pocket-battleships *Lützow* and *Scheer*, and heavy-cruisers like the *Hipper* and the *Prinz Eugen*, all avoided the challenge waiting for them from the ships of the Royal Navy and the United States Navy. So, the casualties suffered by us were a small price to pay for helping to 'bottle up' the enemy's ships.

THE AUTHOR Lieutenant-Colonel Stuart Chant-Sempill, OBE, MC, (below, arm bandaged), served with No. 5 Commando during the St Nazaire raid and was awarded the Military Cross for his part in the action. His personal account of the operation, *St Nazaire Commando*, is published by John Murray.

RADFAN
RECCE TROOP

45 Commando arrived in Aden on St George's Day, 23 April 1960, having seen action at Suez in 1956, followed by two operational tours in Cyprus. In July 1961 the unit was deployed to Kuwait, in response to a threatened invasion of the oil-rich state by General Kassim of Iraq. Within three weeks, 45 Commando, together with a considerable British force that included Royal Marines from 42 Commando, had helped to restore order.

In January 1964, 45 Commando was embarked on the aircraft carrier HMS *Centaur* and sent 1500 miles south to Tanganyika (Tanzania), where the army had revolted. For the marines, this was to be action in their traditional commando role – order was restored within a matter of weeks and the unit returned to its base in Aden.

In April 1964, 45 Commando was reinforced to a group strength of 1500 men, in preparation for operations against rebel tribesmen in the Radfan area, 70 miles north of Aden. The rebels, unlike most of the British troops who spent a maximum of one year in Aden, knew the Radfan like the backs of their hands. Armed with their superior knowledge of the terrain, the tribesmen could set up carefully concealed ambushes and sniping positions, open fire, and then fade into the mountainous surroundings before British reinforcements arrived.

Up to 30 May 1967, 45 Commando had completed 13 operational tours in the Radfan.

One year earlier, Britain had announced its intention to hand over sovereignty to the Federation of South Arabia (FSA) and leave Aden. The Royal Marines of 45 Commando were thus well aware that their days in the tortuous and bleak mountains were numbered. The last of the British forces left Aden on 29 November 1967, with few regrets.

In May 1967, when rebel tribesmen ambushed a sapper convoy in the Radfan, the Royal Marines of Recce Troop, 45 Commando, were airlifted into the area with lightning speed

'SCRAMBLE THE STAND-BY TROOP' came the cry to the Royal Marines of Recce Troop, 45 Commando, as they were washing up their breakfast plates at Khormaksar Camp in Aden. Marine Morgan looked at his watch... the time was 0835 on Tuesday, 30 May 1967. They would be relieved of their 'Stand-by Troop' duties at midday, having been at 15 minutes' notice for the previous 24 hours, and Morgan had planned to play soccer at the main unit camp at Little Aden that afternoon. With the urgent shout from his troop sergeant, however, he wondered whether they would be back in time from whatever emergency this might be... or perhaps it was just another exercise. The dry Aden heat was beginning to make itself felt. As usual, the sky was scrupulously clear and the insects were just beginning to buzz around the 'gash bin' where the left-over food was thrown.

Morgan and the other marines, most of them stripped to the waist after their early morning wash and shave, quickly got themselves ready. Their Bergen rucksacks, which most preferred to the 1944 pattern packs, were already filled with a selection of clothing, rations and ammunition that might be required in the event of a long operation. For the moment, however, the marines had no idea where and for what they were being scrambled.

This was what 45 Commando had been practising for during their long months of fighting in the Radfan

Lieutenant Terry Knott, who commanded Recce Troop, despatched an NCO and three marines in the Scout helicopter, which was already warming up, to act as an airborne emergency picket. He then dashed over to the command post, collecting his gear and Armalite rifle on the way, for a briefing that consisted of little more than the incident and its location. In the background, the monotonous whine of the unit Sioux helicopter was joined by the deeper tones of an armed Scout. Both aircraft were ready for the lift and in the Sioux could be seen the considerable figure of Second-Lieutenant John Meardon, the Forward Air Controller (FAC), whilst alongside him was the pilot, Lieutenant Ian Uzzell, another Royal Marines officer. They knew their territory well, and the Dhala Road in particular. In their minds they were conjuring up a picture of the area in which the incident had occurred. The early morning sun was still fairly low in the east, and they decided to exploit this line of approach.

Lieutenant Knott, still reeling from his swift briefing that had lasted only two minutes, raced across to the Wessex helicopter that had already embarked the remaining marines of his troop. Within five minutes of an up-country ambush being radioed to the unit command post, a composite fighting force was on its way. As the marines became airborne, their radio crackled with more information concerning the present emergency. This was what 45 Commando had been practising for during their long months of fighting in the Radfan area of Aden. The response time was encouraging, and one marine who had been blissfully enjoying his daily

motion, had grabbed his trousers, his kit and his wits to make it to the helicopter with time to spare.

High in the rocky outcrops above the 39th milestone on the Dhala Road, Mohammed bin Zubeidi was feeling well satisfied with his morning's work. He relished the prospect of a little more action as the adrenalin of an early morning success continued to race through his body. He and his 27 tribesmen had been planning this ambush for many weeks. Their information had been filtering in from various sources, particularly from local Adeni workers who were employed in the British Camp at Habilayn, where 'Fort Knox' was the hub of the defences; and also from Commando Camp at Dhala, where marines of 45 Commando had been in almost continuous occupation for seven years. Zubeidi, who had been constantly observing the road for the past week, knew that the Royal Engineers had been doing repair work on the winding road leading south to

Aden, nearly 40 miles away. He reckoned the British would need some heavy plant to complete their job, and this would require the type of convoy that Zubeidi was determined to ambush.

He chose his positions as carefully as he had done his men. They were all veterans of the mountains, and although the British had achieved a measure of success against his marauding band, Zubeidi still

Page 61: Combat exercise. Supported by a third marine carrying a General Purpose Machine Gun (GPMG), two marines from 45 Commando race over the rugged, inhospitable terrain of the Radfan. Despite the intense heat of the Aden climate, regular patrols (left) were vital if British forces were to limit the supply of arms and ammunition that were reaching the dissidents via the Yemen. The use of observation posts and snipers (top left) complemented these patrols and enabled the commandos and paras to set ambushes of their own.
Above: Marines man a 7.62mm GPMG, capable of 200 rounds per minute in the sustained-fire role.

In contrast to the barren hills and rock-strewn gulleys of the Radfan, the area immediately west of the town of Aden comprises a wide expanse of desert known as the sand sea. Using Land Rovers, commando patrols scoured this area and intercepted Arabs running arms and ammunition to the National Liberation Front (NLF). Below: Members of Recce Troop scan the terrain for signs of enemy infiltration. The undersides of the Land Rover have been strengthened with armour plating as protection against the land mines employed by the insurgents in Aden. A variety of equipment would be carried in the vehicle, including rations for 10 days, an infra-red driving aid, helicopter lifting straps and personal weapons for the four-man team.

had a group of trusted and highly trained Arabs about him. They were well armed, with many of their weapons stolen from the bodies of British servicemen they had killed during the preceding months.

After settling into their ambush positions during the moonless Aden night, they had laid their defence using the expertise they had learned at a training camp over the border in the Yemen. As the sun rose slowly, they edged silently and carefully into positions from which they could overlook the narrowest part of the road. But that morning, they had an unexpected bonus when a NAAFI truck came into view around the corner where they lay in wait.

Knott, sitting in the rear of the Wessex, spread out the map on his lap. Listening on the Unit Command Net, he started to piece together the information he had been given. It appeared that a convoy of 39 Field Squadron, Royal Engineers, on its way south from Habilayn, had come under fire close to the dreaded 39th milestone where the Wadi Bilah meets the Wadi Matlah. This area was infamous as one of the most hazardous sections of the notorious Dhala Road – the dusty track narrowed as it wound its way through the valley, and the steep rocky outcrops on either side almost obscured the sun. The morning convoy – consisting of a Saracen armoured car, several Land Rovers and lorries, a tipper and other pieces of heavy engineering plant – had rounded a corner on the tortuous Dhala Road to find the way blocked by a barricade of full beer crates. The Saracen commander had done this trip many times before, but had always dreaded the prospect of an ambush. However, his training had prepared him for this eventuality.

As the convoy came to a halt, it was met by a

fusilade of smallarms fire. The Saracen was hit by a Blindicide rocket, and, as the crew clambered out, two soldiers were shot dead. The gunner, still in his vehicle, returned the fire but was soon hit and wounded, whilst the driver managed to scramble out and take cover amongst the jagged rocks. A Land Rover, hit by smallarms fire, veered off the road and crashed into a ditch. The crew escaped with a few scratches and returned fire in the general direction of their attackers. The noise was horrific in the confined space, and the smoke and dust clouds caused by bullets ripping into the sand around the sappers obscured most of their view. All the advantage lay with the ambushers, skilfully concealed in the rocky outcrops high above the beleaguered convoy.

The enemy were on the high ground to the north and northwest of the 39th milestone

When a grader tried to reverse out of the ambush position, it was hit by another Blindicide and the driver thrown out. The sappers in the following vehicles quickly left their charges and took up defensive positions. They returned the enemy fire blindly. The convoy commander, Second-Lieutenant Conroy, was in the second part of the convoy, some three miles further behind. He came forward to investigate, but almost immediately came under fire and was pinned down.

Lieutenant Knott also learned that earlier that morning a NAAFI truck, on its way north to Habilayn, had been stopped by a number of rebel dissidents and threatened, hence the unusual but effective

adblock. Although Knott's small Recce Troop was
[th]e immediate reaction force, he heard over the
[wi]reless net that already on the road from Habilayn
[w]ere two armoured cars, followed by the reserve
[tr]oop, 7 Troop of Z Company, commanded by his
[gr]eat friend Lieutenant Bob Sankey. In the air, the
[R]oyal Air Force (RAF) had scrambled two Hunters
[fr]om Khormaksar. These were over the target area
[wi]thin three minutes, and their first strike went in at
[09]00 – only 27 minutes after the balloon had gone up.
It was clear from reports on the ground – relayed
[fr]om the ambushed Royal Engineers, through their
[ow]n headquarters at Sapper Camp, and thence to 45
[C]ommando's command post via their defence com-
[p]any at Fort Knox – that the enemy were on the high
[gr]ound to the north and northwest of the 39th mile-
[st]one.

The daring of the RAF pilots resulted in a direct hit and at least one enemy casualty

[Th]e FAC, Second-Lieutenant Meardon, airborne
[in] the Sioux, quickly identified the area where the
[di]ssidents were concealed and brought a Hunter
[st]rike in with devastating effect. It is the art of the
[ai]rborne FAC to be able to identify the enemy and
[br]ief the fighter pilot well out of the latter's sight of the

45 Commando Radfan, May 1967

In January 1964 British and South Arabian Federation troops began operations in the Radfan, a rugged mountainous area to the north of Aden. A poor region, the only source of regular income to the inhabitants of the area was protection money paid by traffic travelling along the road from Dhala to Aden. This challenge to the authority of the South Arabian Federation was met by armed force; and the expedition of 1964 captured an important stronghold of the Radfan tribesmen, the Wadi Misrah, in June. The tribesmen, although defeated, were not beaten. They continued to intercept traffic along the Dhala road, and the British forces in the Federation were forced to conduct constant operations against them. On 30 May 1967, a group of tribesmen attacked a NAAFI truck and a Royal Engineers' convoy at Milestone 39 on the Dhala road. The Royal Marines of 45 Commando's Recce Troop, who were on stand-by at the main British base at Khormaksar, were rushed by helicopter to the scene of the ambush.

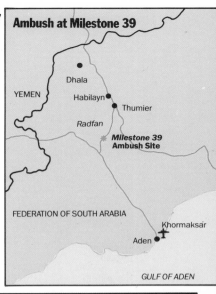

Ambush at Milestone 39

YEMEN
Dhala
Habilayn
Thumier
Radfan
Milestone 39 Ambush Site
FEDERATION OF SOUTH ARABIA
Khormaksar
Aden
GULF OF ADEN

Rebel retreat

0945 The Recce Troop comes under heavy fire from the rebel positions. Despite this, they begin their sweep of the hills above the Dhala road.
1005 7 Troop, Z Company arrives by road with two armoured cars and occupies the cleared area. Y Company also arrives from Habilayn by helicopter and assists the Recce Troop in clearing the ridge.
1138 Serious opposition from the rebels ends. Three of the tribesmen have been killed and several wounded.

Airstrike

0900 The RAF Hunters are directed by the Forward Air Controller on to the rebel positions. These are raked by rockets and 30mm Aden cannon and at least one tribesman is hit. Shortly afterwards, further strikes go in.
0945 The Recce Troop lands to the rebels' left.

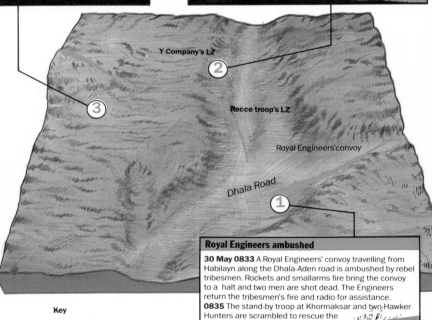

Y Company's LZ
②
③
Recce troop's LZ
Royal Engineers' convoy
Dhala Road
①

Royal Engineers ambushed

30 May 0833 A Royal Engineers' convoy travelling from Habilayn along the Dhala-Aden road is ambushed by rebel tribesmen. Rockets and smallarms fire bring the convoy to a halt and two men are shot dead. The Engineers return the tribesmen's fire and radio for assistance.
0835 The stand-by troop at Khormaksar and two Hawker Hunters are scrambled to rescue the Royal Engineers.

Key
Rebel positions
Royal Marines' advance
Retreat of rebels

Left: A convoy advances into the arid hinterland of the Radfan. Using combined-arms tactics the British security forces proved themselves equal to the determined guerrillas, in spite of the unfavourable mountainous conditions. Cordons and aggressive patrolling by brigade-sized units were often employed, taking full advantage of air support from helicopters and strike aircraft.

target, so that, pulling up steeply at the last moment, the fighter pilot can instantly recognise his target and bring the full force of his rockets and cannon to bear on the enemy. Meardon had practised many times with the RAF and he knew the pilots well. In turn, they recognised his descriptive skills and had every confidence in his ability. The first strike, on a cave situated underneath the overhang of a steep-sided rock formation, was an almost impossible target. Yet the daring of the RAF pilots resulted in a direct hit and at least one enemy casualty. But the pilots could not see the success of their attack, for as they pulled up into the clear air an enormous cloud obscured

The two main nationalist groups that dominated the insurgent effort were the National Liberation Front (NLF) and the Front for the Liberation of Occupied South Yemen (FLOSY). Those dissidents who were captured alive were sent to the town of Aden and interrogated by the intelligence officers before being handed over to the civilian authorities. Here, in the dangerous backstreets of the town, the terrorists employed a variety of methods to undermine the power of the Federal Government of Aden. The first of these methods was to intimidate the local population and security forces using propaganda, death threats against 'collaborators' and the murder of selected individuals. In the alleys of Crater, to the south, terrorists mingled freely with the various ethnic groups, making the task of patrolling the area extremely hazardous. The British Army therefore came to adopt a 90-minute limit for men on patrol. The last 60 minutes of daylight in Aden became known as 'Happy Hour' due to the surge in terrorist activity that occurred during this time. Secondly, by carrying out attacks on the Special Branch and Police Force, the terrorists sought to neutralise the army's intelligence sources. A third method was the use of strikes and demonstrations to cripple the Aden economy. Demonstrations were often exploited by the dissidents, who used the diversion to lure the security forces into 'killing zones'. To combat these tactics the security forces in the town of Aden – never more than two brigades – employed road blocks, aggressive patrolling, cordons, searches and radio-linked observation posts.

their view. Another strike followed soon after, and the pilots were reassured by Meardon that they had done a good job.

However, the bravery of the dissident tribesmen could never be underestimated, and although the Sioux continued its search for more targets at a height of some 1500ft, the helicopter was eventually hit by smallarms fire and forced to limp back to base. Its role was taken over by a Scout from 13 Flight, Army Air Corps, piloted by Captain R.E. Matthews of the Duke of Edinburgh's Royal Regiment. Matthews had already picked up Meardon, and the FAC continued to direct the Hunters. Salvo upon salvo of rockets ripped into the rebel positions and the air was filled with flying rocks and clouds of dust. Recce Troop, in their Scout and Wessex helicopters, continued to orbit the area of Jebel Lahmahr, the highest point of the enemy positions, with Lieutenant Knott finalising his plan and selecting his line of approach. On completion of the air strikes at about 0945, Lieutenant Knott used the settling dust clouds as partial cover and cautiously approached his selected landing area. It was clear from fire being directed at it, that he had chosen the middle of an enemy position. It is an echoing feature of this rocky, arid landscape that it is difficult for anyone on the ground to pinpoint the direction of approaching helicopters using only their sound as a guide. Recce Troop exploited this fact by coming in as low as possible, the helicopters hugging the outcrops and lifting only at the last moment to deposit their load at the chosen landing site.

Leaving his marines to cover him, Knott crawled up the steep outcrop to one side of the cave

The Wessex hovered over the landing point but could get no lower than 10 to 12ft above it. Knott ordered his men to jump, prepared to risk injury for the sake of speed. As they hit the jagged and precipitous rocks, the marines came under heavy fire, not only from the enemy in whose midst they had landed, but also from other rebel positions high in the outcrops of Jebel Lahmahr. One dissident was killed as the 15 marines moved into a steep gulley to avoid the withering fire. As they gathered themselves, the leading marine drew Knott's attention to a small cave 20yds away. Even as they were watching, a rebel emerged from the cave and fired two rounds from an automatic rifle at Knott at almost point-blank range. He returned the fire and the dissident withdrew into the cave. Leaving his marines to cover him, Knott crawled up the steep outcrop to one side of the cave. He took out an American M26 grenade. Recce Troop preferred this to the Mills 36 grenade which tended to break up on impact with rocks – the M26, with its tin casing, had more of a blast effect. Knott pitched the grenade into the cave, but, astonishingly, it was picked up by the dissident and thrown back at him. Avoiding the blast, Knott jumped down from the rocks and charged into the cave, shooting the rebel dead.

Recce Troop continued to sweep up the hill to the main enemy position, while 7 Troop, who had arrived by road, occupied the cleared area. It was still only 1005 hours. The acting commanding officer, Major

Alan Jukes, who had arrived over the scene by helicopter, realised that the enemy positions were larger than his immediate reaction force could deal with. He therefore alerted Major Ted Carroll's Y Company, who left Habilayn by Wessex helicopter with one section of 3in mortars. A 105mm gun was also moved into the Wadi Matlah by road. Y Company landed on the 800ft ridge and scoured the area for enemy, just after another Hunter strike went in. But, as so often happened in these skirmishes, the rebels had simply disappeared into the rugged hinterland. By 1138 all serious opposition on the high ground had ceased. But it was not until 1450 that the whole ridge had been searched and cleared. Signs of recent occupation and blood trails were apparent as well as equipment and food that had been abandoned by the rebels. Only now did the full extent of the British sapper casualties become known. Two had been killed and 10 wounded, all being evacuated by Scout helicopters to Aden. Three rebels had been killed and it was later reported that a further two had died and many others wounded. Ironically the rifle that was recovered from one of the dead dissidents, and which had been fired at Lieutenant Knott, was an SLR taken from Gunner Cane of the Royal Horse Artillery. Cane had been killed in a helicopter crash in December 1966.

There was no doubt that this had been a well sited and executed ambush, possibly sprung a little early before the main convoy had time to reach the 39th

Above right: Lieutenant Knott (right of picture) leads a 45 Commando patrol through the Wadi Dhupson hillside of the Radfan. Right: British equipment, recaptured during Recce Troop's assault on Zubeidi's guerrillas above the Dhala Road.

milestone. Once again, it demonstrated the resourcefulness of the Radfan rebel tribesmen. However, it was also a superb example of the prompt action that a well-trained quick-reaction force was capable of. Recce Troop, containing a number of marines who had not seen action before 30 May, could be proud of its performance.

For his outstanding example of courage and leadership, Lieutenant Terry Knott was awarded the Military Cross, and the citation adds that his coolness and judgement under continuous heavy fire inspired his troop. His determination had effected the relief of the wounded sappers, all of whom later recovered. Marine Morgan missed his football match that afternoon, but he had the satisfaction of knowing that his side won both the morning and the afternoon 'skirmishes'.

THE AUTHOR Captain Derek Oakley, MBE, served with the Royal Marine Commandos in Malaya, Hong Kong, the Middle East, Northern Ireland, Brunei and Borneo. He recently retired as the editor of *The Globe and Laurel*, the journal of the Royal Marines.

Below left: As a Recce Troop vehicle winds up the Dhala Road, marines (below) conduct an up-country patrol, laden with ammunition and supplies. Bottom: An RAF Hunter strike in the Wadi Dhupson area.

Supporting US Special Forces units in Vietnam, the Air Commandos had a vital role in the early stages of the war against the Viet Cong

FEW OF THE professional, combat-wise airmen of the Western world would question the dedication, expertise and legendary accomplishments of the American Air Commandos in the early years of the Vietnam War. Skilfully flying ageing World War II aircraft, the pilots of this small, relatively unknown unit laid the foundations of the sophisticated USAF Special Operations Wing of today, and presented their modern successors with an enviable military heritage. Deceptively casual in appearance, they were a tight-knit, dependable and thoroughly organised body of men. For the US Air Force, they constituted an important bridge between the American flyers in the Southeast Asia of World War II and the superb US Special Operations airmen of the 1980s.

The public image of the original Air Commandos was formed, not by their actual performance, but by a popular comic strip by Milton Caniff called 'Terry and the Pirates', which was supposedly based on the exploits of the Commandos. In the cartoon, Terry was one of a band of devil-may-care airmen who led romantic, dangerous lives battling the Japanese, and its flamboyant leader, Colonel 'Flip Corkin', was advertised to represent Colonel Phil Cochran, com-

manding officer of the Air Commandos. There was, however, little in common with the American newspaper cartoon and the reality. Cochran was more interested in competence than romance, and his pilots were selected from the most experienced and dedicated group of professionals in the USAAF, the flight instructors.

The rebirth of the unit in 1961 came about under the rather lacklustre title of the 4400th Combat Crew Training Squadron (CCTS), nicknamed 'Jungle Jim', and it was not until 1962 that the expanded unit was redesignated the First Air Commando Group. The aircraft that they possessed made them seem virtually a reincarnation of the first Air Commandos, for they were operating C-47s and light aircraft, this time L-19s instead of L-1s. B-26 bombers with nose armament had replaced the B-25s and the P-51 Mustangs of the original unit were replaced by the armed version of the T-28 Trojan, a US training aircraft which had first been used in the combat role by the French in Algeria. There were no gliders and, initially, no helicopters.

Just as the aircraft lined up at Hurlburt Field in Florida resembled those of Cochran's World War II unit, the squadron's personnel seemed a throw-back as well. In the spring of 1961, Colonel Ben King began to prepare the 4400th for deployment to Southeast Asia, and he selected his volunteers in much the same way that Cochran had done, picking only the most skilled professionals. Again, the chosen pilots were required to carry out staff functions, preventing the unit from becoming administratively top-heavy

THE AIR COMMANDOS

The first Air Commandos were raised in 1943 to support Major-General Orde C. Wingate's 1944 Burma offensive, in which his 'Chindits' were to be inserted far behind Japanese lines in some of the most inaccessible areas of the Burmese jungle. The Commandos were to provide Wingate's transportation, reconnaissance, supply and heavy firepower. All of this was accomplished with about 270 aircraft.

The unit's commander, Colonel Phil Cochran, shared with Wingate a belief that the air element in Burma could be much more than a supporting arm. Their theory was that, once the Chindits had been air transported to a location that would attract enemy forces, the air arm would not only provide the wherewithal to supply the ground element, it would also use its firepower to destroy the enemy. Cochran was determined to bring this concept to life, and he created a small, efficient staff, often tasking his pilots with administration in order to ensure that the planning took full advantage of operational capabilities. He relied on innovation, putting multiple 0.5in machine guns in the nose of his Mitchell bombers, staging the first combat use of helicopters, and developing novel glider pick-up techniques. The Air Commandos served Wingate's Chindits well, establishing traditions that were to be renewed by their successors some 18 years later in 1961.
Above: The badge of the First Air Commando Group. the successors of the original Air Commandos, in Vietnam.

AIR
COMMANDOS

DOUGLAS A-1 SKYRAIDER

Having lost the US Navy's competition to find a successor for their excellent Douglas SBD Dauntless dive bomber, the design team at Douglas El Segundo division, led by Ed Heinemann, began work on a radical new design. After an extraordinary effort by the whole division, the prototype flew on 18 March 1945, a mere nine months from the decision to begin again from scratch. Capable of an impressive 375mph at medium altitude and a climb of 3680ft per minute, the Skyraider was to become a very popular machine. One reason was that Heinemann had extensively researched the needs of carrier-based pilots and had incorporated many of their preferences into the design. The plane was robustly built with a large, comfortable cockpit and generous internal space, largely due to the fact that all ordnance was carried externally on 15 pylons. A ruthless simplification of design also significantly reduced the aircraft's fuelling, arming and maintenance times. Arriving too late for World War II, the Skyraider did not immediately go into large-scale production, but orders increased as the US Navy realised its virtues and within four years 22 variants were in service. Production ended in 1957 with 3180 aircraft completed.

With the advent of the Vietnam War, the Skyraider proved itself the best close ground support aircraft that the Americans possessed. It could lift huge payloads and remain over the target area for long periods of time, and its control at slow speeds made it ideal for counter-insurgency warfare in densely forested terrain. The Navy Department even considered reopening the Skyraider assembly line, but the cost was found to be prohibitively high.

Below left: Jack Salyards of the 1st Air Commando Squadron at Pleiku in Vietnam and (page 68, top) in the cockpit of his Douglas A-1 Skyraider. By the mid-1960s the slow, piston-engined Skyraider had often proved itself more effective as a ground-attack aircraft over jungle than its jet-propelled rivals. Left: A Skyraider seeks opportunity targets, while (page 68, bottom) an A-1 drops napalm. In the earliest days of their involvement in Vietnam the Air Commandos operated T-28 Trojan armed trainers (page 68, centre) and World War II B-26 Marauders (page 69) which were rebuilt and reclassified as the Douglas AC-26K Invader.

and ensuring that operational skill was being injected into the planning and development of the unit.

The Air Commandos of the 1960s were fewer in number than their World War II predecessors, trained in a different manner and intended for a different mission. Initially equipped with 16 C-47s, eight B-26s and eight T-28s, they were to liaise with Third World air forces, teaching them tactics and techniques suitable for counter-insurgency campaigns. The crews spent long hours training in languages, survival and escape skills, and they also began to adopt techniques designed to cope with the growing insurgency in Vietnam. In late 1961, as the 4400th CCTS rounded out their training, the South Vietnamese Air Force began to be overwhelmed by the increasing success of the Viet Cong (VC). Equipped with ageing F-8 Bearcats, C-47s, armed T-6 Texans and three squadrons of L-19 light aircraft, the Vietnamese force could not keep up with the growing requests for emergency air supply, and the pilots were not sufficiently competent to fly close air support when they were most needed, at night. Consequently, the communists were able to block the roads and seize control of village after village.

In November 1961, Colonel King and the first contingent of the Air Commandos brought eight T-28s, four C-47s and four B-26s to Vietnam, where the aircraft were given Vietnamese markings. The Air Commandos' tasks were to train Vietnamese airmen and perform combat missions, the latter only when the Vietnamese could not carry them out on their own, and only when at least one Vietnamese airman was aboard the aircraft. However, such was the intense pressure from the Viet Cong in late 1961 and early 1962 that King could not commit his men to training missions alone – the 4400th were obliged to assume a direct role in the war.

In 1962 the American and Vietnamese strategy was to wrest control of as many villages as possible from the Viet Cong. US Special Forces personnel were inserted into the Vietnamese Central Highlands, each 12-man detachment attempting to establish a network of up to 30 armed villages amongst the primitive Montagnard tribes in the mountainous jungle. As this programme started to succeed, the VC began a concerted effort to destroy the small units of American Green Berets. The attacks invariably came at night and were almost always executed by company-sized units of the VC using an assault wave supported by mortars and machine guns. Special Forces detachment commanders quickly learned to call on the Air Commandos to help them survive the night attacks.

In the late summer of 1962, I had the opportunity to see the Air Commandos exercising their skills at close range. The assault came without warning at

Above: The Douglas A-1 Skyraider has the record number of 15 ordnance pylons. Top: Air Commando Skyraiders are bombed up at Bien Hoa airbase in Vietnam.

about midnight, preceded by a rain of mortar shells. My Special Forces soldiers and diminuitive Mnoung tribesmen managed to beat off the first wave of VC infantry, and I dived for the radio to call up air support. As we waited for the sound of the aircraft engines, the enemy began to probe our village defences, looking for weaknesses, and we were beginning to lose control of one corner when an Air Commando C-47 roared over the mountain tops.

Each defended village in the mountains had a 12ft 'fire arrow', designed to be easily visible from the air and usually constructed of bamboo with a wooden stake as a pivot. We quickly lit gasoline cans fixed to the edges of the arrow and pointed it at the enemy clustered to the east of the village. The C-47 pulled up to 3000ft, then slowly began dropping 750,000-candlepower flares, two at a time: the parachute flares drifted down and the village and surrounding jungle were bathed in an eerie light. As two Martin B-26 Marauders darted into the valley and began circling our beleaguered camp, we used our radio contact with the C-47 'flareship'. We explained the situation on the ground, giving the estimated position

of the VC mortars. Behind the controls of the leading B-26, First Lieutenant Bob Dutton rolled in on the first run. Two 500lb bombs silenced both the VC anti-aircraft fire and the mortar attack. When the smallarms fire died down, the three Air Commando aircraft flew in lazy orbits over what was left of our camp, ready to resume the argument. Over the next few hours the C-47 occasionally dropped further flares, but when dawn broke the VC were nowhere to be seen.

The Air Commandos flew some 45,000 sorties in 1962 and lost four of their aircraft. One B-26 and a T-28 fell to ground fire. A C-47 was shot down while dropping leaflets during a psychological-warfare mission. The fourth loss was an L-28, a single-engine light reconnaissance aircraft, which was brought down while Montagnards and a Special Forces detachment attacked a VC stronghold. The detachment's commander, Captain Terry Cordell, died in the crash. Despite these losses, 1962 was a successful year for the Commandos. Techniques were being

Below left: A C-47 lies shattered after a successful Viet Cong mortar attack. Bottom left: The 4th Air Commando Squadron lines up in front of a 'Spooky' AC-47 gunship. Below: The three miniguns of an Air Commando gunship unleash a storm of fire. Bottom right: A customised Air Commando jeep, bearing the sawn-off heads of three bombs.

eveloped that helped deny the VC their nightly rains, and in the last months of 1962, Saigon's control f the countryside began to grow.

The South Vietnamese situation had improved, not nly through the Air Commandos' night activities, ut also because they had the capacity to supply the emote positions and outposts which the VC were ttempting to isolate with their road-cutting cam aign. In 1961, only 15 of the 176 airstrips in South

ietnam had control towers and were considered to e secure. The Commandos' first task, therefore, vas to open up a line of air communications to the reviously closed, remote airfields. Meanwhile, day fter day, the Commandos supplied isolated South ietnamese and Special Forces units, flying over 'C-occupied road nets and landing on short, bumpy irt strips with ammunition, food and fuel. During 962 and 1963, the Commandos flew 77,000 tons of

supplies and airdropped some 4000 tons more, effectively defeating the VC 'strangulation strategy'. Although this ability to supply the remote regions was important logistically, the greater impact was psychological. Able to count on American backing, the South Vietnamese forces gained confidence in their ability to survive and succeed against the VC.

An example of the kind of support Saigon's ground elements could expect from these US airmen occurred on the night of 20/21 July 1963. Captain Warren Tomsett was flying a C-47 flareship mission in the Mekong Delta when he was alerted to a grim and desperate situation developing 100 miles to the north at the abandoned French rubber plantation of Loc Ninh. Located on the northern edge of the infamous War Zone C, very near the Cambodian border, the American Special Forces camp at Loc Ninh had come under a strong VC attack. The enemy effort had started several days before with an ambush that had killed two Special Forces officers. The remaining Americans and their Cambodian irregulars had defeated the first VC assault in the early hours of the night, but six Cambodians were critically wounded and near death. The young Special Forces lieutenant in charge had requested an air evacuation, despite the fact that the camp was still receiving fire. Captain Tomsett completed his flare run and hurried his aircraft northwards.

Ramming the throttles forward, Tomsett pulled his ageing aircraft towards the moon

Arriving over Loc Ninh, he gained radio contact and was informed that the small airstrip would be outlined by blazing petrol-soaked rolls of toilet paper impaled on stakes. The Special Forces troopers burst out of their defensive perimeter in the darkness and set up a hail of fire, at the same time planting and lighting their improvised torches. Swooping downwards, Tomsett gauged from the 60ft rubber trees lining the pock-marked runway that he was approaching too high and too fast. Ramming the throttles forward, Tomsett pulled his ageing aircraft towards the moon and began to set up his second approach. Slamming down hard, he stamped on the brakes and pivoted the old transport sharply to avoid the massive trees at the end of the runway.

The six wounded Cambodians were placed in the C-47, accompanied by a Special Forces medic. Tomsett thrust the throttles forward, saw muzzle flashes on the side of the strip, and suddenly all of the lights on the instrument panel went out. His co-pilot quickly shone his flashlight on the instruments as the C-47 lurched forward and, gathering speed, the loaded plane sped down the runway. Barely clearing the tall rubber trees, Tomsett set his course for the nearest medical base. The word of this exploit spread throughout South Vietnam. It was this sort of courage and unflagging American support that inspired the South Vietnamese to continue their fight against the VC.

The Air Commandos lost twice as many aircraft in 1963 than in the previous year. Nine planes had been shot down. For example, in February of that year, Major Jim O'Neill's B-26 had been crippled by ground fire while he was supporting a hamlet under attack. O'Neill tried to get the bomber back to his base at Bien Hoa but he began losing altitude. He ordered his crew to bale out and held enough height to ensure their safe exit, but he failed to gain enough time for himself. The B-26 crashed with O'Neill still at

A DIMINISHING ROLE

In 1961, just as the Air Commandos were arriving in Vietnam, Secretary of Defense Robert MacNamara approved the deployment of one C-123 Provider squadron to that country. The C-123 could lift 16,000lb of cargo, 5000lb more than the C-47 could get off the ground. It could handle a shorter and rougher airstrip, and experience showed that it possessed a remarkable ability to absorb punishment – one of them was hit 47 times in May 1962, yet its mission availability was unaffected. Based on a glider design, the C-123 had rear ramp access that could accommodate vehicles and artillery pieces that were beyond the carrying capacity of the Air Commandos' C-47s. With such advantages, it is little wonder that the C-123 Providers were soon taking the lion's share of the US airlifting effort. The Air Commandos' share was further diminished by the arrival of the US Army's own twin-engine C7A Caribou companies, which began to take over some of their air-supply missions to the Special Forces camps.

Although the South Vietnamese C-47s were now being used more efficiently, thanks to an odd group of USAF trainer pilots nicknamed the 'Dirty Thirty', the Air Commandos' task gradually passed to the growing number of C-123 units, which were codenamed the 'Mule Train'.

Commandos was the lack of volunteers. The war w[as] changing, and with the introduction of jet atta[ck] aircraft into the Vietnam conflict in 1964 the lure [of] adventure in the Commando 'air museum' was wa[n]ing. By late 1963, half of the pilots were not voluntee[rs] and there seemed little need for such a specialis[t] force in the growing Vietnam conflict. The aircr[aft] were also suffering from the years of hard flying, a[nd] by late 1963 the Commandos were maintaining onl[y a] 59 per cent aircraft availability rate, primarily due [to] their austere, 150-man organisation. The USA[F] cured that problem by adding more maintenan[ce] personnel in 1964, but by then most of the

Left: A-1 Skyraiders roar ov[er] Vietnam. The flight contain[ed] both single-seat and two-se[at] versions and the latter may well have served as trainin[g] aircraft for South Vietnames[e] pilots. While the Air Commandos' A-1s were lan[d] based, the US Navy and US Marine Corps fielded hundreds of them from aircraft carriers lying in the South China Sea.

the controls.

The Air Commandos' increased losses were a reflection of their stepped-up level of activity. They flew some 56,000 sorties in 1963 and; together with the growing South Vietnamese Air Force, they were credited with inflicting some 13,000 casualties on the enemy. Their success did not go unnoticed in Hanoi.

In the autumn of 1963, the Hanoi Politburo despatched a 13-man assessment team southward to carry out an inspection tour of VC units. In December their leader, Colonel Bui Tin, reported to Hanoi that the VC were losing the war, citing the Saigon regime's growing control of the countryside. In response, the Politburo decided to shift to the mobile warfare phase of Mao Tse-Tung's protracted war concept, organising the North Vietnamese regulars and VC units into regiments and division-sized formations wherever possible. The 'Big Unit' era of the war was about to begin.

In Saigon, meanwhile, the Americans were unaware of the coming shift away from the enemy's guerrilla tactics. However, changes were already taking place in the organisation of US airpower in Vietnam, for its commitments had grown at such a rapid pace that it was no longer practical to rely on a small volunteer force. Moreover, the Air Commandos' aircraft were steadily nearing obsolescence, and the USAF was alarmed by a growing number of accidents with the B-26. The Commandos were literally flying the wings off the World War II light bombers, and while most of the crashes occurred at the Air Commandos' Florida training base, some happened in the war zone. The USAF decided to switch to the Douglas Skyraider, which could carry about the same bomb load as the B-26, but had up to nine hours of loiter time. Armed with four 20mm cannon, the Skyraider was a good choice, but the Air Commandos went into limbo during the transition.

Another aspect of the diminishing role of the Air

transport sorties, training of Vietnamese pilots, a[nd] close air support missions were being performed [by] other USAF and US Army organisations. The w[ar] simply outgrew the capacity of the Air Command[os.] Before they were eclipsed by events, however, t[he] Air Commandos made a notable contribution to [the] firepower in Vietnam, the fixed-wing gunship, and became the most effective weapons system on t[he] Ho Chi Minh Trail.

Created to instruct the air elements of Third Wo[rld] states, the Air Commandos' most important contrib[u]tion to the Vietnam War turned out to be the traini[ng] of American aircrews. Although they did much wo[rk] in the developing nations of Africa and Latin Am[er]ica, the concepts behind their foundation we[re] inadequate in the context of the large-scale confl[ict] in Vietnam where, in some ways, the Air Comma[n]dos fell victim to their initial success. Together w[ith] the US Special Forces, they had been instrumental [in] persuading the North Vietnamese leadership [to] change strategy in 1963. Hanoi had perceived th[at] the American and South Vietnamese counter-[in]surgency effort was gaining ground, and had there[fore] proceeded to stand-up battles with regu[lar] forces, a strategy which ultimately succeeded.

THE AUTHOR Colonel Rod Paschall served six years [in] Laos, Vietnam and Cambodia during the Seco[nd] Indochina War. Afterwards, he was the Delta For[ce] commander.

In the war against the rebels in Algeria, intelligence played a key role, and while the Commandos de Chasse gathered information on the ground (bottom), observation aircraft (right) were crucial for the reconnaissance of more inaccessible areas.

MOUNTAIN LIONS

When General Maurice Challe assumed operational control in Algeria, he took the war to the enemy with a new unit – the Commandos de Chasse

THERE IS AN OLD Arab proverb that states that 'the mountain lion must be hunted with the mountain lion.' Today, this maxim has become firmly entrenched in the tactical doctrine of any security force engaged in operations against guerrillas. Special forces, familiar with the tactics and operational methods of the guerrilla fighter, have become stock-in-trade to armed forces the world over, and experience has shown that to defeat such an adversary men must be trained to take the war to the enemy and fight him at his own game.

When General Maurice Challe of the French Air Force assumed command of operations against the elusive guerrillas of the National Liberation Front (FLN) in Algeria in December 1958, he found himself in charge of an army weary of five years of an entrenched war and demoralised by the ineffectual strategy of the French high command and its continuing lack of success in the field. When Challe arrived in Algeria he found two very different types of soldier under his command. First, he had the paras and legionnaires of the 'general reserve' – highly disciplined, professional and well-armed troops who also had helicopters at their disposal for rapid deployment. The remainder of his command was made up of 'sector' troops – young conscripts with only six months training behind them, who were led by inexperienced officers. The sector troops were tasked with the routine military grind of protecting strategic points, opening up roads, escorting convoys and the 'pacification' of the civilian population. They were not organised for war or the active pursuit of the enemy and their control of the terrain was largely illusory: the FLN political cadres moved freely among the people and FLN military units were able to operate at night and sometimes even in broad daylight without being intercepted.

The paras and legionnaires, the cutting edge of the French military effort and a very effective fighting force, were hampered by their lack of knowledge of the local situation, and major offensive operations, mounted hours or even days after a sighting of the enemy, invariably resulted in a failure to make contact.

All were infused with a fresh spirit and a renewed determination to get to grips with the enemy

Challe was quick to see the problem and realised that to break the stalemate he would need to introduce a new strategy. To his fresh eye, the solution to the problem was very simple: intelligence. The sector troops deployed through the country were in a perfect position to gather the necessary information and such a new assignment would strengthen their flagging morale and give them a more active role in the war against the FLN. The old strategy of sealing off an area and then combing it thoroughly – dull, foot-slogging work with very little to show for the effort at the end of the day – was to be abandoned. New units would be formed to implement a new approach and to bridge the gap between the paras and the legionnaires, with their tireless spirit of attack, and the weary foot-sloggers tied up in the

boring and fruitless duties of passive defence. Thus came into being the Commandos de Chasse – Challe's 'mountain lions'.

Notice of the formation of the Commandos de Chasse was posted to all units in early 1959 and the news of Challe's decision was greeted with great enthusiasm in every quarter. Even though few men were actually to serve in the new units, all were infused with a fresh spirit and a renewed determination to get to grips with the enemy. The Commandos were formed as small units of about 60 men of which two-thirds were young native Algerians or Arab volunteers, known as *harkis*, many of whom had come over from the FLN and had no desire whatever to renew contact with their erstwhile colleagues in arms, unless backed by French military might. Most of the European element of the new units was made up of young conscripts, men who volunteered for the Commandos to get away from the static, day-to-day routine of their bases and who were looking for 'action and adventure' in the field. Being a member of a Commando put them one cut above their comrades in the more ordinary companies and a definite 'Commando style' was encouraged. This served to foster an esprit de corps and helped to smooth over any racial or religious tensions that might otherwise have marred a unit of such mixed ethnic origins. The commandos also had their own distinctive style of dress – a camouflage cap was worn during operations in the field while a black beret was worn back at base. But the most important symbol of their elevated station was that they always carried an American M8 knife, so as to be armed even when drinking a beer or a soda in the canteen!

Below: General Maurice Challe (right) formed the Commandos de Chasse as part of a more aggressive strategy in Algeria. The ranks of the Commandos (right) included a high proportion of native Algerians. Right, above: Commandos examine the corpse of a rebel soldier after a successful skirmish. Far right, above: An intelligence officer questions an Algerian villager.

AA52 LMG

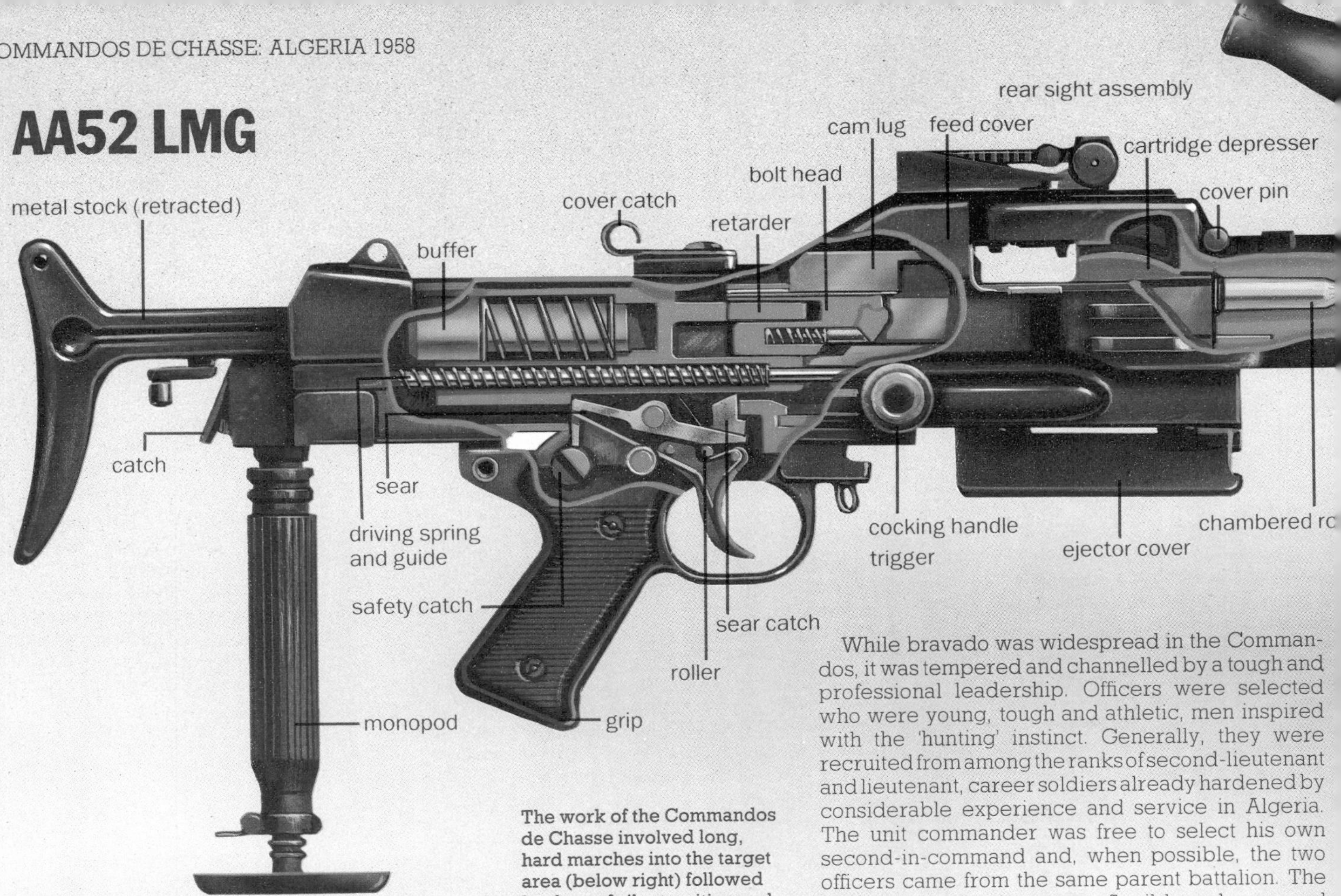

- metal stock (retracted)
- buffer
- cover catch
- retarder
- cam lug
- bolt head
- feed cover
- rear sight assembly
- cartridge depresser
- cover pin
- catch
- sear
- driving spring and guide
- safety catch
- sear catch
- roller
- grip
- cocking handle
- trigger
- ejector cover
- chambered ro
- monopod

The work of the Commandos de Chasse involved long, hard marches into the target area (below right) followed by days of silent waiting and watching (left). While many of their patrols drew a blank, when they did spot an enemy force on the move they would call in the paras and legionnaires of the 'general reserve' to deal the enemy a devastating blow.

While bravado was widespread in the Commandos, it was tempered and channelled by a tough and professional leadership. Officers were selected who were young, tough and athletic, men inspired with the 'hunting' instinct. Generally, they were recruited from among the ranks of second-lieutenant and lieutenant, career soldiers already hardened by considerable experience and service in Algeria. The unit commander was free to select his own second-in-command and, when possible, the two officers came from the same parent battalion. The structure of the unit was very flexible and command of the smaller component groups of a Commando always went to the best soldier, whether a European or a native Algerian.

The unit CO also had to sort out the question of weapons and equipment for his Commando. He would try and swap his four or five M1924/29 light machine guns for AA 52s, despite the fact that the increased rate of fire on the AA 52 meant carrying extra ammunition belts during operations. Most important, however, was communications equipment and the CO would do his best to get his hands on the

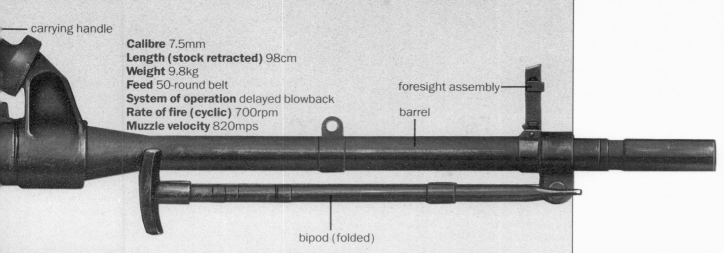

— carrying handle

Calibre 7.5mm
Length (stock retracted) 98cm
Weight 9.8kg
Feed 50-round belt
System of operation delayed blowback
Rate of fire (cyclic) 700rpm
Muzzle velocity 820mps

foresight assembly —

barrel

bipod (folded)

NPRC 10 radio, a lighter and more powerful piece of kit than the antiquated American SCR 300s left over from World War II and the war in Indochina.

Commandos operating in rebel-contested areas often adopted local dress – the Algerian shepherd's *jellabah*, a thick woollen garment with a large hood that could be pulled down to cover the face. Thus attired, they were able to pass themselves off as rebels and sometimes they even went so far as to wear the FLN insignia – a green and white rectangle with red crescent and star – to further the deception.

Out in the field, the Commandos de Chasse also adopted enemy operational methods: small, lightly equipped units would march for several days on a packet of army biscuits, a few onions and lemons and a can of sardines, drinking from wadis and stagnant pools and sleeping rough among the rocks.

Before setting out on an operation, the Commandos would be briefed by the battalion staff officer on the area they would be going into. The intelligence officer would give them what details he could, based on informers' reports and information gleaned from the interrogation of prisoners. The unit would then move out.

Secrecy was essential. The Commandos always went into a hostile rebel zone at night and on foot, and usually made a wide detour around the area between their base and the target. Security was further enhanced by the fact that only the commander and his second-in-command knew the point where the unit would lie up before the sun came up.

The long night approaches were physically strenuous and extremely nerve-racking – there was always the danger of an enemy ambush and the troops had to be alert at all times. Navigation in the dark and over the rough terrain was also very difficult and experienced commanders would lead their men as much by instinct as by military training. The whole object of the stealthy approach was to establish several camouflaged observation dug-outs, linked by radio. There was only one basic rule: to be in position and completely camouflaged before daybreak.

With the first streaks of dawn light, the long vigil began. In the observation dug-outs the men remained silent and motionless – smoking and talking were strictly forbidden, but the men not engaged in direct observation were permitted to read, and *livres de poche* ('pocket' paperbacks) were extremely popular. Long, endless waiting was the very stuff of the commandos' life, for they were the 'eyes and ears' of the barren mountains. If nothing was spotted on the first day, the Commando would often move to a new position during the following night, which involved a hazardous and arduous march and the construction of new look-out positions. Many missions, on the face of it, seemed a waste of time but even though the Commando might not have located a

AA 52 MACHINE GUN

The Arme Automatique Transformable Mle 1952 (AA 52) is designed for use as both a light and heavy machine gun. In the light machine-gun role it is known as the 'fusil mitrailleur' or automatic rifle and is fitted with a light barrel, a bipod and a stock support. For sustained fire, the AA 52 can be mounted on a US M2 tripod and is fitted with a heavy barrel. The AA 52 is designed for cheap manufacture and a great many stampings are used. The weapon features an unusual delayed blowback system, similar in principle to the Spanish CETME rifle but with a locking lever rather than two roller bearings for locks. It also has fluted chamber walls to assist with the extraction of expended cartridges.

The AA 52 was introduced to replace the old M1924/29 which had a considerably slower rate of fire. The weapon is fed by a 50-round, metallic, nondistintegrating link belt and when used in the light machine-gun role a single belt is fed from a box mounted on the left side of the receiver.

rebel force, the men would have become very familiar with their hunting ground, getting to know each path, cave, dry-stone wall and freshwater spring of the area.

Despite their strict precautions against discovery, the Commandos were sometimes spotted by an enemy look-out. This, however, was not such a bad thing since it had a profound psychological effect on the rebels: a sense of enemy eyes and ears all around them undermined the guerrillas' confidence in their ability to move at will. By the summer of 1959, the FLN were well shaken and realised that the days of running circles around clumsy regular troops were over.

But the success of the Commandos de Chasse was not confined merely to unsettling the enemy. There were lucky days. Suddenly, out of nowhere, a rebel *katiba* (company) would appear.

On one particular operation in 1959 a Commando was in position on a rugged bluff overlooking a track. For several long, hot days they had kept watch when, suddenly, an enemy force came into view. The second-in-command spotted them first and seized the radio to report to his CO:

'Black One from Black Two.'
'Received. Five out of five.'
'Here are the customers.'
'How many?'
'Big one. Around a hundred.'

The CO thought fast. The incoming force was probably a rebel *katiba* coming over from Tunisia and the FLN were obviously unaware of the Commando's presence. He radioed back to his number two:

'Where are they?'
'Filing along below me. East to west on the path above the Wadi Kebir. You'll see them soon.'
'Received. On no account fire.'

Without a moment to lose, the CO radioed back to battalion operational command, giving details of the strength and, through the use of codenames, the location of the rebel unit:

'One hundred rebels on the track between Montmartre and Montparnasse. Suggest we turn on the fans at once.'
'Received. Leave it to us.'

At an airstrip 30 or 40km away a Foreign Legion battalion was standing by for a helicopter transfer. Seizing their kit, the legionnaires dashed for the Piasecki 'bananas' and one after another the helicopters lifted off. At the same time, two T6 combat aircraft took off to provide close air support and strafe the enemy as soon as they made contact. The assault force commander jumped into an Alouette

Below: During the war in Algeria, Piasecki H-21 helicopters, known as 'bananas' because of their shape, were used for the rapid deployment of troops across the inhospitable mountain terrain. The combination of accurate and up-to-date intelligence, mobility and firepower was the cutting edge of Challe's strategy against the FLN. Right, above: From his vantage point high in the mountains, an officer of the Commandos de Chasse surveys the landscape for signs of rebel movement. Right: After sighting a rebel company, a Commando sniper keeps the enemy in his sights while waiting for the main French combat force to arrive.

chopper and joined the legionnaires in the air. At the same time, several Mystères were put on standby in case the legionnaires ran into trouble and were unable to dislodge the rebel force. Like a tightly choreographed ballet, the airborne operation swung into action.

Back at the Commando observation point, the CO switched his radio on to an Air Force channel, ready to direct the T6s when they reached the battle area. Then the rebel *katiba* came into view, moving at a leisurely pace, in single file, towards his look-out point. He followed them with his binoculars. They were well-organised with scouts out front but, as yet, they had failed to spot the commandos hiding in the thorn bushes on the slopes leading up to the look-out point.

A distant roar . . . and then, suddenly, the T6s thundered in, shaving the ridges as they fell on the enemy column with a blaze of machine-gun and rocket fire. The whole mountain shook with the crash of exploding ordnance. As the rebels broke off in all directions, searching for cover, the choppers arrived. The legionnaires were dropped in combat groups, some to form a cordon around the battle zone, others lifted in directly to take on the rebels at close quarters. In the sky above, the T6s continued to pass back and forth like angry wasps, spitting bursts of fire into the dark lines of vegetation in the bed of the wadi where the rebels had holed up.

High above the battlefield, the commander of the Commando de Chasse watched the unfolding scene with satisfaction when, suddenly, he caught sight of a small group of rebels moving up from the wadi onto

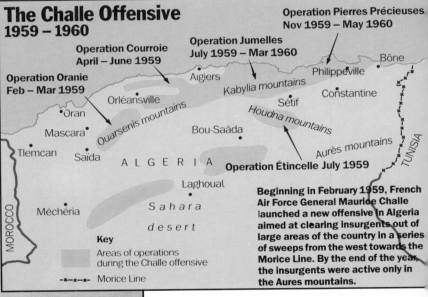

The Challe Offensive 1959 – 1960

Operation Courroie
April – June 1959

Operation Oranie
Feb – Mar 1959

Operation Jumelles
July 1959 – Mar 1960

Operation Pierres Précieuses
Nov 1959 – May 1960

Bône

Aigiers

Philippeville

Kabylia mountains

Constantine

Orléansville

Sétif

Oran

Ouarsenis mountains

Houdna mountains

Mascara

Bou-Saâda

Tlemcan

Saïda

A L G E R I A

Aurès mountains

TUNISIA

Operation Étincelle July 1959

Laghouat

S a h a r a

Méchéria

d e s e r t

MOROCCO

Key

Areas of operations during the Challe offensive

–x–x–x– Morice Line

Beginning in February 1959, French Air Force General Maurice Challe launched a new offensive in Algeria aimed at clearing insurgents out of large areas of the country in a series of sweeps from the west towards the Morice Line. By the end of the year, the insurgents were active only in the Aures mountains.

the slopes of the bluff. They were clearly trying to slip through the net that was rapidly closing in around them, but they had not seen the commandos hiding among the bushes and rocks directly ahead. As soon as they came into range, the commandos opened up, raking the slopes with bursts of automatic fire. The rebels dived for cover and were lost from view. The CO was none too happy – his men had blown it by opening up too soon.

But little had been lost. The legionnaires had encircled the FLN *katiba* and half the force was destroyed. Enemy corpses lay abandoned among the thorn bushes as the rest of the rebels struggled to make their escape. As the shooting died down, the

legionnaires moved through the wadi, gathering up
the weapons of the fallen rebels – 30 rifles, two
automatic weapons and a brand new anti-tank rocket launcher, still in its packing case. A few grenades
were also taken back to the store at base, but no
pistols – the legionnaires kept them as souvenirs.

Later in the day, the assault force boarded its
helicopters and lifted out. As always, the Commando
de Chasse returned on foot. They had not knocked
out a single rebel or picked up a single weapon, but
they had done their job.

THE AUTHOR Jean Mabire is one of France's best-
known military historians. He served with distinc-
tion in the Commandos de Chasse during the war in
Algeria.

THE CHALLE OFFENSIVE

When General Challe
arrived in Algeria he
determined to take the
initiative away from the FLN
rebels and go onto the
offensive. The essence of
his plan was that the country
should be combed through,
area by area, with
overwhelming force.
One after the other the rebel
strongholds were taken on,
starting with the Ouarsenis
mountains which were
cleared out during
Operations Oranie and
Courroie between February
and mid-June 1959.
Challe's next objective was
to subdue the Hodna
mountains and in July 1959
Operation Etincelle was
launched and the rebels
were severely mauled. He
then turned his attention to
the Kabylie mountains in the
northeast and scored a
striking success with
Operation Jumelles.
By late October, the French
claimed to have inflicted
3746 casualties in the
Kabylie and smashed the
rebel organisation.
In November 1959, Challe
moved onto the area north
of Constantine and by the
end of the year rebel troops
remained active only in the
Aurès; and Challe already
had plans for this area.
Before he could embark on
his final mopping-up
operation, however, Challe
lost the political confidence
of General de Gaulle for not
dealing firmly with the
Europeans in Algiers during
the troubles of 'Barricades
Week' in January 1960.
Three months later Challe
was recalled and command
was assumed by General
Crèpin.
Above: the insignia of the
Commandos de Chasse.

THE SMALL-SCALE RAIDING FORCE

In terms of the conventional forces and personnel fielded by the British Army and by Special Operations Executive (SOE), the Small-Scale Raiding Force (SSRF) was neither fish nor fowl. Instigated by SOE, Britain's Secret Service, operational command of this special band of raiders first belonged to SOE and then to Combined Operations Headquarters (COHQ). In its earliest days, SSRF was regarded with suspicion by the Admiralty, which refused to sanction the use of its Brixham trawler in cross-Channel forays, and later it even fell foul of the Foreign Office. Even when the force was put under the control of Lord Louis Mountbatten it continued to run into difficulties.

It was given, as the SOE archives report, 'very much of a free hand' when operating across the Channel, but the same source also notes that its raids on the Breton coast were 'divided rather ambiguously between SOE and Combined Operations HQ' until an agreement was eventually signed between the two parties on 17 December 1942. Unfortunately, this did not solve the problem of who had strategic responsibility for the areas raided, for the Special Intelligence Service (SIS) needed the Breton coast to be left undisturbed, while COHQ regarded it as its job to harass the Germans at every available opportunity.

This conflict of interest eventually spelled the end of the SSRF. Although the unit went through a period of considerable expansion, and under its cover name of No.62 Commando began to shelter such vital units as the Combined Operations (Assault) Pilotage Parties (COPP) and the Special Boat Squadron, in January 1943 the Chiefs of Staff gave instructions which rendered cross-Channel raiding on the French coast by the SSRF virtually impossible. Without a proper task to perform the Small-Scale Raiding Force was disbanded in April 1943.

During World War II, the courageous commandos of the Small-Scale Raiding Force launched lightning attacks against Axis objectives

IN JANUARY 1942 a small group of highly trained men executed one of the most extraordinary operations of World War II. So secret was their undertaking – and so potentially damaging to relations between the countries involved – that even now, 45 years on, some of the official files concerning it remain closed. The small band of elite commandos involved in the mission was the Small Scale Raiding Force.

The impetus for forming this very special group of men came from three sources: a young commando officer, Captain March-Phillipps, or Gus as everyone called him, a subaltern in No. 7 Commando, Gus's unit, named Jan Nasmyth, and Brigadier John Gubbins, the head of the London group of Special Operations Executive (SOE). In an essay entitled 'How to win the war' Nasmyth had shown how troops could be maintained in enemy territory without making contact with the local population to gain food or shelter. When Gus read Nasmyth's proposals he knew immediately that this was just the type of force he wanted to lead – a small group of highly skilled individuals wreaking destruction on enemy-held soil.

As it happened, Gubbins needed just such a group to liaise with and help train his expanding number of agents working in occupied territory. After reading Nasmyth's essay, he recruited Gus, with Lieutenant Geoffrey Appleyard as his second-in-command, to form a small force which would operate across the English Channel under SOE's command. Gus hit upon the idea of using a wooden-hulled vessel that would not be vulnerable to magnetic mines, and a Brixham trawler called *Maid Honor*, which had been converted into a yacht, was requisitioned and sailed to a hidden part of Poole Harbour in Dorset. There Gus set up his headquarters in a nearby pub and launched into a vigorous training programme.

Appleyard was the first into action. He and another member of Gus's group, a Free Frenchman called Andre Desgranges, were taken by submarine to land in the Bay of Biscay and pick up two agents. The night was rough and one of their two canoes was swept away before it could be launched. Appleyard decided to go in alone, and despite the fact that his canoe was only built to hold two men he managed to bring both agents safely back to the submarine. For this action he was subsequently awarded the MC.

After some months of waiting, the whole force was at last deployed on just the kind of operation for which it had been training. SOE suspected that German U-boats were operating out of creeks and rivers in West Africa, where their supply ships could easily be hidden. It was decided that Gus and his men should sail to the area, track down the supply vessels and destroy them. *Maid Honor* was converted for this task with the installation of a collapsible deckhouse which concealed a Vickers Mk 8 2-pounder gun, while in her stern four depth-charges were concealed underneath a pile of fishing nets. When questioned about these, Gus replied cheerfully that, 'if we can't knock out a sub any other way, we shall heave these into the ocean. The sub will then proceed to perdition, closely followed by ourselves'.

While Appleyard and the main body of 'Maid Honor Force', as it was now called, went ahead by troopship, Gus and his crew sailed the trawler to Freetown in Sierra Leone. There, the two parties met and set up camp. In the following months Gus and his men carefully and discreetly combed the area for possible U-boat supply hideouts, but while they searched, SOE found an even more important task for them.

The *Nuneaton,* under the command of Lieutenant Graham Hayes, approached the two German merchantmen

Sheltering in the neutral harbour of Santa Isabel, on the Spanish-owned island of Fernando Po, in the Gulf of Guinea, were two small German merchant ships and a larger Italian vessel. In London there was mounting concern that they might soon be used for re-supplying U-boats operating in the area, and it was decided that they must be captured. Code-named Operation Postmaster, this plan was at first opposed by the Foreign Office, which was worried about infringing Spanish neutrality, but eventually Gus received orders to sail for Lagos in Nigeria.

As *Maid Honor* was unsuitable for such an undertaking, two tugs were obtained to carry the party from Lagos to Santa Isabel. Gus and about 20 men left Lagos on 11 January 1942, arriving off Fernando Po on the night of 15 January. On the stroke of midnight, after waiting for the harbour lights to be turned off, the two tugs entered the harbour. The *Vulcan*, with

Left: Some of the leading lights of the Small-Scale Raiding Force against the background of their base, Anderson Manor. Anti-clockwise from the top, they are Gus March-Phillipps, Anders Lassen, Tom Winter, Graham Hayes and Geoffrey Appleyard. Below: The SSRF in West Africa, before the attack on the *Duchessa d'Aosta*.

Gus and Appleyard aboard, headed for the largest enemy ship, the *Duchessa d'Aosta*, while the *Nuneaton*, under the command of Lieutenant Graham Hayes, approached the two German merchantmen, which were moored alongside one another.

As planned by local Allied agents, all the ships' officers were ashore at a dinner party, and it took no time to overpower the crews. One of the raiding party, however, thought that he had come into violent contact with the enemy when with a knife in one hand and a pistol in the other, he jumped onto the deck of the Italian ship. As he moved forward in the darkness he felt something rush between his legs. He thought that it was a panicking member of the crew, but it turned out to be one of several pigs kept on board by the Italians.

Charges were used to sever the mooring cables and soon both tugs, with the three ships in tow, were on their way back to Lagos. Only then did the Spaniards, who had thought that the explosions had been caused by an air raid, realised what was happening. The operation was a total triumph, with the *Duchessa d'Aosta* being up to that time the biggest prize of the war. Subsequently, Gus was awarded the DSO, Appleyard a bar to his MC, and Hayes the MC.

The month after Operation Postmaster, Lord Louis Mountbatten, at that time Chief of Combined Operations, proposed to the Chiefs of Staff that an amphibious sabotage force of about 50 men should be formed for operations under his personal direction. This was approved, and Gus and his men were returned to England to form its nucleus. Gus set up his

The yacht *Maid Honor* (right) was refitted for SSRF use (top) with a 2-pounder gun installed in a collapsible deckhouse. Above: The *Maid Honor*, after arriving in West Africa, undergoes repairs before the mission on Fernando Po.

Top right: Captain Blake Glanville, original skipper of the Brixham trawler *Maid Honor*, who taught the SSRF everything they needed to know about the handling of the craft. Below: On board the *Maid Honor*. Right: The harbour of Saint Isabel in which the *Duchessa d'Aosta* (inset) was captured by the SSRF during Operation Postmaster.

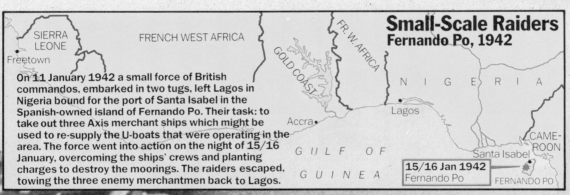

Small-Scale Raiders
Fernando Po, 1942

On 11 January 1942 a small force of British commandos, embarked in two tugs, left Lagos in Nigeria bound for the port of Santa Isabel in the Spanish-owned island of Fernando Po. Their task: to take out three Axis merchant ships which might be used to re-supply the U-boats that were operating in the area. The force went into action on the night of 15/16 January, overcoming the ships' crews and planting charges to destroy the moorings. The raiders escaped, towing the three enemy merchantmen back to Lagos.

SIERRA LEONE
Freetown

FRENCH WEST AFRICA

GOLD COAST

FR. W. AFRICA

NIGERIA

Accra

Lagos

CAMEROON

Santa Isabel

15/16 Jan 1942
Fernando Po

FERNANDO PO

GULF OF GUINEA

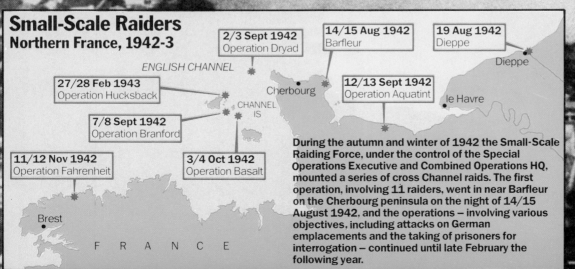

Small-Scale Raiders
Northern France, 1942-3

ENGLISH CHANNEL

2/3 Sept 1942
Operation Dryad

14/15 Aug 1942
Barfleur

19 Aug 1942
Dieppe

Dieppe

27/28 Feb 1943
Operation Hucksback

Cherbourg

12/13 Sept 1942
Operation Aquatint

le Havre

CHANNEL IS

7/8 Sept 1942
Operation Branford

11/12 Nov 1942
Operation Fahrenheit

3/4 Oct 1942
Operation Basalt

Brest

FRANCE

During the autumn and winter of 1942 the Small-Scale Raiding Force, under the control of the Special Operations Executive and Combined Operations HQ, mounted a series of cross Channel raids. The first operation, involving 11 raiders, went in near Barfleur on the Cherbourg peninsula on the night of 14/15 August 1942, and the operations – involving various objectives, including attacks on German emplacements and the taking of prisoners for interrogation – continued until late February the following year.

training headquarters at Anderson Manor near Bere Regis in Dorset, and began recruiting extra members for the new group, now officially called the Small-Scale Raiding Force (SSRF). Most of the new recruits were officers, the idea being that they would gain practical raiding experience before training other bands of raiders. Tragically, this was never to be.

In SOE – which now shared responsibility for the new force with Combined Operations Headquarters – Anderson Manor became known as Station 62, while the SSRF assumed the cover name of No. 62 Commando. The training was hard and thorough, and much experimentation was done with various types of weapons. For example, Lieutenant Anders Lassen, a young Danish officer who was later awarded a posthumous VC, was a crack shot with the bow and arrow, a silent and lethal weapon which he handled with great accuracy. However, the authorities forbade him to use his bow in action, describing it, somewhat ironically one might have thought, as an 'inhumane weapon'.

The men also learned to handle boats in all weathers, and they constantly practised covert beach insertions from the two Motor Launches (MLs) which had been assigned them. It was soon found that the MLs were too slow, and they were replaced by a modified Motor Torpedo Boat, *MTB 344*, which Gus and his men affectionately called 'the little pisser'.

The SSRF's first operation was mounted on the night of 14/15 August 1942, when 11 raiders led by Gus set out to destroy an anti-aircraft gun site south of Barfleur. Despite landing in the wrong place, Operation Barricade was counted a success as the raiders clashed with the Germans and killed at least three of them.

The following week, six members were sent on the abortive Dieppe raid, and in September three operations were mounted, the last of which had tragic consequences for this elite force. The first, Operation Dryad, was launched on the night of 2/3 September, when 10 officers and two other ranks led by Gus raided the lighthouse on Les Casquets near the Channel islands. The MTB was anchored 800yds out and the party then paddled ashore in a Goatley boat. Two officers were left with the boat while the rest clambered up an 80ft cliff. A way was found

round the defensive wire and the whole party got into the courtyard of the lighthouse without being challenged. According to the pre-arranged plan, the men now split up and rushed their objectives. Seven prisoners were taken without a shot being fired, the radio was destroyed and codebooks were seized. While re-embarking, Appleyard injured his ankle and another officer, Captain Peter Kemp, was accidentally stabbed in the backside, but the prisoners were got aboard and later proved to be a valuable source of information.

A reconnaissance of the Ile Barhou in the Channel Islands took place five nights later and then, on the night of 12/13 September, Operation Aquatint was launched. This entailed landing east of St Honorine, climbing some cliffs, approaching the village from the rear, and capturing a prisoner. However, the night was so dark that the spot where the cliffs could be climbed was not to be seen, so Gus decided to land at St Honorine itself. His party of 11 men went ashore in a Goatley boat and clashed almost immediately with a German patrol. Gus and his men were heavily outnumbered and were forced to attempt a withdrawal, but the Goatley overturned and Gus, who had been wounded, was drowned. Some managed to struggle ashore undetected, but the rest were captured or shot. Only Desgranges managed to get back to England. Hayes remained free for some time before being captured and thrown into Fresnes prison where, nine months later, he was shot by the Gestapo.

They surprised some Germans in a hotel annexe and bound their hands to prevent them from escaping

The loss of its commander and so many of its best men was a heavy blow to the SSRF, but both Appleyard, who had been forced to stay aboard the MTB because of his injured ankle, and the authorities were determined that operations should continue. On the night of 3/4 October, a raid was mounted on the island of Sark; it was codenamed Operation Basalt. Seven men from the SSRF and five from No. 12 Commando led by Appleyard were landed by dory on a deserted part of the coast with the objective of taking prisoners. They surprised some Germans in a hotel

CAPTAIN GUS MARCH-PHILLIPPS

A regular soldier with an irregular outlook, Gus March-Phillipps had no patience for peacetime military routine and in 1931, at the age of 23, he resigned his commission to write novels. Though possessing a volatile temper and a bad stutter, he was a natural leader of men, and when the war came he immediately volunteered and was again commissioned. In 1940 he found himself on the beach at Dunkirk next to a young officer, Lieutenant Geoffrey Appleyard. 'I f-feel a b-b-bloody coward,' he said to the younger man. It was the start of a firm friendship, and when the British Army formed its Commandos, Gus, as a Troop commander in No. 7 Commando, chose Appleyard as one of his subalterns.

Gus's theories for training commandos soon won him praise, and by forming and leading 'Maid Honor Force' and then the Small-Scale Raiding Force into action he was able to put them to the test.

The devotion he inspired in his men became legendary, and the idealism which he brought to the Allied cause made him extraordinarily courageous. 'He's the first army officer I've met so far,' wrote Appleyard, 'who kneels down by the side of his bed for 10 minutes before he goes to sleep. He died as he would have chosen, at a moment of great danger, fighting the enemy in just the kind of encounter he believed would eventually help win the war.'

Below: A photograph taken in 1983 of two survivors of SSRF operations at their first reunion since the war. On the left is Leslie 'Red' Wright shaking hands with Tom Winter.

Below: *MTB 344*, known to her crew as the 'little pisser'. The *Maid Honor*, unseaworthy for the long voyage home, had to be left behind in West Africa and the SSRF took to raiding from the MTB. Right: On the bridge of the 'little pisser'. The two swastika symbols denote two German E-boats destroyed, while the vertical lines bear witness to eight Commando raids undertaken by the craft.

annexe and bound their hands to prevent them from escaping. However, on the way back to the boat their captives tried to break free and in the ensuing fracas two were shot and Lassen knifed a third. A fourth one escaped but the fifth was bundled into the boat and the raiders made their escape with the Germans close on their heels.

The prisoner yielded some vital information and Appleyard was awarded the DSO. However, the raid had an unpleasant repercussion in that the Germans, furious at finding their men dead with their hands tied, shackled the prisoners they had taken during the Dieppe raid as a reprisal. Nevertheless, the authorities were otherwise delighted with the operation and that same month orders were given to expand the SSRF from one Troop to four. The group's HQ remained at Anderson Manor, but three other houses were requisitioned for the new members, who were all from No. 12 Commando, and the number of naval craft available to the larger force was also increased. The idea, a logical development of Gus's own theories, was for small groups of commandos to be attached to the SSRF for training and then to take part in a raid. For a time it looked as if Gus's dreams really would come true, even if he was not there to see them.

By now Appleyard had been promoted to major, one of the youngest in the army, but with a much larger force in the process of being formed he had to hand over his temporary command to Lieutenant-Colonel Bill Stirling, brother of David Stirling, the founder of the Special Air Service. The first operation under Stirling's command was an attack, codenamed Operation Fahrenheit, on the signal station at Pointe de Plouezec. It took place on the night of 11/12 November and was led by Peter Kemp.

In addition to their usual commando weaponry, which included Brens and silenced Sten guns, the party of 10 was issued with two hand grenades known officially as 'Grenades P.E., No. 6'. These had a thin metal casing and contained a heavy charge of plastic explosive. They burst on impact with a very heavy blast and could be used to blow a path through the heaviest barbed-wire entanglement.

The party landed in a rocky cove and soon found that, due to minefields, they could only make a direct assault on the signal station. They managed to reach the defensive wire undetected, and both of the sentries were killed when one of the No. 6 grenades was thrown to clear a path through it. The guardhouse was empty, and when a third German ran out of the darkness firing a light automatic rifle, he was shot and killed. Another German, who foolishly silhouetted himself in the doorway of the signal station ahead,

was also shot. Kemp now planned to storm the build- ing, but the remaining Germans reacted quickly and began pouring heavy fire down on the raiders Wisely, Kemp withdrew the force before it incurred casualties and without further incident it reached the dory to paddle out to the waiting *MTB 344*.

Only one more raid was accomplished before the SSRF was officially disbanded in April 1943. This took place on the night of 27/28 February and was code named Operation Huckaback. Its object was to discover whether artillery could be put ashore in support of an invasion of Guernsey. This the raiders were able to confirm, but they were unable to make contact with the Germans before returning.

The ideas which Gus March-Phillipps had used in the creation of the SSRF were to be developed by other specialist commando raiders in both the Mediterranean and the English Channel as the war progressed, and they helped shape such elite units as the Special Air Service, the Special Boat Squadron and the Combined Operations (Assault) Pilotage Parties. Sadly, however, few of the men who had worked with Gus lived to see his ideas come to fruition. Dispersed into combat units after their unit's disbandment, most of them were to die in the fighting for Sicily, Italy and France.

THE AUTHOR Ian Dear served as a regular officer in the Royal Marines, 1953-56. He is now a professional writer on military and maritime subjects and author of *Ten Commando*, a book on No. 10 (Inter Allied) Commando, which is to be published in 198 by Leo Cooper Ltd.

In September 1943 the dashing
German special forces commander,
Otto Skorzeny, led a daring
commando raid to rescue Mussolini.

THROUGHOUT HIS lunch, Captain Otto Skorzeny, chief
of Germany's special forces, had had a nagging
feeling that something was wrong. Leaving his
coffee, he placed a call to his headquarters at
Friedenthal. His nagging thoughts were answered:
all of Berlin was trying to find him. He had orders to be
at Tempelhof airfield by 1700 hours, ready to fly to
Hitler's wartime headquarters, the 'Wolf's Lair'.

A Ju 52 was waiting to deliver Skorzeny in isolated
splendour and his second-in-command, Lieutenant
Karl Radl, had his dress uniform ready for him. The
only light that Skorzeny could throw on this sudden
call to visit Hitler was that the Italian government had
fallen and that Mussolini was missing.

The aircraft touched down at Lotzen in East Prus-
sia, where a Mercedes staff car was waiting. The car
took Skorzeny to the HQ, stopping many times for his
papers to be examined. At last, after waiting in an
ante-room, he was summoned into Hitler's presence.
The Führer informed Skorzeny that Mussolini had
been arrested and that it would be up to him to rescue

GRAN SASSO
RESCUE

Il Duce. He carried on, telling the young captain that
it was to be a secret mission, only a small group of
people would know of it, and that he would be
nominally under the command of General Kurt Student, chief of airborne troops.

Skorzeny then spent several hours itemising the
men and equipment that he might need in Italy, and
had the requirements sent to his own HQ. He requested 50 men and included a shopping list that
ranged from machine guns to priests'.robes. The
following morning, he flew with General Student to
Rome. Three days later the rest of his team arrived
and the search for Mussolini moved into top gear. For
several weeks, rumours abounded and were followed up, only to disappear as quickly as they had
surfaced. Then, finally, the whereabouts of Mussolini
was pinned down.

In Rome, Skorzeny and his staff had toured the bars
and cafes hoping to overhear any information that
might give them a new clue. It was an intercepted,
coded message, 'Security measures around the
Gran Sasso completed', from a General Cueli to the
Italian Ministry of the Interior, that put them on the

Above left: Mussolini is led to safety by German paras on
12 February 1943. In a daring swoop on his hotel prison
(left), commandos, under Otto Skorzeny, freed the
dictator without firing a shot in anger.

TRACKING THE QUARRY

After three fruitless weeks in Rome discounting rumours, Skorzeny was presented with the first hard facts: Mussolini (below) had been moved from Rome on 27 July and taken to the naval base at Gaeta, some 120km south of the capital. From there, he had been transferred onto a corvette, the *Persefone*, which sailed for the island of Ponza on the 28th.
However, before Skorzeny could prepare any rescue plans, other intelligence sources indicated that Mussolini had been moved again, to La Maddalena, an island off the northeast coast of Sardinia. On 18 August, Skorzeny carried out a reconnaissance flight over the island to gather detailed photographic evidence. On the 20th, Skorzeny began his preparations for the rescue mission, scheduled to take place on 27 August. In readiness for the raid, the commandos moved to the port of Anzio and Skorzeny ordered a more detailed look at the villa. Reaching the island on the 26th, Skorzeny and a fellow officer, Lieutenant Warger, tricked one of the Italian guards into revealing that Mussolini had been moved by seaplane to the Italian mainland. After landing at Braccianno, a lake in the mountains east of Rome, he had been placed under house arrest at Albergo-Rifugia, a hotel situated 6500ft above the valley.

scent. This was the break that they had been after – it was known that Cueli was in charge of Mussolini.

It soon became obvious that the Hotel Albergo-Rifugio on the Gran Sasso, a mountainous ridge northeast of Rome, had been turned into a military camp, with the only approach being by cable-car. Several of Skorzeny's men were sent into the area around the mountain hotel, but they could not get through the cordon of Italian troops. Skorzeny decided to fly over the area in an He 111 to see the hotel for himself. He was accompanied by Radl and the corps intelligence officer. The plan was to photograph the whole of the area, but when they tried the main camera, they found that it was jammed. The

only way they could take any pictures was to hang out of the rear turret and use a hand camera. This method was not to be recommended when dressed in light tropical uniform. On the first run, Skorzeny was dangled out, with Radl holding his legs. When he was hauled back into the aircraft, half frozen, he discovered Radl roaring with laughter. Pulling rank, he soon got rid of Radl's hilarity by ordering another run, this time dangling Radl out of the back.

On the return trip, Skorzeny must have thought that the Allied air force had a personal vendetta against him. His aircraft was forced to hug the ground a

American bombers and fighters attacked the German headquarters and the commando barracks at Frascati. The place was a wreck and the photo lab had been destroyed, as had a lot of the men's kit. It was 8 September 1943, Italy had surrendered and on the 9th the Allies landed at Salerno.

The pictures were developed and printed, confirming what Skorzeny and Radl had seen from the air. The squat hotel was situated on a small plateau; a small triangle of clear ground with the top station of the cable-car on one side. Final confirmation of their intelligence came when it was reported that the local trade union was complaining that the hotel staff had been evicted, 'Simply to accommodate that Fascist, Mussolini.' He was there.

General Student would supply 90 men for the landing and the commandos the rest. A second group of commandos and paras would, at the same time as the main assault, take control of the lower end of the cable-car. A third team would free Il Duce's wife and family from house arrest at their country residence near Rocca della Cominata. Student ordered 12 DFS 230 gliders and their tugs to carry the commandos, but it would take at least three days to get them from the south of France. D-day was fixed for dawn on 12 September. Skorzeny and Radl fleshed out the bare bones of the operation: each

Below, far left: Smiling paras check over their weapons and equipment prior to boarding their DFS 230 assault gliders for the short flight to Gran Sasso. Once at the target (bottom), they fanned out for the dash to the hotel where Mussolini was confined.
Below left: After the action, paras stand around one of their DFS 230s waiting for the order to withdraw.

glider could take a section of 10 men plus the pilot. The para intelligence officer would fly in the first glider and act as pathfinder. Skorzeny would travel in the third glider and Radl in the fourth.

The launch had to be put back several hours because the gliders had been delayed. It was also decided, at the last minute, that it would be a good idea to take an Italian officer, General Soletti, along to help with the guards. When he arrived, Student, through an interpreter, told the general that, at Hitler's own request, he was to go on the raid and help reduce the possibility of bloodshed. Soletti was very impressed and agreed to go along. As the morning progressed, the tugs and gliders arrived

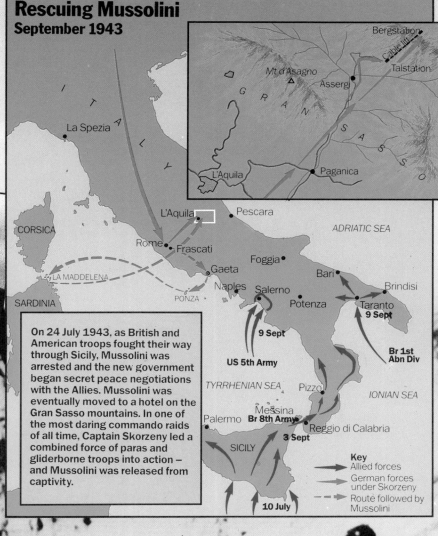

Rescuing Mussolini
September 1943

Bergstation
Cable lift
Mt d'Asagno
Talstation
Assergi
GRAN SASSO
L'Aquila
Paganica

La Spezia

CORSICA

L'Aquila
Pescara
ADRIATIC SEA

Rome
Frascati
Foggia
Gaeta
Bari
Naples
Salerno
Brindisi
LA MADDELENA
Potenza
Taranto
9 Sept
PONZA
9 Sept
SARDINIA
Br 1st
Abn Div
US 5th Army
TYRRHENIAN SEA
Pizzo
IONIAN SEA
Palermo
Messina
Br 8th Army
Reggio di Calabria
3 Sept
SICILY
10 July

On 24 July 1943, as British and American troops fought their way through Sicily, Mussolini was arrested and the new government began secret peace negotiations with the Allies. Mussolini was eventually moved to a hotel on the Gran Sasso mountains. In one of the most daring commando raids of all time, Captain Skorzeny led a combined force of paras and gliderborne troops into action – and Mussolini was released from captivity.

Key
→ Allied forces
→ German forces under Skorzeny
--→ Route followed by Mussolini

Bottom left: Mussolini is escorted to the waiting Storch. Left: Paras, including Second Lieutenant Schwerdt (far right), salute Skorzeny before take-off. Bottom right: Second Lieutenant Berlepsch, (right) greets the leader of the valley assault force, Major Mors (left). Below: Hitler welcomes Mussolini to Germany.

and were at once refuelled. Final briefings were held, and Student told the glider pilots that under no circumstances were they to crash-land.

At 1230 hours the air-raid sirens went off, and everyone dashed for shelter. By 1300, the raid was over – the assault aircraft had been missed, but the runway had several holes along its length. The order was given for an immediate take-off. Skorzeny and Soletti shared a seat in a cramped glider. With a ceiling of 9000ft, the armada was ordered to assemble above the clouds.

Skorzeny's pilot reported that the first two gliders had not made the rendezvous. Disaster had struck. Both of them never left the ground, running into craters on the runway. Skorzeny freed his knife and hacked away at the flimsy canvas that clad the glider. Through this small hole, he was able to get his bearings and shout the route to the glider pilot, who then passed it on to the tug. As the hotel came into view he ordered the glider to release the towing line.

The Italian guards just stood in amazement as the gliders landed. No-one fired a shot.

As the glider banked to the right, it became obvious to both the pilot, Lieutenant Meyer, and Skorzeny that the landing site was not flat, but a steep slope. Meyer looked at Skorzeny for help. All that he could do was to order the pilot to bring the glider down. Disobeying General Student's express order, the young pilot crash-landed within 30ft of the hotel. Never one for half measures, Skorzeny thrust himself through the canvas and wood of the glider, and raced for the hotel. The Italian guards just stood in amazement as the gliders landed. No-one fired a shot.

Dashing through an open door, Skorzeny found a signaller frantically trying to transmit a warning. A well-aimed boot sent the man flying and the butt of Skorzeny's machine pistol neatly fixed the transmitter. Discovering that the room was a dead end, the commandos retraced their steps. Rounding the corner of the hotel, they were faced with a nine-foot wall. Using Corporal Himmel's back, Skorzeny was quickly over, followed by the rest of his squad. Total chaos reigned as the Germans pushed their way through

the front door, while the Carabinieri tried to escape in the opposite direction. Later on, Skorzeny was to be amazed that not a single shot was fired during the first, crucial moments of the raid.

The commandos rushed up the main stairs and, opening the first door on the right, found Mussolini and two officers. Second Lieutenant Schwerdt escorted the two officers out of the room, leaving his boss and Mussolini alone. They were not to remain by themselves for long: the heads of two commandos, who had climbed up a lightning conductor, appeared at the window.

Watching the remaining gliders coming in to land, Skorzeny was horrified to see the eighth glider, caught by a warm thermal, picked up like a paper plane and then sent crashing into the mountain side. Sickened by the sight and hearing distant gunfire, he shouted for the senior Italian officer. A colonel was produced, and the surrender of the garrison demanded. The man asked for time to consider. Skorzeny allowed him exactly one minute. The colonel left the room and quickly returned with a glass of wine, which he offered to Skorzeny, and formally surrendered. A white bedspread was hung out of the window. The guards placed their weapons in the dining room; the officers were allowed to keep their pistols. As the first Germans reached the hotel by the cable-car, a message was sent to General Student, informing him that the raid was a success.

It had been planned that a Fieseler Storch should land in the valley, with Skorzeny and Mussolini flying out from there. Unfortunately, the Storch damaged its undercarriage when it landed and would take some time to repair. This meant the only other possibility was for Captain Gerlach, who had been acting as a spotter, to land his Storch near the hotel itself.

A short landing strip was prepared by rolling the larger boulders to one side. The aircraft landed safely enough, but the captain was not amused by the idea of cramming in both Mussolini and Skorzeny. He was finally convinced by the use of the Führer's name. Once the aircraft had taken off, the rest of the troops would descend to the valley by cable-car. To guard against any trouble, two Italian officers would go with each load.

Mussolini sat in the rear seat, with Skorzeny squeezed in the luggage space behind. Commandos held onto the aircraft as the pilot built up the revs. Suddenly, the aircraft raced forward and tried to rise. It bounced down on its left landing wheel, then shot over the edge of the cliff. The pilot fought with the aircraft and got it under control barely 100ft from the valley floor. At Rome, the Storch had to make a two-point landing because of the damaged wheel.

Skorzeny and Mussolini, after receiving a formal greeting from senior staff, boarded an He 111 and flew straight to Vienna. It was here that the celebrations and phone calls started. Just before midnight, there was a knock at Skorzeny's door; it was the chief-of-staff of the Viennese garrison. Entering the room, he congratulated Skorzeny on the success of the mission. Removing the Knight's Cross from his own neck, he presented it to Skorzeny. By order of Hitler, he was the first man to be presented with the Knight's Cross on the day he had won it.

THE AUTHOR Mike Roberts runs a major picture library that deals with military subjects and has worked in defence research for television.

THE MOST DANGEROUS MAN IN EUROPE

Born in Austria in 1908, Otto Skorzeny (above) was an early member of the Nazi Party and, with the Waffen-SS, fought in France, Yugoslavia and Russia. In 1943 he transferred to Hitler's Security Office where he began working in an undercover capacity.

Skorzeny first rose to prominence in the following September when he led the small group that freed the Italian dictator, Benito Mussolini from his hotel prison at Gran Sasso in Italy. Much admired by Hitler for his daring exploits, Skorzeny was empowered to raise No.502 Special Services Battalion and, later, a number of Jagdverbände – anti-partisan units.

In late 1944, Skorzeny and his men were responsible for ensuring the continued loyalty of the Hungarian government to the Nazi cause by the simple expedient of capturing the buildings on Castle Hill in Budapest that housed the offices of the wavering ministers.

Skorzeny also organised and led the forces involved in Operation Greif in the winter of 1944. Disguised as US Army personnel, his troops worked in advance of the German forces involved in the Battle of the Bulge to sow confusion behind enemy lines. In the event, the mission was only a very limited success.

91

From Sicily to Anzio the men of the Naval Commandos were at the forefront of the Allied amphibious landings

THE LONE, single-engined British fighter swooped down as it approached the southeast coast of Sicily, just to the west of Cape Passero. On the final run-in the pilot banked and turned sharply. To an observer of the defending Italian 206th Coastal Division, the British plane would have been just another of the many enemy fighters that were flying missions over Sicily at that time, headed perhaps for Pachino airfield a few kilometres to the north. But this fighter's mission was no ordinary one. Moreover, its pilot – Lieutenant John Russell, RN – was no ordinary pilot. An ex-Fleet Air Arm flyer, Lieutenant Russell was one of the Royal Navy's highly trained beachhead commandos, the Beachmaster of No.1 Section, N Commando.

Following his orders, Russell was taking careful note of the pattern of offshore sandbars and runnels beneath the shallow waters before continuing inland. Avoiding contact with the enemy, he regained height, re-crossed the coast further along and headed for home – the North African base where N Commando was training hard for its next operation.

It was the spring of 1943. The last pocket of Axis resistance in North Africa, in Tunisia, had been cleared by 12 May, and plans for the next operation – the seizure of Sicily, codenamed Operation Husky – were already well advanced. The invasion of Sicily was scheduled for early July: two naval task forces incorporating convoys from Britain, the US, the Middle East and North Africa were timetabled to arrive simultaneously in the central Mediterranean south of Sicily, forming an armada of some 2500 vessels. While covering forces stood by to counter enemy naval activity, the invasion fleet would deliver two Allied armies – totalling over 180,000 men – to their designated beaches.

H-hour was set at 0330 on 10 July. The US Seventh Army, under General George S. Patton, was to land in the Gulf of Gela and push north into central Sicily, securing the Axis airfields around Gela itself, thus neutralising any effective enemy aerial counter-attack. Meanwhile the British Eighth Army, commanded by General Bernard L. Montgomery, was tasked to land on the stretch of coast between the Cape Passero peninsula and Syracuse, some 60km to the east of the American beaches. Montgomery's objectives included the airfield at Pachino and, crucially, the ports of Syracuse and Augusta. Against Axis forces numbering some 315,000 Italian and over 50,000 German troops, the fighting was going to be tough – and until a major port was in Allied hands, men and supplies would have to be brought ashore

BEACHHEAD COMMANDOS

The training regime of the Naval Commandos was vigorous and extremely demanding to prepare the men for every aspect of their vital role in the spearhead of an amphibious landing. The commandos had to be all-rounders, and were well-practised in coming ashore from landing craft (above), storming beach defences (right), hand-to-hand combat (right, centre), and scaling cliffs and sea walls (far right, above). Their training was based at the Royal Navy 'stone frigate' HMS *Armadillo* in Scotland (far right, below).

BEACH INVADERS

The urgent need for standing naval beach organisations was the subject of a meeting at Combined Operations HQ as early as December 1941, when it was decided to form eight permanent Beach Parties by the end of 1942. The structure of these units was eventually set at 55 all ranks each, with a Commander or Lieutenant-Commander as Principal Beachmaster, responsible for 48 ratings organised into three sections, each of which was to be commanded by a Beachmaster and Assistant Beachmaster.

An appropriate name was needed and, after various alternatives such as 'Beach Assault Pioneers' had been considered, Mountbatten's suggestion that they be called Naval Commandos met with the approval of Brigadier Laycock, and the RN Commando shoulder flash (shown above), designed to be worn above the Combined Operations badge, was adopted. In order to eliminate confusion between the Army, Royal Marine and Naval Commandos, each Naval Commando was to be identified by a letter instead of a number.

By the spring of 1942, C and D Commandos had formed (the designations A and B were reserved for units forming in Madagascar). By the time the Dieppe operation was launched on 19 August, E, F and G Commandos had also formed.

However, the Naval Commandos still lacked their own training camp, and the scheme of specialised instruction that was to be given to them had yet to be finalised.

across the beaches, making the operation vulnerable to enemy counter-attack. Husky was going to be an operation of appalling complexity; and in the early stages much would depend on securing the beachheads and then organising them so that stores could be brought to land, and troops deployed, as rapidly as possible.

Controlling the movement of assault craft, men and material at the beachhead during amphibious landings had been the responsibility of the Royal Navy from the outset. But during the first two years of war, no permanent specialised beach organisations existed. The Beach Parties (naval elements of an amphibious assault assigned to work ashore) had been chosen from shore or ship-based units as the need arose, and they were normally returned to their parent units after the beachhead had been secured. As the amphibious raids mounted by Combined Operations grew in scale, involving purpose-built landing craft, more equipment and increasing numbers of men, it quickly became apparent that, if the landing areas were to be secured and chaos on the beachheads minimised, a new kind of beach organisation was needed.

The new organisation would consist of highly trained specialists who could land during the first waves of an amphibious assault, seize the beach, seek out and mark suitable landing places for infantry and armour, and control the movements of landing craft so as to ensure the most rapid turn-round

practicable. On a heavily defended beach, this could turn out to be, as Special Service Brigade commander Brigadier Laycock put it, 'the toughest job of the lot'. These Beach Parties, soon to be renamed Naval Commandos, would be responsible for clearing the landing areas of anti-personnel mines and submerged obstructions, co-operating with the military in securing the beachhead and – where necessary – eliminating snipers and taking out enemy strongpoints. As the assault got under way, the Commandos would be expected to cordon off 'drowned' vehicles, mark out food and ammunition dumps, and assist their opposite numbers in the military by guiding troops and vehicles forward to assembly points.

The main tasks of the Naval Commandos had been clearly defined, following the confusion and failure of the amphibious assault on Dieppe on 19 August 1942. The Dieppe raid was the largest of the Combined Operations to be mounted so far, involving the

Below: 10 July 1943, D-day on 'Queen' beach in Sicily. This landing area was consolidated by M Commando for the main amphibious force of men from the 51st (Highland) Division. Below left: A Sherman tank comes ashore at Anzio in January 1944 in the wake of a Naval Commando operation which encountered heavy opposition from Axis defences.

entire 2nd Canadian Division, with two Army Commandos, Nos. 3 and 4, securing the Canadian flanks. The main landing in Dieppe itself was met by withering fire; the Canadians were pinned down on the beaches and, despite showing great courage, suffered appalling losses. In terms of men and materials the raid was a disaster; its saving grace lay in the lessons that were learned, and put into practice in future Combined Operations.

For most of the personnel of the navy's newly formed beach units, the Dieppe raid was their first taste of Combined Operations. The raid highlighted the urgent need for finalising the Naval Commando training scheme, and as a direct result the RN Commando camp at Ardentinny on the shores of Loch Long, in the west of Scotland, was set up; eventually it was commissioned as one of the Royal Navy's 'stone frigates', HMS *Armadillo*. The course at

Ardentinny combined arduous physical exercise, general commando assault and weapons training, and specialised training for the beach commando role.

By now, the Commandos were forming at the rate of one a month. The twelfth, and the first to emerge from HMS *Armadillo,* was M Commando, which formed in November 1942 as its sister units went into action on the North African coast at Algiers and Oran in support of the Operation Torch landings on 8 November. With the end of fighting in North Africa early in May, plans for Operation Husky were soon finalised. M Commando had already been shipped to Algiers in March to begin working up for the operation, and it was followed soon afterwards by N Commando. K Commando, which was to accompany one of the convoys from the Middle East, had landed at Aqaba on the Red Sea and was training intensively

Below: Leading Seaman Ray Bromley, a Lewis gunner with N Commando, who was obliged to take on a number of enemy positions on the beach at Pachino during the invasion of Sicily. Bottom: Officers and petty officers of M Commando pose for the camera. Bottom left: A little rest and relaxation after the Sicily landings.

Italian campaign: Sicily to Anzio

July 1943 – Jan 1944

The war in the Mediterranean entered a new phase in May 1943 when the last pocket of Axis resistance in North Africa was overcome.

The Allied landings in Sicily in July 1943 marked the beginning of a hard fight for possession of Italy. With the capitulation of the Italian government on 3 September, only two weeks after the fall of Sicily, the German 10th Army continued to put up a stubborn resistance against the Allied advance. The Allied armies carried out a series of amphibious operations, involving major landings at Reggio di Calabria, Salerno, and later at Anzio. Accompanying the British divisions on their amphibious assaults, the RN Commandos undertook the hazardous job of landing with the first waves and staking out the landing beaches.

From Sicily to Anzio the RN Commandos were in the forefront of the action on beaches that were often heavily-defended, and they made a large contribution to the success of the drive through Italy.

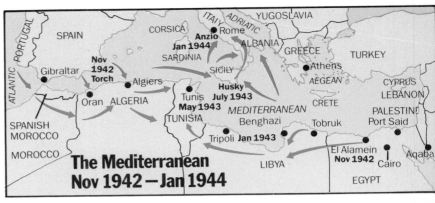

The Mediterranean Nov 1942 – Jan 1944

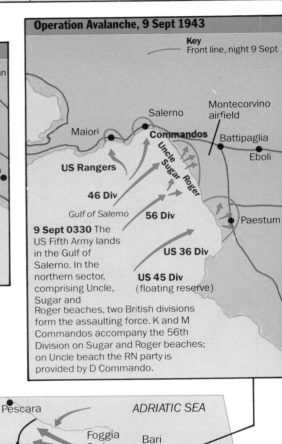

Operation Avalanche, 9 Sept 1943

Key
Front line, night 9 Sept

9 Sept 0330 The US Fifth Army lands in the Gulf of Salerno. In the northern sector, comprising Uncle, Sugar and Roger beaches, two British divisions form the assaulting force. K and M Commandos accompany the 56th Division on Sugar and Roger beaches; on Uncle beach the RN party is provided by D Commando.

Operation Shingle, 22 Jan 1944

Key
Front line, 24 Jan

22 Jan 0200 The US 3rd Division and part of the British 1st Division land at Anzio in an attempt to outflank the Germans holding the Allies at Cassino. N and K Commandos land with the 1st Division on Peter beach.

Key
Allied forces

Operation Baytown, 3 Sept 1943

3 Sept 0430 The Allied landings near Reggio di Calabria are spearheaded by N and G Commandos.

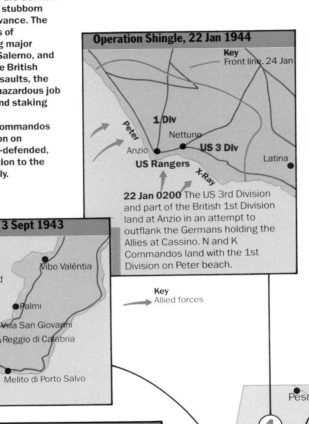

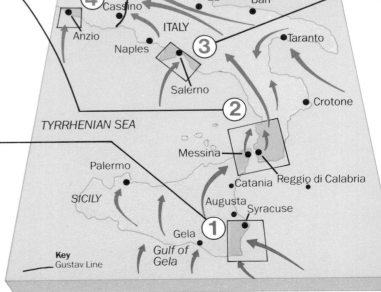

Operation Husky, 10 July 1943

Key
Gun emplacements

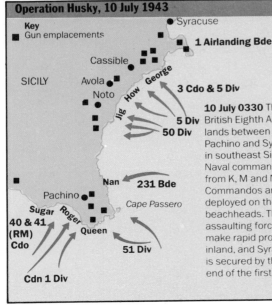

10 July 0330 The British Eighth Army lands between Pachino and Syracuse in southeast Sicily. Naval commandos from K, M and N Commandos are deployed on the beachheads. The assaulting forces make rapid progress inland, and Syracuse is secured by the end of the first day.

Key
Gustav Line

96

...preparation.

For the Sicily landings, K, M and N Commandos were assigned to the British assault beaches in the Bark East, Bark South and Bark West sectors, which surrounded the Pachino-Cape Passero peninsula. N Commando were to accompany the 1st Canadian Division and 40 and 41 (RM) Commandos in their assault on the 'Roger' and 'Sugar' beaches on the west side of the peninsula. The men of the 51st (Highland) Division, assaulting the 'Queen' beach near Cape Passero, were to be accompanied by M Commando, while to the north K Commando would land on the 'Jan' beaches, in the area of Marzamemi, accompanying the 231st Brigade.

On 9 July 1943, the day before D-day, the weather deteriorated as the wind freshened to a half-gale. Under the command of the convoy's Senior Naval Officer Landing, Captain Lord Ashbourne, the British Landing Ships, Infantry (LSIs) *Otranto, Keren* and *Strathnaver*, with the 231st Brigade embarked, drew near to the end of their voyage from Suez. Already, as the evening drew in, the mass of Mount Etna was visible in the distance.

As M Commando concentrated on consolidating the beachhead, the highlanders went into action

Early the following morning, after a tot of army rum all round, transfer to the Landing Craft, Assault (LCAs) began. Although the weather had eased a little, and Ashbourne's force was in the lee of the peninsula, the sea remained rough. At 0245, H minus 45, the first waves of landing craft – including those bearing K Commando – moved off from the ships, hitting the beaches approximately on time. Opposition, largely from a coastal battery behind Marzamemi, was light. Lieutenant Portman's group gained the shore and, without taking casualties from enemy fire, secured and staked out their beach. Other members of K Commando had a more difficult time. Able Seaman Sidney Worden and some others were set down at 0330, but they were half-a-mile to the north of the intended landing-point and had to make their way back under fire:

'We had to watch out for land mines; we could see them in the sand, wooden boxes about nine inches by nine, but rather deadly...I felt very apprehensive, and we were being fired on!'

By 0400, men of the Dorset and Hampshire Regiments were fighting their way inland towards the coastal battery. At daybreak, *Flores* and *Soemba*, two Dutch gunboats, lent supporting fire and the battery was soon silenced. The Beach Group was augmented by marines from the 7th Battalion, RM, and K Commando established a beach headquarters in a small house near Marzamemi harbour. It turned out to be a wine store, but the wine was rough and little of it was drunk. Some shelling was experienced, and during the afternoon an Italian counter-attack was launched using French M35 tanks. By this time, however, Shermans had arrived, strengthening the Allied force, and the attack was soon broken up. A more potent threat was from the air: the Italian Air Force sent in Aeromacchi fighter-bombers in an attempt to halt the build-up of Allied stores. The mines continued to be a hazard, as Able Seaman Worden recalled:

'We had some bombing, but not much shelling really. Where a pile of those wooden mines had been stacked, quite a number of them, some fellows (I don't know where from) were messing about near them with sticks of cordite and set the whole lot off – went up like a Roman candle, blokes with it.'

On 'Queen' beach, to the south, M Commando had an easier time. The first waves of the assault hit the beaches as early as 0245, meeting only light resistance and suffering few casualties. As M Commando concentrated on consolidating the beachhead, the highlanders went into action, driving the Italian coastal troops inland, to the sound of bagpipes and bloodthirsty yells.

Bark West sector was destined to be a more difficult landing: both 'Sugar' beach, where 40 and 41 (RM) Commandos comprised the assault force, and 'Roger' beach, the landing area for the 1st Canadian Division, were plagued by the dangerous sandbars and runnels that Lieutenant Russell had already surveyed from the air. Now, along with the rest of N Commando, Russell put his observations to the test.

Bark West was more exposed than the other British beaches, and a heavy swell delayed the transfer of troops onto the landing craft. At 0315 on D-day the first wave moved out. Leading Seaman Ray Bromley of N Commando recalled the journey in:

'We landed at Pachino and came under fire from German howitzers on our way. (There was interference from coast defence and shore batteries after daylight had come, but these were silenced by ships' gunfire.) At first we thought the shells were from one of the bombarding British cruisers falling short...Shells were dropping all round us!'

In fact, the batteries continued to fire even after Task Force vessels, *Hilary* and *Roberts*, moved in closer along a freshly-swept channel at around 0425: it took a further 90 minutes of bombardment to silence them. The first assault troops reached the beaches at 0455, and on landing encountered resistance from Italian machine-gun positions.

He remained just offshore in a small rubber dinghy – exposed and often under fire

While fire support craft gave some assistance in suppressing the enemy, N Commando were obliged to deal with a number of positions themselves, some of which were located on the beach assigned to Lieutenant Russell's section. Leading Seamen Bromley remembered:

'a troublesome Italian machine-gun pit sited close to a small hut. This pinned us down for a while until I was called forward with my stripped Lewis gun to deal with it. My Number Two, Able Seaman Dodds, positioned himself among some grape vines, and Sub-Lieutenant Harris, RANVR, took up position on my right to direct my fire. I opened up on the hut and spotted the machine-gun post, which was duly attended to. On my ceasing fire Petty Officer Letby, Leading Seaman Lamb and Able Seaman Pete Lightfoot charged from the left as Lieutenant Russell and Leading Seaman Sam Gregory came in from the right.'

One of the Italian soldiers who abandoned the position to Lieutenant Russell's commandos left behind him a 'Red Devil' – an impact grenade concealed in a greatcoat – intending it to explode upon impact with the floor when the coat was disturbed. Russell saw the grenade drop, and with deft footwork managed to break its fall.

After the initial landing, Russell left Harris and Bromley to deal with the Italian positions while he...

LIEUTENANT JOHN RUSSELL

Lieutenant John Russell, RN trained as a Fleet Air Arm pilot before World War II, but at the outbreak of hostilities he saw service on Home Fleet destroyers. He was then appointed as First Lieutenant on a destroyer in the Mediterranean theatre. Returning to the United Kingdom after contracting pneumonia, he was eventually posted to the RN Commandos.

Russell's unit, N Commando, was sent to North Africa to prepare for the invasion of Sicily, and Russell flew a series of reconnaissance patrols over the Sicilian coast before participating in the main invasion. N Commando went on to take part in the 'Baytown' crossing to mainland Italy early in September.

Less than a week later, the US Fifth Army landed at Salerno and Russell was present as an observer, after which he was withdrawn to Kabrit in Egypt with the rest of N Commando.

On New Year's Eve 1943, Russell, now commander and Principal Beachmaster of N Commando, set sail with his unit in the British cruiser *Phoebe* for the beaches at Anzio. N Commando landed on 'Peter' beach under heavy shelling on D-day, 24 January 1944. The Allied bridgehead at Anzio was contained by German counter-attacks for over four months, and Russell's commandos remained on the beaches. German shelling and air attacks were a constant problem, and on one occasion, when a British destroyer had been sunk by a glider-bomb attack, Russell took a DUKW out to pick up survivors. Eventually, Russell lost a leg in the blast from a German railway-gun shell, and he was later awarded a Bar to the Distinguished Service Cross he had earned during his destroyer days.

remained just offshore in a small rubber dinghy – exposed and often under fire – taking soundings in order to mark out the landing area as soon as possible. Russell unfortunately saw plenty to confirm his earlier suspicions about the treacherous nature of the beach. Afterwards he recounted seeing 'several drowned Canadians hauled out of the water at Pachino on the next beach to the one I was running . . .' These deaths were an inevitable result of the sandbars which rose to within a couple of feet of the water's surface, causing landing craft to ground, and infantrymen, weighed down with equipment, to drown in several feet of water nearby. While air attacks constituted a serious hazard for the disembarking troops, their main obstacle was the unfavourable nature of Bark West's beaches.

By the end of D-day, British forces further north had secured the port of Syracuse, and the defending Italians were in retreat. The following day it was decided to close Bark West and concentrate on landing supplies on easier beaches and harbours. For the beachhead commandos the war had moved on and the excitement of the assault gave way to routine – at least until the next operations were in sight.

By mid-August, the whole of Sicily was in Allied hands, and early in September the Allies were ready to move onto the Italian mainland. Two major operations were involved, with Naval Commandos playing a vital role in both: on 3 September, the Eighth Army crossed the Straits of Messina, and six days later, the US Fifth Army landed at Salerno. The landings at Anzio, in January 1944, again saw Naval Commandos

Below: Members of a German mortar crew prepare for action against the incoming Allies on the coast of Sicily. It was not long, however, before many of their comrades were on their way to captivity (bottom).

in the forefront of the action. But by that time, sever[al] RN Commando units were preparing for the greate[st] amphibious operation of all: the Allied invasion [of] Normandy.

THE AUTHOR Barry Smith has taught politics at Exet[er] and Brunel Universities. He is a contributor to t[he] journal *History of Political Thought* and has written [a] number of articles on military subjects.

FIRE
SUPPORT

148 BATTERY

148 (Meiktila) Commando Forward Observation Battery, Royal Artillery, is the last surviving World War II commando unit to recruit from both the Royal Navy and the British Army, and it retains the wartime Combined Operations insignia of an anchor, a Thompson sub-machine gun and an eagle.

For many years there were two amphibious observation batteries, one based in Singapore and the other at Hamworthy in the UK. A single regiment, 95 Forward Observation Unit (95 FOU) was formed, and the two batteries were consolidated at Hamworthy as part of Royal Marines Poole.

In 1975, 95 FOU was reduced in size to become 148 Battery in 29 Commando Regiment, the artillery regiment of 3 Commando Brigade. The battery was to provide observation teams to support both the parachute and commando brigades, the Allied Mobile Force (Land) and the Special Boat Squadron, but the smaller unit found it impossible to cover all these commitments. Prior to the Falklands campaign, cuts to 3 Commando Brigade were being discussed, and 148 Battery seemed the most likely victim.

Operation Corporate radically altered 148 Battery's position. Commanders in the field quickly realised the inestimable value of carefully controlled naval gunfire and also of men trained to insert themselves by small boat or parachute to forward observation positions. In the event, demand for the 148 Battery teams far outstripped supply, and teams had to be rushed from unit to unit.

The men of 148 Commando Forward Observation Battery blasted Argentinian targets that threatened the San Carlos beach-head

FOLLOWING THEIR landings at San Carlos on East Falkland on 21 May 1982, the British Special Forces immediately set about planning and carrying out operations in preparation for the ultimate attack on Port Stanley. Reconnaissance teams were despatched to key locations on the islands, and the Special Air Service (SAS) mounted patrols to push into the centre of East Falkland towards Mount Kent.

Meanwhile, the anchorage at San Carlos wa under constant threat from a large Argentinian garr son on West Falkland. Based at Fox Bay, in the sout of that island, was an infantry brigade, a larg battalion group with at least one field artillery ba tery, several anti-aircraft batteries and a number helicopters. Another battalion group was based Port Howard to the north, and the remote wester islands also had small Argentinian garrisons.

Although it was clearly essential that this powerf force should be kept bottled up and away from th San Carlos beach-head, most of the Special Force

FORWARD OBSERVATION

The complement of 148 Battery consists of radio operators recruited from the Royal Navy, gunners from the Royal Artillery, and radio and vehicle maintenance staff from the Royal Electrical and Mechanical Engineers. No man is accepted for training before he has successfully completed the Royal Marines' commando course, followed by The Parachute Regiment's P Company selection course and the parachute course at RAF Brize Norton. Those who are selected for the battery begin a mentally taxing six months of basic naval gunfire team training.

At the end of the basic course, the naval gunfire assistant (NGA) is required to be able to send and read morse at over 18 words a minute cope with a very wide range of sophisticated code systems, operate the complete range of service radios in all terrains and over all distances, and adjust both naval and artillery fire, as well as maintain a high standard of weapon handling and personal camouflage. The course finishes with a gruelling test exercise during which the recruits cover long distances on foot and put into practice all that they have learned. They start parachuting with steerable 'chutes (the 22ft steerable) from the tailgate of Hercules aircraft (as opposed to normal jumps from the side doors). They also

Page 99, from top: The guns of HMS *Plymouth* unleash a salvo; Bombardier Nick Allin, commander of the forward observation (FO) team that directed naval gunfire onto Port Howard; Forward Observation Team No. 1 (FO1) on Beagle Ridge late in the Falklands campaign. Top left: An FO team in the process of training in the Arctic ice. Below: The Gemini raider, a smaller version of the rigid inflatable boat used in the raid on Fox Bay. Bottom: Forward Observation Team No. 1, from left to right- Gunners Tim Bedford and Des Dixon, RO1 Steve Hoyland, Captain Hugh McManners and Bombardier Nick Allin.

learn to do a 200ft abseil from a helicopter.

The more promising NGAs, once they have proved themselves as members of a forward observation (FO) team, are trained as divers, and join one of the amphibious operations teams. They train as coxswains and learn to parachute as a team into water, following a Gemini assault boat (under its own 'chute) out of the aircraft and landing in the water as close to the boat as possible. Amphibious training also includes long surface and sub-surface swims, and small-boat work. This takes place mostly at night, using compass, charts and tide tables.

Each FO team consists of five men; an artillery captain, a bombardier (the Royal Navy equivalent of a corporal), an RO or RO1 (radio operator Royal Navy), a lance bombardier and a gunner. The team can be split in two, with the bombardier able to perform all the tasks of the officer and each member able to bring down artillery or naval gunfire.

MAJOR HUGH McMANNERS, RA

Major Hugh McManners was commissioned from the Royal Military Academy Sandhurst into the Royal Artillery in 1973. After passing the commando course at the Commando Training Centre, Lympstone, he was posted to 8 (Alma) Commando Battery of 29 Commando Regiment, Royal Artillery. As part of 41 Commando Group, the battery served in Malta and the Mediterranean, and six months were spent with United Nations Forces Cyprus in the wake of the Turkish invasion of the island in 1974.

After reading geography at St Edmund Hall, Oxford, and passing the P Company parachute selection course and the basic parachute jumps course at RAF Abingdon, he was posted to 148 Battery. Following two years' service, during which he ran a jungle warfare training school for eight months in Belize and took part in military exercises all over the world, he was made responsible for the 148 Battery amphibious warfare teams, becoming a diving supervisor and taking part in training and exercises with the SBS. He spent several winters in Norway and parachuted regularly as part of the battery's parachute programme.

Returned from the Falklands campaign, he was posted to the Ministry of Defence in London, and then to the Army Staff Course at Camberley, passing out in December 1984. He now works in a staff appointment in London, and in 1985 he was elected a Fellow of the Royal Geographical Society.

Captain Hugh McManners, 148 Commando Forward Observation Battery, Royal Artillery, Falklands 1982

Over a padded, quilted suit, Captain McManners is wearing a DPM Arctic windproof smock and trousers with a black balaclava, civilian gaiters, and waterproof ski-march boots. His rifle is a 5.56mm Colt Commando, and a 9mm Browning pistol is attached to the lanyard tied to the front of his smock. His pockets are stuffed with ammunition and field dressings, and a vacuum-packed field dressing is also taped to the stock of the rifle. The webbing is basically '58 pattern, and a bergen rucksack would be carried when moving into a new observation post.

The 148 Commando
Forward Observation
Battery took part in nearly
every Special Force
operation in the South
Atlantic. Both the Special Air
Service and the Special Boat
Squadron had teams
attached to 148 Battery, and
the battery also operated on
its own ahead of the main
landing force, observing
Argentinian positions and
directing artillery, naval
gunfire and Harrier attacks
onto them.
Early in the campaign, naval
gunfire played a crucial part
in Operation Paraquat,
which led to the surrender
of the Argentinian garrison
on South Georgia. The
gunfire was controlled by
two heliborne 148 Battery
observers, while teams from
the battery took part in the
ground assault. Heliborne
observers also adjusted the
naval bombardments of Port
Stanley, and their
helicopters were damaged
by concentrated fire from
Argentinian fast patrol boats
and anti-aircraft guns.
Forward observation teams
were inserted into the San
Carlos area ahead of the
main invasion force, one by
Gemini assault craft one
week prior to the landings,
and another the night before
as part of an SBS fighting
patrol. The second team
attacked an Argentinian
'heavy weapons company'
with gunfire from HMS
Antrim. Later, a team with
2 Para at Goose Green
controlled the Harrier strike
that precipitated the final
surrender of that garrison.
During 3 Commando
Brigade's attack on Port
Stanley, 148 Battery teams
often deployed ahead of the
assaulting units, taking out
sniper positions and
bringing down artillery and
naval gunfire. A 148 Battery
team was inserted onto
Beagle Ridge one week
before the main assault to
guide the bombardment of
Argentinian gun batteries,
radar sites and rear
positions.

were already deployed on other pressing tasks. Therefore, with only one Special Boat Squadron (SBS) section (the equivalent of a troop) available, it was decided that the major garrisons at Fox Bay and Port Howard should be subjected to heavy attack by closely observed and directed naval gunfire. The two garrisons were located in strong defensive positions, sheltered from the sea by high ground which also offered excellent fire positions against raiding landing craft or helicopters. It was plain that a pre-emptive attack could save a great deal of very costly fighting in the future.

The task of directing the ship's guns onto target fell to 148 Commando Forward Observation Battery. As commander of the forward observation (FO) team, I decided to split the team into two parties, the second one under Bombardier Nick Allin being kept in reserve to raid Port Howard after the initial raid on Fox Bay. The FO teams were to go in at night by boat with SBS coxswains and heavily armed sentries, in order to infiltrate the Argentinian positions, find observation points close enough to adjust the gunfire, and then assess the damage achieved.

The first raid was put into Fox Bay on the night 25/26 May. The gunship for the raid was HMS *Plymouth*, commanded by Captain David Pentreath, RN. We would be dropped by boat five miles south of the entrance to Fox Bay. *Plymouth* would then unleash her twin-barrelled Mark 6 4.5in guns (firing a 50lb high-explosive shell over a range of up to 18,000yds) as ordered by me.

On board *Plymouth* was Warrant Officer 2 'Brum' Richards, the 148 Battery Liaison Officer, whose expert interpretation of radio transmissions from the shore would be critical, not only to the success of the mission, but to the lives of those of us in the raiding team if things should begin to go wrong.

We all wore full combat clothing and thick woollen sweaters under lightweight black rubber dry-suits. In addition to black balaclavas, camouflage cream and woollen mountaineering hats, we wore combat waistcoats containing spare ammunition magazines, pistols, grenades, emergency flares, rations, medical packs and fighting knives.

The RIB's engine started first time and we vanished into the darkness towards West Head

On 25 May *Plymouth* left the safety of San Carlos at last light and steamed, flat out, southwards down Falkland Sound towards the drop-off point. The sound is notorious for bad weather and there was already a stiff wind and a heavy swell. *Plymouth's* decks were straining with the vibration as she cut through the black rising seas, throwing a freezing spray across the upper decks where the raiding team was huddled by the davits, clutching Armalite and Colt rifles and waiting for the signal to move.

Five minutes before the drop-off (timed for 0030 Zulu, 26 May) we clambered into the suspended RIB (rigid inflatable boat – a larger version of the Gemini). The ship shuddered and wallowed as her engines went into reverse and she suddenly slowed. The sound of the winches was lost in the noise of the wind and the waves crashing against the side of the ship. The RIB's engine started first time and we vanished into the darkness on a compass bearing towards West Head.

The RIB was heavily laden. Indeed, burdened with weapons, ammunition and equipment, each man would have been too heavy for the inflatable

assault lifejackets to support in the event of a cap[...]. There was also a 7.62mm GPMG (general pur[...] machine gun) in the bow of the RIB with box [...] ammunition, and several 66mm anti-tank ro[...] launchers. With them were the vital radios, care[...] waterproofed.

The sea was freezing cold, and we were [...] chilled to the bone as waves washed over into the[...] as we moved towards the distant shore. A Forc[...] to Seven gale suddenly hit us and water starte[...] seep in from leaking bungs near the engine, w[...] died several times as huge waves swept ove[...] stern. The coxswain steered into the heavy s[...] minimise its force, and at 0130 we arrived in the [...] West Head, further west than we had intended[...]

Looking through the mist, our nightscopes [...] showing only a green haze. Although we were n[...] the lee of West Head where the bay was relat[...] sheltered, the sea was still rough. Hugging the sh[...] we moved carefully along, scanning the high gr[...] and dark shoreline with our nightscopes. A thick[...] of kelp lined the shore and was slowly cloggin[...] the propeller. We could see that a landing a[...] pre-determined spot would not be possible, [...] decided to get onto a small knoll – Knob Island –[...] conduct the bombardment from the top.

The two sentries swam ashore and searche[...] waist-high tussock grass of the 50ft high knoll, sv[...] covering the 100yd diameter of the island. The[...] boat was brought in close enough for the rest of [...] wade ashore. Knob Island sits at the mouth o[...] river at the head of Fox Bay, with Fox Bay Settle[...] on either side. It would have been an ideal spot f[...] Argentinian sentry position and we were care[...] search it fully before landing.

Radio Operator 1 Steve Hoyland contacted[...] ship and then I brought down the bombardment [...] fuel dump and trench positions on the foresh[...] using airburst shells (which produce a sho[...] effect). Unfortunately, the soaking of the boat tri[...] affected the radio and it began to function inter[...] tently as water short-circuited the leads.

The tide was receding, revealing an ever gre[...] barrier of seaweed, so the coxswain recalled [...] the boat in order to get back out into the centre c[...] bay. The RIB engine revved suddenly. The coxs[...] reached down below the waterline and annour[...] that the propeller had been wrenched off by ke[...] and there was no spare.

On the shore our shelling had been accurate; [...] tanks were burning and there was panic firing [...]

Raid on Fox Bay
26 May 1982

Occupying a defensive position which could be taken by amphibious assault only at great cost, the Argentinian garrison at Fox Bay on West Falkland was selected as a target for the guns of HMS *Plymouth*. Two men from 148 Commando Forward Observation Battery and an SBS combat team were inserted by small boat to adjust the fire.

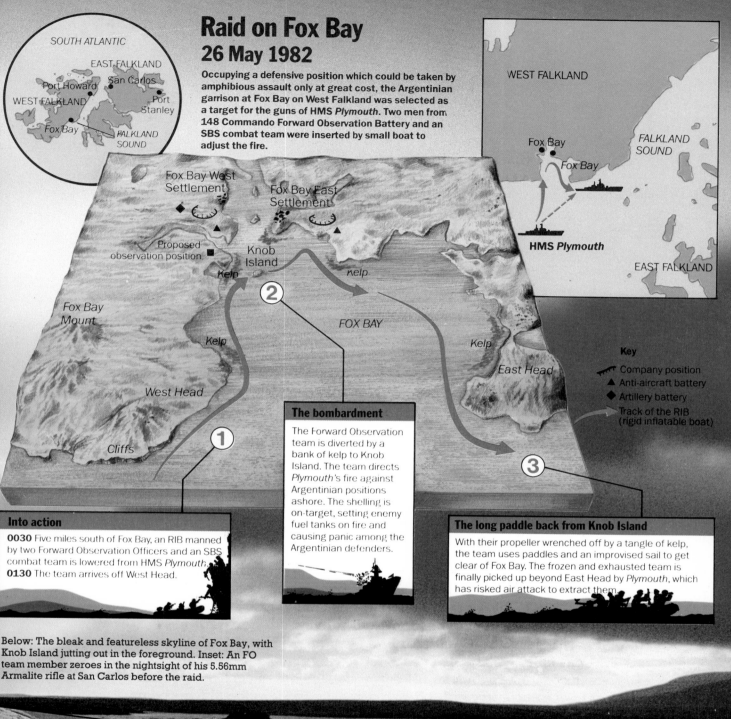

SOUTH ATLANTIC

EAST FALKLAND

Port Howard   San Carlos

WEST FALKLAND   Port Stanley

Fox Bay   FALKLAND SOUND

WEST FALKLAND

Fox Bay   Fox Bay

FALKLAND SOUND

EAST FALKLAND

HMS *Plymouth*

Fox Bay West Settlement

Fox Bay East Settlement

Proposed observation position   Knob Island

Kelp

Fox Bay Mount

Kelp

FOX BAY

Kelp

East Head

West Head

Cliffs

Key
- Company position
- Anti-aircraft battery
- Artillery battery
- Track of the RIB (rigid inflatable boat)

Into action

0030 Five miles south of Fox Bay, an RIB manned by two Forward Observation Officers and an SBS combat team is lowered from HMS *Plymouth*.
0130 The team arrives off West Head.

The bombardment

The Forward Observation team is diverted by a bank of kelp to Knob Island. The team directs *Plymouth*'s fire against Argentinian positions ashore. The shelling is on-target, setting enemy fuel tanks on fire and causing panic among the Argentinian defenders.

The long paddle back from Knob Island

With their propeller wrenched off by a tangle of kelp, the team uses paddles and an improvised sail to get clear of Fox Bay. The frozen and exhausted team is finally picked up beyond East Head by *Plymouth*, which has risked air attack to extract them.

Below: The bleak and featureless skyline of Fox Bay, with Knob Island jutting out in the foreground. Inset: An FO team member zeroes in the nightsight of his 5.56mm Armalite rifle at San Carlos before the raid.

Left: Just before the main landings at San Carlos, FO1 and an SBS fighting patrol neutralised an Argentinian heavy weapons company on Fanning Head and took the first prisoners on East Falkland (below left). Far left: Operating undetected on enemy-occupied Beagle Ridge, FO1 was able to photograph the 2 Para attack on Wireless Ridge almost from the receiving end. Bottom: Captain Hugh McManners, looking in no mood for a photograph.

away. The naval shells that followed promptly silenced it.

The night was very dark. The ship's muzzle flashes could be seen far out in the sound, followed by the sinister hiss of shells coming in overhead. Each faint report from the guns (delayed by distance) was followed by a heartless crash close by as the shells landed, then a dull echo as the explosions reverberated in the darkness of the surrounding hills.

Our boat was now being blown onto the eastern shore of the bay. We took down the sail and began paddling again to cover the mile-and-a-half back around East Head, out to sea where *Plymouth* (which dared not enter the bay for fear of land-based Exocet missiles) could pick us up. There was a cut-off time by which she had to sail if she was to reach the safety of the anti-aircraft missile screen of San Carlos before first light. Already *Plymouth* had detected Fledermaus radar emissions from Fox Bay and enemy aircraft in the vicinity. Another anti-aircraft battery started firing, the flak cannon shells bursting overhead and uncomfortably close to our water-logged boat.

The cut-off time elapsed and the ship was due to leave to avoid daylight and the danger of air attack. Captain Pentreath announced over *Plymouth's* tannoy that as far as he was concerned we were part of his ship's company and the ship would not be leaving Fox Bay without us – in spite of the risk from the usual dawn Argentinian air raid. In the water-filled RIB we were making our own contingency plans, firstly, for landing in the midst of the enemy and then, when the wind shifted, for landing on the east side of the bay.

As we paddled painfully towards East Head, *Plymouth* launched her Gemini to rendezvous and give a tow, and we vectored ourselves together using red lights. The RIB was so heavy and full of water that we had to continue paddling even after the Gemini had begun to tow us, right round the headland and out to sea to make the rendezvous with the ship. It was broad daylight, well after the agreed cut-off time, when we came alongside and clambered wearily up the rope scramble net to the welcome of the waiting gunship.

The assault by *Plymouth's* guns crippled the Argentinian base at Fox Bay, damaging a precious stock of fuel and killing or wounding several of the garrison. Argentinian prisoners questioned after the war described in detail the demoralising effect of this and subsequent naval gunfire raids. It was also reported that the commanding officer at Fox Bay had committed suicide with his pistol after the raid. Perhaps, if he had known the plight of the 148 Commando FO team out in the bay, he would have stayed his hand.

Argentinian positions, the tracer giving away their exact locations. With the propeller gone, a stiff wind was blowing us onto the shore which we had just been shelling. The Argentinian sentries were wide awake, firing bursts of tracer sporadically out to sea.

We began to paddle in earnest to keep the boat from being blown onto the shore. Although we were chilled and shivering from the long wet passage, we were soon drenched with sweat inside the rubber suits. Vigorous bailing was also needed as the leaks were becoming serious. The coxswain then detected a wind change, away from the Argentinian positions and towards the eastern side of the bay, but as all the planned emergency rendezvous were on the western side (the side where the landing should have been made) this was small improvement.

By using parts from the spare radio it was possible to get through to the ship, but on VHF and not an HF circuit. Warrant Officer 2 Richards on *Plymouth* identified the transmissions on VHF and worked out what had gone wrong. I was able to carry on with the bombardment, adjusting the fall of the shells in between periods of bailing furiously. I could use only the most rudimentary procedure as I dared not use a torch to look at the written fireplan for the proper target numbers. Warrant Officer 2 Richards was thus obliged to translate messages like, 'Ten salvoes on the far right-hand target,' into proper calls for fire.

The radio had become the most important piece of equipment to us now, essential to our safe recovery. The GPMG and the 66mm rockets lay ignored in the ankle-deep water at the bottom of the RIB. The coxswain then made a mast and sail from the paddles and a poncho and it was held up by two of us balancing precariously in the bow. The wind was now blowing the boat sideways, across the shoreline rather than directly onto it.

The shelling was increasing the Argentinians' excitement – and their firing. The anti-aircraft battery to the east – towards which we were being blown – opened up with flak shells, giving its position

THE AUTHOR Major Hugh McManners, as a captain, was one of the Naval Gunfire Forward Observers of 148 Commando Forward Observation Battery in the Falklands campaign of 1982, where he received a Mention in Despatches. He has subsequently written a book entitled *Falklands Commando*.

The division of Korea along the 38th parallel in 1945 led to the outbreak of war on 25 June 1950, when North Korean communist forces crossed the border and invaded the South.

At the Royal Marines Commando School near Dartmoor, orders were received to form an Independent Commando unit to serve with the United Nations forces deployed to Korea. The Commando was to be used for special raiding tasks, in support of US forces, behind enemy lines. In the space of a few days during August, 41 (Independent) Commando was raised, under the command of Lieutenant-Colonel Douglas Drysdale. The force totalled a mere 219 all ranks, inclusive of medical personnel.

Wearing their civilian clothes, the commandos were flown to Japan, where they were equipped with American weapons and kit. However, in keeping with marine tradition, the proud commandos kept their green berets.

Following intensive training at Camp McGill during September, 41 performed a number of successful raids on the northeast coast of Korea, before being placed under the command of the 1st US Marine Division and shipped to Hungnam. After the perilous retreat from the Chosin Reservoir, the unit moved to Yodo island and made a number of raids which wreaked havoc on the main coastal railway. 41 Commando was withdrawn from Korea in December 1951, some elements being incorporated into the 3rd Commando Brigade in Malaya. 41 was eventually disbanded in Plymouth, Devon, in February 1952. Above: The 41 Commando insignia.

Originally tasked to disrupt enemy supply lines, 41 Commando was to cover the US 1st Marine Division in its perilous withdrawal from Chosin

NOVEMBER IN KOREA is bitterly cold and wet, and the inhospitable terrain creates a breeding ground for sickness and injury. As winter set in, the US marines in the Chosin area were totally unprepared for the intolerable conditions. While their North Korean and Chinese counterparts were equipped with thick quilted clothing, the marines lacked adequate protection; even their sleeping bags provided no respite from the cold. When nightfall came, the temperature dropped dramatically and a full night's sleep was a rare luxury.

On the night of 27 November 1950, the Chinese Communist Forces (CCF) began to advance against the US X Corps in the Chosin area, making exploratory probes at Koto-ri, Yudam-ni and Hagaru. The following night they attacked Hagaru in force, inflicting heavy casualties on the American forces. The 1st US Marine Division was in urgent need of reinforcements and Lieutenant-Colonel Douglas Drysdale was ordered to take a relieving force to Koto-ri, and then proceed north to Hagaru. At 0700 on 29 November the column set off along a winding road which snaked between the steep hillsides. Drysdale's force totalled 992 men and 141 vehicles, made up of the British 41 (Independent) Commando, a company of US marines and a US army company under command. During the previous night the Chinese had blocked the column's route in over 17 places, and enemy troops held most of the high ground. The relieving force was easy prey for an ambush.

Serious resistance was soon encountered from a large Chinese force pouring withering fire down on the beleaguered column from a hill to the north, and 41 Commando were tasked to take out the enemy strongpoint. Despite the extreme cold and driving snow flurries, the commandos prised the frozen Chinese from their hastily concealed fox-holes, allowing the US marines to pass through and secure a second hill. The commandos then continued on to a third rise, while the army company remained with the main transport column. The heavy weapons group, under the command of Lieutenant Peter Thomas, helped to keep the enemy pinned down with 81mm mortars and A4 Brownings.

The relieving force was augmented by the arrival of 17 tanks in the early afternoon. Drysdale had

Right: Deep inside enemy territory, commandos prepare to demolish the main railway line south of Songjin. A series of 40lb charges are being placed in holes (top) blasted out by 'beehive' explosives (bottom). Top right: Second-in-command, Major Dennis Aldridge (right) is seen here with the unit's doctor, Surgeon Lieutenant Douglas Knock.

COMING OUT FIGHTING

RAILWAY SABOTAGE

On the night of 1/2 October 1950, Lieutenant-Colonel Drysdale led the men of 41 Commando on their first raid, only six weeks after the unit had been raised. Their target was Sorye Dong and the railway that ran along the northeast coast of Korea. The commandos were transported to the raid by the submarine USS *Perch*, living in spaces formerly taken up by torpedo tubes. After avoiding patrol boats, the submarine launched a landing craft that had been housed in the conning tower and this towed the commandos, in 10 10-man inflatables, the four and a half miles to shore. With the enemy unaware of their presence, the raiders placed their anti-tank mines on the railway and returned to *Perch* without incident. The mines were soon detonated by a train, and 41 Commando returned to its base in Japan.

The Commando's second raid was made by C and D Troops on 7 October. The target was an important supply line, eight miles south of Songjin. The force comprised 130 all ranks, and it was towed towards the shore by landing craft launched from two US destroyers. A swimmer, sent ahead to recce the beach, encountered no enemy patrols and signalled the main party to land. Again, their target was the railway line, their objective being to cut off supplies bound for North Korean divisions. An 88mm bazooka was sited at the entrance of the tunnel, and the raiders spent two hours hauling explosives from the landing craft to the target. Thirty-minute fuzes ensured the commandos enough time to reach the beach, before a thunderous explosion and a ball of flame signalled their mission's success.

Following 41 Commando's action in the withdrawal from the Chosin Reservoir, the unit operated from Yodo island in Wonsan Bay in strikes against the North Korean coast. By the summer of 1951 it possessed a strength of 300, and the Commando's lightning efficiency forced the communists to divert troops away from the main battle area in order to defend the railway. Large-scale landings gave way to raids conducted by sections of 20 men, towed ashore in inflatables by landing craft, with canoeists making recces prior to each operation.

By late 1951, air strikes had destroyed most of the railway bridges and 41 Commando, its task complete, was ordered to withdraw.

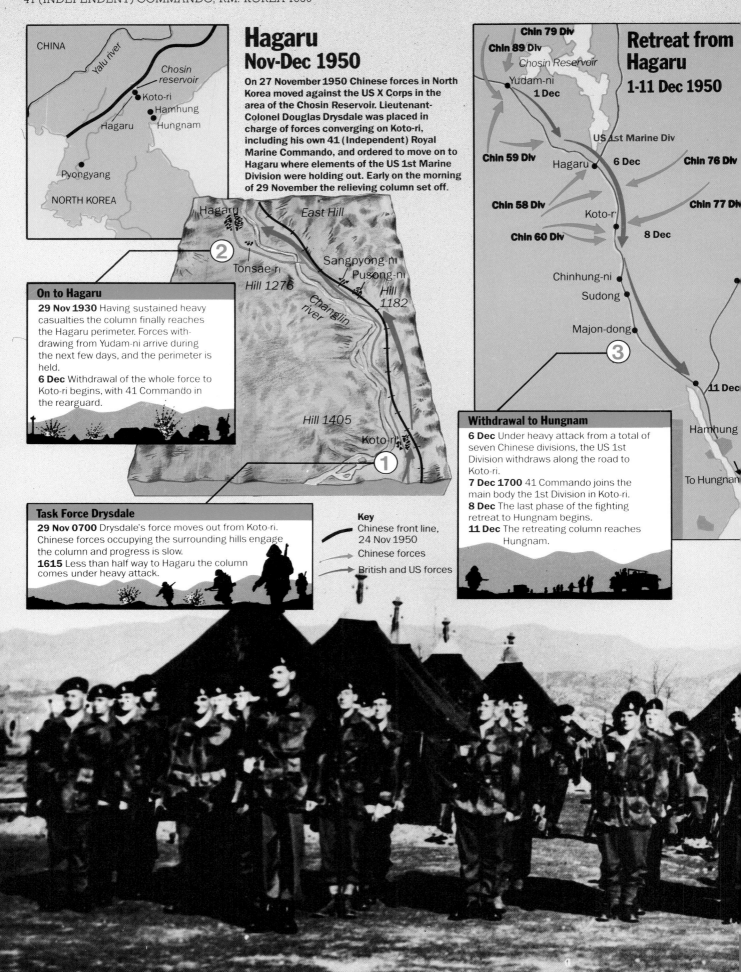

Hagaru
Nov-Dec 1950

On 27 November 1950 Chinese forces in North Korea moved against the US X Corps in the area of the Chosin Reservoir. Lieutenant-Colonel Douglas Drysdale was placed in charge of forces converging on Koto-ri, including his own 41 (Independent) Royal Marine Commando, and ordered to move on to Hagaru where elements of the US 1st Marine Division were holding out. Early on the morning of 29 November the relieving column set off.

Retreat from Hagaru
1-11 Dec 1950

On to Hagaru

29 Nov 1930 Having sustained heavy casualties the column finally reaches the Hagaru perimeter. Forces withdrawing from Yudam-ni arrive during the next few days, and the perimeter is held.
6 Dec Withdrawal of the whole force to Koto-ri begins, with 41 Commando in the rearguard.

Task Force Drysdale

29 Nov 0700 Drysdale's force moves out from Koto-ri. Chinese forces occupying the surrounding hills engage the column and progress is slow.
1615 Less than half way to Hagaru the column comes under heavy attack.

Withdrawal to Hungnam

6 Dec Under heavy attack from a total of seven Chinese divisions, the US 1st Division withdraws along the road to Koto-ri.
7 Dec 1700 41 Commando joins the main body the 1st Division in Koto-ri.
8 Dec The last phase of the fighting retreat to Hungnam begins.
11 Dec The retreating column reaches Hungnam.

Key
— Chinese front line, 24 Nov 1950
→ Chinese forces
→ British and US forces

Map labels: CHINA, Yalu river, Chosin reservoir, Koto-ri, Hamhung, Hagaru, Hungnam, Pyongyang, NORTH KOREA

Chin 79 Div, Chin 89 Div, Chosin Reservoir, Yudam-ni, 1 Dec, US 1st Marine Div, Chin 59 Div, Hagaru, 6 Dec, Chin 76 Div, Chin 58 Div, Koto-ri, Chin 77 Div, Chin 60 Div, 8 Dec, Chinhung-ni, Sudong, Majon-dong, 11 Dec, Hamhung, To Hungnam

Terrain map labels: Hagaru, East Hill, Tonsae-ri, Sangpyong-ni, Pusong-ni, Hill 1276, Hill 1182, Changjin river, Hill 1405, Koto-ri

wanted to split these down the column's length to ensure adequate protection, but was overruled by the tank commander who insisted that they should be kept together at the front. This was to prove disastrous. As the tanks set off, their progress was impeded by innumerable potholes and icy patches along the road. The column was repeatedly held up by frontal and right-flank fire and, with all the tanks concentrated at the front, it was extremely vulnerable.

By 1615, the column had only moved four miles along the road to Hagaru, and the icy winter night was setting in. No sooner had one hill been cleared of snipers and mortar positions, than the next dominating feature required similar treatment. Unprotected, the soft-skinned vehicles were fired upon unmercifully and burning trucks lit up the winter gloom. With flames licking the night sky, it was an easy task for the Chinese to range their guns onto worthwhile targets. Very soon, the tanks ground to a standstill; Drysdale was tempted to withdraw to Koto-ri and renew the journey to Hagaru the following day. However, an urgent message from the besieged American division at Hagaru forced him to press on.

After moving only one mile further, the column was again under serious threat. The CCF had dominated a defile and, after letting the vanguard through, they split the column. Among those cut off was Captain Pat Ovens with his assault engineers and some of Commando HQ. Altogether, 25 marines were led skilfully over the snowbound hills back to Koto-ri by Ovens. That night the temperature dropped to minus 10 degrees; wet gloves froze on the marines' hands, making any attempt to fire their weapons virtually impossible.

Since Drysdale was leading the main force his second-in-command, Major Dennis Aldridge, was left to command 41. At one point he saw hordes of Chinese infantry streaming down a hill towards the column. Hopelessly outnumbered, Aldridge called up support from American ground-attack fighters. Conspicuous against the white snow, the enemy

were relentlessly mown down.

Under heavy fire, the main column pushed on to within one mile of Hagaru. Here it was confronted by an abandoned tank and other burning vehicles blocking the narrow road. In the distance, illuminated by arclights, US engineers could be seen working frantically to construct a runway out of the frozen earth. Enemy fire was still being poured onto the relieving force from both sides, and it was only by hand-to-hand fighting that the British and American marines managed to forge their way through. Casualties had been heavy: 65 men of 41 Commando were either killed, wounded or missing in action.

'To the slender garrison of Hagaru was added a tank company and some 300 seasoned infantry'

By pushing on slowly, allowing the Chinese to come at them and then mowing them down in their hordes, the column eventually reached the Hagaru perimeter around 1930 on the 29th. In the two days of continuous fighting, 321 casualties had been sustained and 75 vehicles lost. But as the official US Marine Corps history states: 'To the slender garrison of Hagaru was added a tank company and some 300 seasoned infantry.' Less than 100 men of 41 Commando had got through, in temperatures that had dropped to minus 24 degrees. Only when they had reached Hagaru did they learn that three Chinese regiments had been ranged against them.

Operating as a mobile reserve, 41 Commando was immediately placed under the command of the 3rd Battalion, 1st US Marines, which was responsible for securing the Hagaru perimeter, some six miles in circumference. Despite having been on their feet for over 48 hours, few of the commandos managed to sleep that night. Huddled together for warmth, they were gripped by the twin enemies of the CCF and the bitterly cold conditions. During the days that followed, many of the wounded were flown out from the hastily constructed airstrip. One plane crashed just outside the perimeter and 41 Commando was given the unsavoury task of trying to locate the survivors. It was one of the few occasions when the

By the end of September 1950, the collapse of the North Korean People's Army (NKPA) seemed inevitable. Seoul had been captured by UN and Republic of Korea (ROK) forces, which were now sweeping up towards the 38th parallel. By mid-November, the NKPA had been driven back to the Chinese border.

The 1st US Marine Division, under command of X Corps, had established itself in the mountains around the Chosin Reservoir, and there was a strong feeling among the troops that they would be 'home for Christmas'.

Then, suddenly, a new element entered the picture. China had already expressed her unwillingness to see her Korean neighbour overrun by UN forces, and elements of the Chinese Communist Forces (CCF) had attacked isolated ROK units in late October.

Then, between 25 and 27 November, the CCF launched a major offensive – 18 divisions attacked UN forces west of the Chosin mountains, smashing three ROK divisions and threatening to encircle the entire US Eighth Army. As the CCF drove southwards into the X Corps zone, five Chinese divisions were then used to attack the 1st US Marine Division positions at Yudam-ni, Hagaru and Koto-ri. The US marines were completely isolated. Hagaru, with its airstrip, had to be held, but there was not much more than a battalion there to defend it.

Against this background, 41 Commando, sent in as part of a relief force, was to become embroiled in one of the bloodiest battles fought during the early stages of the Korean War.

Included in 41 Commando were several veterans of World War II commando operations. Below: On parade at Koto-ri, the men of 41 demonstrate how they acquired their reputation as an immaculately turned-out unit under the most arduous conditions.

enemy did not attempt to interfere. On the night of 30 November, the perimeter was breached and B Troop, under Lieutenant Gerald Roberts, was ordered to secure the area. Over unfamiliar ground and with scarcely any protection against the extreme temperatures, the commandos went in. The Chinese were no match for the highly trained men of 41, and by 0400 the perimeter had been restored.

The days were now relatively quiet. The marines cleaned their semi-automatic M1 Garand rifles, having preferred these to the M1 lightweight carbines which had proved unreliable in the freezing temperatures of North Korea. Unlike their American counterparts, the British marines took great pride in shaving each morning, giving them at least a clean appearance 'up top'. Capped with their prized green berets, this did much for discipline and morale considering the appalling conditions. Several fighting patrols were sent out to assess the enemy's

Right: Hell at Chosin. The perilous Hagaru-Koto-ri breakout was the first time that the British and American Marine Corps had fought alongside each other since the defence of the Peking Legations at the turn of the century. Guarding the main column, marines were called upon to take out many enemy strongpoints on high ground above the road (below).

Commando, Royal Marines, North Korea 1950

This commando wears US M43 combat dress issued to the unit upon their arrival in Japan. The web equipment incorporates a US marine first aid pouch. The commandos retained their green berets (minus the unit badge), their rubber-soled boots and '37 pattern blackened web anklets. This commando carries the .30in M1 Garand rifle, and a clasp knife.

strength and on 4 December the depleted Commando, with tanks in support, was sent to recover some 155mm howitzers that had been abandoned on the Yudam-ni road. Sniper fire failed to impede their progress and they reached the guns without loss. However, the howitzers were impossible to recover and, to prevent them from falling into enemy hands, they were destroyed.

Meanwhile, casualty evacuation continued. By nightfall on 5 December, 4312 men, including 25 Royal Marines, had been flown out, and 500 men had come in from outlying positions. On 6 December, orders arrived for the withdrawal to Koto-ri; 41 Commando was placed under command of the 5th US Marines, recently withdrawn from Yudam-ni, who were to form the rearguard of the column. The extreme temperatures were unremitting as this weary force began its withdrawal– down the road over which they had fought so recently – but the resolve of the Royal Marines remained intact. Indeed, before the main party moved out just after dawn, Colonel Drysdale ordered an inspection of 41 Commando – much to the astonishment of the Americans.

Comprising 10,000 troops and 1000 vehicles, the column was led by the 7th US Marines with air support from US navy and marine corps pilots. Flying World War II Corsairs, these brave pilots were constantly in the air, monitoring the column's progress and providing much-needed close air support.

At the rear of the column, entrenched at Hagaru, 41 Commando awaited its turn to move, but constant enemy attacks all along the road meant that progress was painfully slow. The rear perimeter around Hagaru gradually receded in the face of relentless Chinese attack. To the commandos of 41, it seemed as if the resources of their enemy were without limit. For most of the day, the British and American marines fought a desperate battle against vast odds, sending out patrols to bolster the perimeter and under constant threat of sniper and mortar fire. Eventually, as dusk settled, the column began to move forward and the rearguard withdrew from Hagaru. However, 41 Commando only managed to move a miserable 400yds before being forced to halt.

During the interminable night to follow, rest was impossible due to continuous probing by the CCF. The crackle of gunfire and the dull thud of mortars engulfed the beleaguered column. Silences, which came infrequently, were even worse – somehow there was comfort in the rattling of smallarms fire. Numb fingers tightened around waiting triggers, and tired eyes imagined a steady stream of enemy forces pouring down the dark, snow-covered hills. Silences were often broken by the surreal sound of Chinese bugle calls echoing around the countryside. The effect was spine-chilling. Only firm disci-

Air support was used to destroy CCF roadblocks (left) and cover the retreating troops (below). Below left: A hot meal for the commandos of 41.

Top: Their sustained effort over, members of 41 (Independent) Commando are able to wind down at their camp at Hungnam after the battle. Now that their American outer garments are removed their British battledress is much in evidence, including the distinctive flashes and green berets of the Royal Marine Commandos. Above: Exhausted but jubilant, commandos pause in their combat gear next to a trailer piled with equipment for a victory photograph.

and flushed their opponents from their well-dug positions, without any loss to themselves.

This was almost the final incident of the withdrawal, and at 1700 hours the rearguard rejoined the main divisional column and marched into Koto-ri. The arduous 10-mile journey from Hagaru had taken them a sleepless 38 hours. En route they had recovered some of 41 Commando's dead, killed only ten days before; ten days which now seemed like a lifetime. On 8 December these were duly buried with full military honours. That night Captain Ovens and his party of marines rejoined the unit, having been cut off during the battle on 29 November.

But the struggle was not over yet; the next 'breakout', from Koto-ri to Hungnam, had already started. Just two miles south of Koto-ri, 41 Commando was ordered to occupy the high ground to the east, in order to prevent infiltration by Chinese infantry. They climbed the steep slope, sometimes in more than two feet of snow, with a blinding storm obscuring their view and lending hazard to each step. The unit spent that night perched on the bleak mountainside, chilled by a temperature of minus 15 degrees, wondering if dawn would ever come. Luckily, the enemy decided to stay in that night.

With heads held high and a stiffening of their backs, the Royal Marines of 41 Commando fell in

The depressing thought of a 23-mile march to the Hungnam bridgehead, having had little sleep for the past fortnight, was a daunting prospect. Nevertheless, the young officers and their more experienced NCOs, with typical British resolve and humour, had maintained a high level of morale. As dawn broke, morale was further boosted by the welcome news that trucks were awaiting them five miles ahead at Majon-dong. With heads held high and a stiffening of their backs, the Royal Marines of 41 Commando fell in, stepped out almost as though they were on parade at their depot at Deal, and set off at a speed which left the Americans astonished. The sweet ride into Hungnam was due reward for the small, highly trained and independent unit, which at that time was the sole representative of British forces in the 1st US Marine Division. By 11 December the whole of the division had come out fighting, bringing their wounded and equipment with them. In doing so, they had inflicted a major defeat on the CCF, which had sustained over 37,000 casualties.

As a result of their heroic exploits in the Chosin area, 41 Commando received a US Presidential Citation, which they proudly wear on their colours in the form of a streamer. Fourteen American gallantry awards were made, and a number of British medals were awarded to the marines of 41. But 41 Commando suffered dearly – 98 casualties, 39 wounded and 27 missing – a very high percentage from the 219 men who had set out from Koto-ri.

The citation reads as testimony to the bravery of 41 (Independent) Commando RM:

'The valiant fighting spirit, relentless perseverance and heroic fortitude of the officers and men of the First Marine Division, Reinforced, in battle against vastly outnumbering enemy, were in keeping with the highest traditions of the United States Naval Service.'

THE AUTHOR Captain Derek Oakley, Royal Marines, was a staff officer of 3 Commando Brigade, Royal Marines, in 1962.

pline and controlled bravery prevented those men defending the perimeter from opening fire – and disclosing their positions to the enemy.

By now, seven Chinese divisions were concentrated against the 1st US Marine Division, and under a moonless night the enemy closed in. Remarkably, they were driven off with only a few casualties to the column. Next morning the bodies of over 600 Chinese soldiers were strewn in front of their positions.

It was a cold and weary rearguard column that got underway on the morning of 7 December, only to discover that they had been cut off from the main divisional column during the night. Marching for two hours under constant fire, they were halted at 1100 hours by an enemy road block. After the marines had cleared this obstacle, the withdrawing force was obliged to hedge-hop along the high ground overlooking the winding road – seeking to avoid enemy ambush. The support provided by the Corsairs was invaluable; flying in atrocious conditions, they helped the ground forces to take out enemy strongpoints as they retreated.

At 1600, C Troop was called upon to dislodge an enemy position on the high ground to the east of the road. Crawling silently up the steep, snowbound hillside, the commandos manoeuvred into a vantage point overlooking the enemy machine guns and snipers. Fixing bayonets, they stormed down the hill

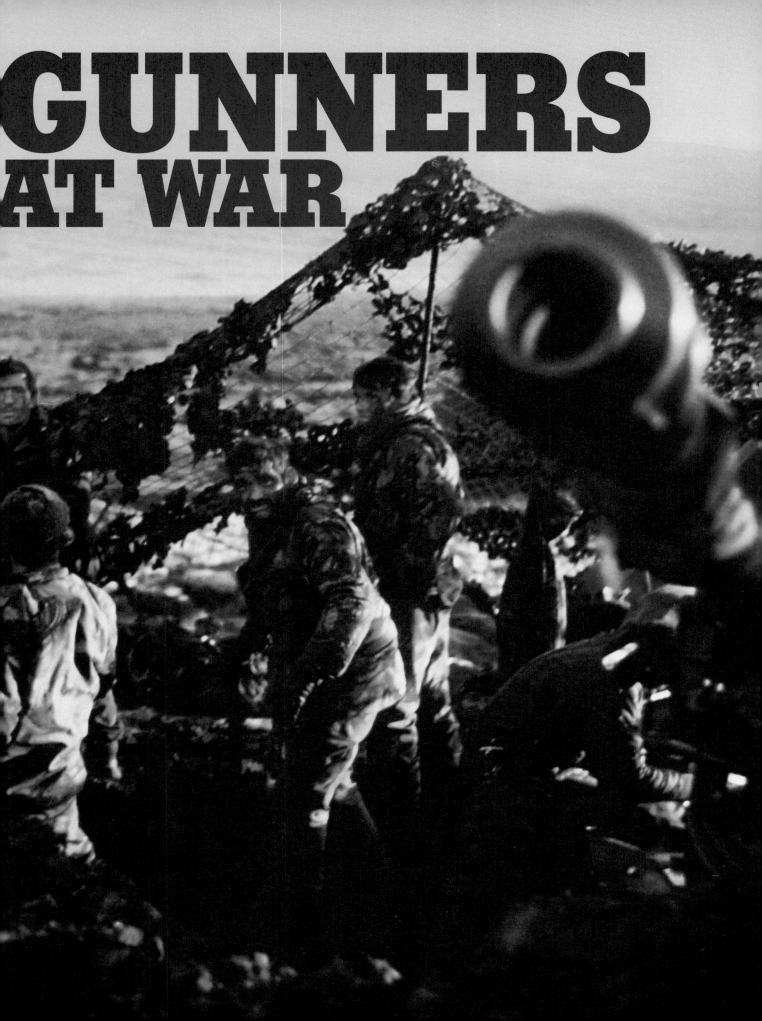

GUNNERS
AT WAR

ROYAL ARTILLERY

Despite its permanent attachment to 3 Commando Brigade, 29 Commando Regiment remains part of the Royal Artillery and, as such, can trace its history back to the fifteenth century. It was not until the early 1720s, however, that the Royal Artillery was formally brought into existence.

Since its formation, the Royal Artillery has seen action in virtually every major battle fought by British troops. The unit does not commemorate its distinguished career with battle honours, but its motto 'Ubique' ('Everywhere'), on the cap badge above, indicates the central role of the Royal Artillery in British military operations. During the Falklands war the ground forces were supported by 30 105mm Light Guns. 29 Commando provided 79 (Kirkee), 7 (Sphinx) and 8 (Alma) Batteries; each of six guns. Other artillery units present, again equipped with 105mm guns, were 8 and 29 Batteries from 4 Field Regiment. Air defence was provided by the Rapier missiles of T Battery, 12 Air Defence Regiment, and the Blowpipes carried by two troops from 43 Battery, 32 Guided Weapons Regiment. Forward observers were provided by 148 Commando Battery, 4 Field Regiment and 49 Field Regiment.

29 Commando, RA, gave 3 Commando Brigade the firepower they needed to take on the Argentinian defences on the Falklands – but conditions were not easy for the gunners

IN THE late evening of Sunday, 4 April 1982, the commanding officer of 29 Commando Regiment, Royal Artillery, Lieutenant-Colonel M. J. Holroyd Smith, briefed his officers on their mission. As an integral part of 3 Commando Brigade, the regiment with its 18 105mm Light Guns was to join the Royal Navy Task Force preparing to sail to the Falklands. Holroyd Smith stressed that time was of the essence and that preparations had to be completed by the following morning. His orders produced a flurry of hasty action: personal equipment was packed in bergens, and an issue of winter clothing was carried out in quick time. Outside the regiment's barracks at the Citadel in Plymouth, the night echoed to the sound of lorries carrying thousands of artillery rounds and other essential combat supplies to the unit's embarkation points.

Because of its size, the regiment was split between several ships for the journey south: 7 (Sphinx) Commando Battery joined the RFA *Sir Percivale* with part of 8 (Alma) Commando Battery; another part of Alma Battery boarded HMS *Fearless*; and 79 (Kirkee) Commando Battery with T Battery of 12 Air Defence Regiment embarked on the RFA *Sir Geraint*. On 8 April the battery commanders and OP (observation post) parties of 8 and 79 Batteries left Southampton on the *Canberra* with 40 and 42 Commando and 3 Para.

Although conditions on the ships were cramped, the gunners used the journey to Ascension Island to hone their battle skills. Training was intensive and exhaustive: exercises, weapon training and first-aid courses prepared the men for the struggle ahead. Special emphasis was placed on vehicle and aircraft recognition, an essential part of the gunner's art. In early anticipation of victory, every man was taught the correct procedure for handling prisoners. Arriving at Ascension Island on 20 April, the regiment was able to practice off-loading its equipment, and the men had the opportunity to strengthen their leg muscles during an eight-mile march.

Further shore-based training was frustrated after the need to press south became more urgent as the likelihood of a diplomatic solution to the crisis evaporated. On 21 May the spearhead of the landing force, HMS *Fearless* and *Intrepid*, sailed into Falkland Sound, heading for the beach-heads at Ajax Bay, San Carlos and Port San Carlos. First ashore were

OP parties accompanied by Commandos and Paras. Their mission was to prepare artillery positions on the high ground and identify targets. Opposition to the landings was minimal, and at first light the regiment's Light Guns were flown ashore, slung beneath helicopters.

Although the men were thirsting for combat, they were forced to remain in the hills as the essential build-up of men and supplies, occasionally interrupted by Argentinian air attacks, continued. However, on the evening of 27 May, 28 men and three guns of Alma Battery under the control of Lieutenant Mark Waring were despatched to Camilla Creek House in support of 2 Para's attack on Darwin and Goose Green.

Despite the problems caused by a lack of heavy-lift helicopters, the detachment was in position by the early hours of the 28th. At 0715 hours the guns began their deadly work and for the next four hours they rained shells on the enemy's trenches.

Like their comrades in 2 Para, the gunners faced stiff opposition, including counter-battery fire from Argentinian 105mm pack howitzers and, at first light, strafing runs by Pucara ground-attack aircraft.

Previous page: Manned by men from 29 Commando Regiment, Royal Artillery, a 105mm Light Gun points the way to victory. The regiment took three six-gun batteries to the Falklands and, despite the appalling going, all were used to help pierce the Argentinian defences around the islands' capital. Left: Slung beneath the belly of a Sea King, a light gun is rushed forward to Mount Kent. Helicopters were in short supply, but by flying round the clock, those available kept the gunners supplied with ammunition.

However, by 2100 hours, the enemy's will to resist had been broken by the Paras' spirited attacks and the artillery's fire support. In almost continuous action, the three guns had dropped nearly 900 rounds into the heart of the Argentinian defences.

The regiment's first taste of real action in the campaign also highlighted several problems that the unit would have to contend with until the recapture of Port Stanley. In the Falklands, the regiment's usual tactic of digging pits for its Light Guns was found to be impracticable as any hole in the peaty soil quickly filled with water. The other method of protecting the guns, building earth parapets, was an acceptable alternative only when ample camouflage netting was available to hide the emplacement from marauding aircraft.

The volume of fire directed against the Argentinians during the Goose Green battle suggested that large stockpiles of ammunition would be needed in the battles for possession of the enemy's line of defences around Stanley. Already over-worked, the helicopter crews would have to redouble their efforts to bring forward shells and, because of the terrain, the guns themselves. Although a tough job.

L118 105mm Light Gun

Calibre 105mm
Length (firing) 7.01m
Weight 1860kg
Rate of fire (sustained) 3rpm
Elevation −5.5° to +70°
Traverse 5.5° left and right; 360° on platform
Maximum range 17200m
Crew 6

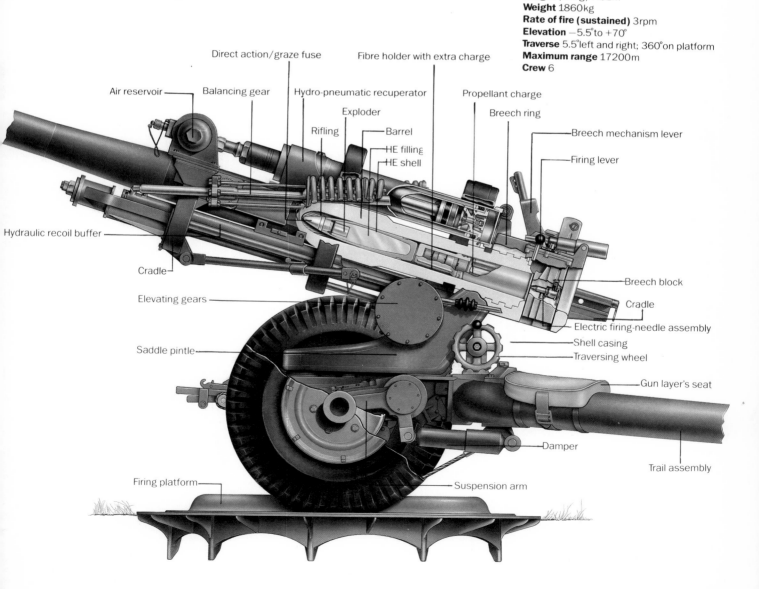

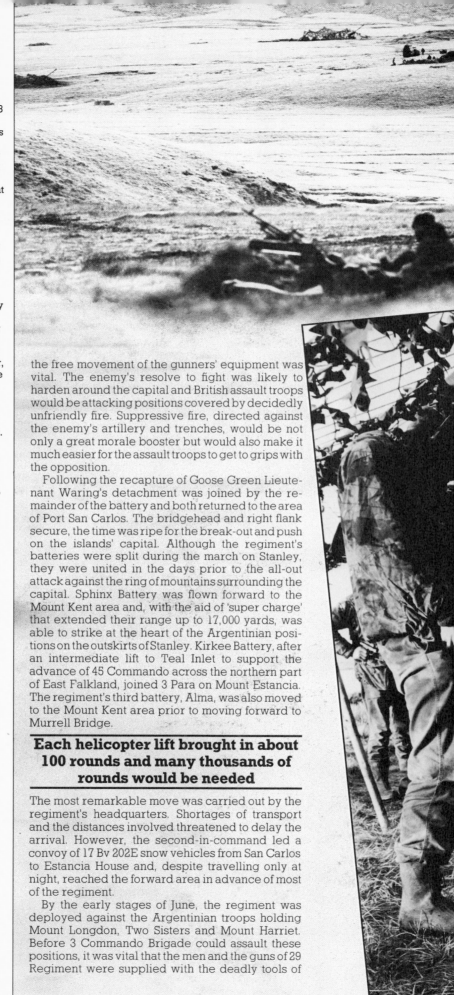

FIREPOWER

Although primarily designed for frontline service in Europe, the L118 105mm Light Gun was ideally suited to the rigours of the battle for the Falklands. After a lengthy period of development at the Royal Armament Research and Development Establishment in Kent during the late 1960s, the gun reached the army in numbers after 1974.

Compact, with a weight of 1860kg, the Light Gun was designed to allow a high degree of battlefield portability. In the air, the Light Gun can be carried by Hercules aircraft or slung under helicopters in either one or two loads. On the ground, the normal towing vehicle is the Land Rover or, under Arctic conditions, the Bv 202E over-snow tractor.

To prevent the gun from turning over during movement its barrel is swung through 180 degrees. This towing aptitude is particularly useful for high speed movement over difficult terrain. If the Light Gun is airlifted in two loads, it can be re-assembled in under 30 minutes by an experienced crew.

The Light Gun packs a considerable battlefield punch and is capable of lobbing shells to a range of 17,200m at a rate of up to eight rounds per minute.

The weapon was also designed to fire a variety of ammunition including high explosive, anti-tank, illuminating and smoke rounds. In action, a limited number of rounds are carried in the Land Rover used by the six-man crew, and another 28 shells are carried in the limber vehicle.

The value of the Light Gun was realised during the battles around Port Stanley. Providing support for infantry assaults or operating against enemy artillery, up to 400 rounds were fired from each gun each day.

the free movement of the gunners' equipment was vital. The enemy's resolve to fight was likely to harden around the capital and British assault troops would be attacking positions covered by decidedly unfriendly fire. Suppressive fire, directed against the enemy's artillery and trenches, would be not only a great morale booster but would also make it much easier for the assault troops to get to grips with the opposition.

Following the recapture of Goose Green Lieutenant Waring's detachment was joined by the remainder of the battery and both returned to the area of Port San Carlos. The bridgehead and right flank secure, the time was ripe for the break-out and push on the islands' capital. Although the regiment's batteries were split during the march on Stanley, they were united in the days prior to the all-out attack against the ring of mountains surrounding the capital. Sphinx Battery was flown forward to the Mount Kent area and, with the aid of 'super charge' that extended their range up to 17,000 yards, was able to strike at the heart of the Argentinian positions on the outskirts of Stanley. Kirkee Battery, after an intermediate lift to Teal Inlet to support the advance of 45 Commando across the northern part of East Falkland, joined 3 Para on Mount Estancia. The regiment's third battery, Alma, was also moved to the Mount Kent area prior to moving forward to Murrell Bridge.

Each helicopter lift brought in about 100 rounds and many thousands of rounds would be needed

The most remarkable move was carried out by the regiment's headquarters. Shortages of transport and the distances involved threatened to delay the arrival. However, the second-in-command led a convoy of 17 Bv 202E snow vehicles from San Carlos to Estancia House and, despite travelling only at night, reached the forward area in advance of most of the regiment.

By the early stages of June, the regiment was deployed against the Argentinian troops holding Mount Longdon, Two Sisters and Mount Harriet. Before 3 Commando Brigade could assault these positions, it was vital that the men and the guns of 29 Regiment were supplied with the deadly tools of

Left: In a featureless landscape, dispersal and an ample supply of camouflage netting were the batteries' best defences against sudden air attack. The ground was usually too boggy for the gunners to dig emplacements, and most positions were surrounded by a low earth parapet. Carefully sited machine guns gave a measure of protection against strafing runs by the enemy's ground-attack aircraft.

GOOSE GREEN

During the attack by 2 Para on Goose Green, fire support was provided by three 105mm guns from 8 (Alma) Commando Battery. The detachment's Gun Position Officer, Lieutenant Mark Waring, fought throughout the action:

'At 0715 hours [GMT, 28 April] the first fire mission took place. The sound of battle could be heard clearly in the background as FOOs [Forward Observation Officers] sent their fire orders. The section fired almost continuously for the first four hours, and cartridge cases and salvage began to pile up inside the cam nets to proportions never before experienced. The observers would simply give a fresh direction and correction to the previous target as more targets appeared in front of them. Often they would order "check firing" as the Paras came too close to the enemy positions for us to engage.

'With the arrival of dawn at 1100 hours [GMT], it was time to worry about our major threat – air attack. The main concern was several Pucara aircraft, operating from Goose Green airstrip. It was not long before two appeared, heading straight down the valley to our front. When the leading aircraft was within 200 yards of the front gun and seemed ready to open fire, it was engaged by Blowpipe. The aircraft veered to the left firing its full broadside of rockets into the right of the gun position. The second aircraft did not approach further. An hour later another Pucara approached, to be engaged this time by our own smallarms fire.

'Throughout the day, the guns fired some 850 rounds, mainly at specific targets such as bunkers, anti-aircraft guns, and most memorable of all, chasing a Pucara up and down the airstrip as it was attempting to take off. By nightfall it became clear that 2 Para had taken all their objectives except Goose Green itself. The Argentinians were bottled up with the sea to their backs and the Paras to their front. Our guns fell silent, allowing detachments a well-earned rest.

'The following morning, 29 May, the remainder of the battery with another 800 rounds were flown in to join us. By early afternoon we were ready for a possible firepower demonstration. This was going to take place on Goose Green airstrip, if the Argentinian troops refused to surrender. We had received reports that negotiations were underway and by mid-afternoon the official ceremony had taken place. Some 1400 Argentinians surrendered.'

Left: Gunners from 79 (Kirkee) Commando Battery prepare to engage targets on the high ground to the west of Port Stanley from Mount Kent. To maintain a constant barrage, each six-man crew had to work as a well-oiled machine. Here, one man rams home the shell while another gunner stands ready to load the charge. Working full out, each team could fire up to eight rounds per minute. During the campaign 79 Battery fired a total of 2700 shells.

their trade. Ammunition was the chief worry; each helicopter lift brought in about 100 rounds and it was believed that many thousands of shells would be needed to conclude the campaign. The loss of valuable helicopters on the *Atlantic Conveyor* reduced the rate of forward supply, but the pilots and logistical service were flexible enough to minimise the disruption.

During this lull the men on the ground prepared for action: Forward Observation Officers accompanied patrols or watched enemy movements to identify key targets while the gunners improved their earthen emplacements and stockpiled ammunition within easy reach.

Given the nature of the first stage of the proposed attack, a three-unit assault along a broad front, the role of the artillery had to be planned to the smallest detail. Particular attention was paid to the timing of the barrage to avoid hitting friendly troops as they went in under the cover of darkness. Whilst the discussions continued, the regiment harassed the enemy with gunfire to sap their will to resist by denying them the luxury of sleep. Conversely, the reassuring blast of the regiment's Light Guns did much to raise the spirits of the British forces in the area as they endured the misery of wearing sodden clothing and eating unappetising rations. During the day, opportunity targets were engaged at every occasion. Many times observers were able to pinpoint Argentinian troops in the open and call up an artillery strike. Frequently, the enemy were sent scurrying back to Stanley by a well-aimed salvo.

By 10 June the regiment had completed its preparations: over 600 rounds per gun were available, target co-ordinates had been processed and the men had regained their stamina. For the first time in the campaign 29 Regiment was operating as a single unit. Each of its three batteries had been given a priority call: 7 Battery was to support 42 Commando's attack on Mount Harriet, 8 Battery was assigned to 45 Commando assaulting Two Sisters, and 79 Battery's

Falklands Campaign
29 Commando Battery, Royal Artillery
May – June 1982

FALKLAND SOUND

On 28 May 1982, a week after the landings at San Carlos and Ajax Bay, Alma Battery of 29 Commando, RA, went into action in support of the men of 2 Para, bombarding Argentinian positions to devastating effect using the British-built 105mm Light Gun. During the long march across East Falkland, 29 Commando's guns were flown forward to Teal Inlet, Mount Kent and eventually to the Murrell Bridge. From these forward positions they were able to give much-needed fire support during the crucial battles against enemy defences around Stanley.

Port San Carlos

Douglas

Teal Inlet

Ajax Bay

San Carlos

Big Mt

Mt Simon

Mt Estancia

Murrell Bridge

Mt Longdon

EAST FALKLAND

Mt Usborne

Estancia House

Mt Kent

Two Sisters

Wireless Ridge

Stanley

Camilla Creek House

Wickham Heights

Bluff Cove
Fitzroy

Mt Harriet

Sapper Hill

Goose Green

Darwin

CHOISEUL SOUND

Key
Main axes of British advance

firepower was deployed against Mount Longdon, the objective of 3 Para. The three attacks were to be silent and artillery support provided if it was requested.

On the night of 11/12 June, the final stage of the Falklands war began. From their start lines the three battalions climbed the rock-strewn slopes of their objectives. Two Sisters was taken, the final attacks on its summit supported by harassing fire from 8 Battery that landed within 100 yards of the assault parties. 42 Commando called on fire support as they reached the upper slopes of Mount Harriet. In both cases very close support helped to prevent the enemy from manning their trenches and enabled the marines to close on their objectives. By daylight all the positions had fallen.

Their capture was of enormous advantage to the gunners: observers now had a clear view of Stanley and were able to identify the enemy's artillery around the capital. For the next two days the guns thundered forth around the clock, neutralising enemy artillery and troops with high explosive, airburst and phosporus rounds.

As the shells struck home, the enemy's defences and his morale both crumbled

As the guns continued to pepper the Argentinian defences around Stanley, the plans for the final attacks of the war were laid. Five Infantry Brigade was tasked with breaching the final ring of hills held by the enemy: the Scots Guards were to act against Mount Tumbledown, supported by the Gurkhas deployed to attack Mount William; and the Welsh Guards were ordered to run the enemy off Sapper Hill. To the north, 2 Para had Wireless Ridge to deal with. These assaults were to go in at night on 13/14 June.

The full weight of 29 Regiment's Light Guns was to be used to soften the enemy positions as the main assault groups fought their way up the mountain slopes. Illumination rounds would aid the climb, while explosive shells would be used to silence fire from bunkers. If, as seemed likely, the enemy fled, the artillery was to harry them back to Stanley.

Although the attacks went in as scheduled, the fierceness of the enemy's resistance on Wireless Ridge and Mount Tumbledown came as a surprise, and both the Scots Guards and 2 Para met with stiff opposition. Until the battalions' own firepower was augmented by the artillery, the battles remained in the balance, but then the Argentinians began to flee. The way to Stanley was open. However, the work of the artillery continued and shells were lobbed onto the very edge of the capital until the news came that surrender flags flew over the enemy's positions.

The final days of the campaign had seen the gunners working at fever pitch: 7 Battery had fired over 3500 rounds, 8 Battery had unleashed 5180, and 79 Battery had used another 2700 shells against the enemy. Despite being faced with air attack and heavy counter-battery fire, casualties were few and only one gun suffered any damage. The volume of fire directed against the enemy was decisive; as the shells struck home, the enemy's defences and his morale both crumbled.

THE AUTHOR William Franklin is a military historian who has contributed to numerous publications. His particular interest is the history of elite forces of World War II.

Below: Flanked by two Royal Marines, the crew of a Light Gun make their last-minute adjustments before going into action. Harassing fire against enemy sangars, trenches and artillery was the gunners' main priority before the assaults on the Argentinian positions around Stanley. Forward observation officers ensured that every battery knew the precise co-ordinates of each potential target.

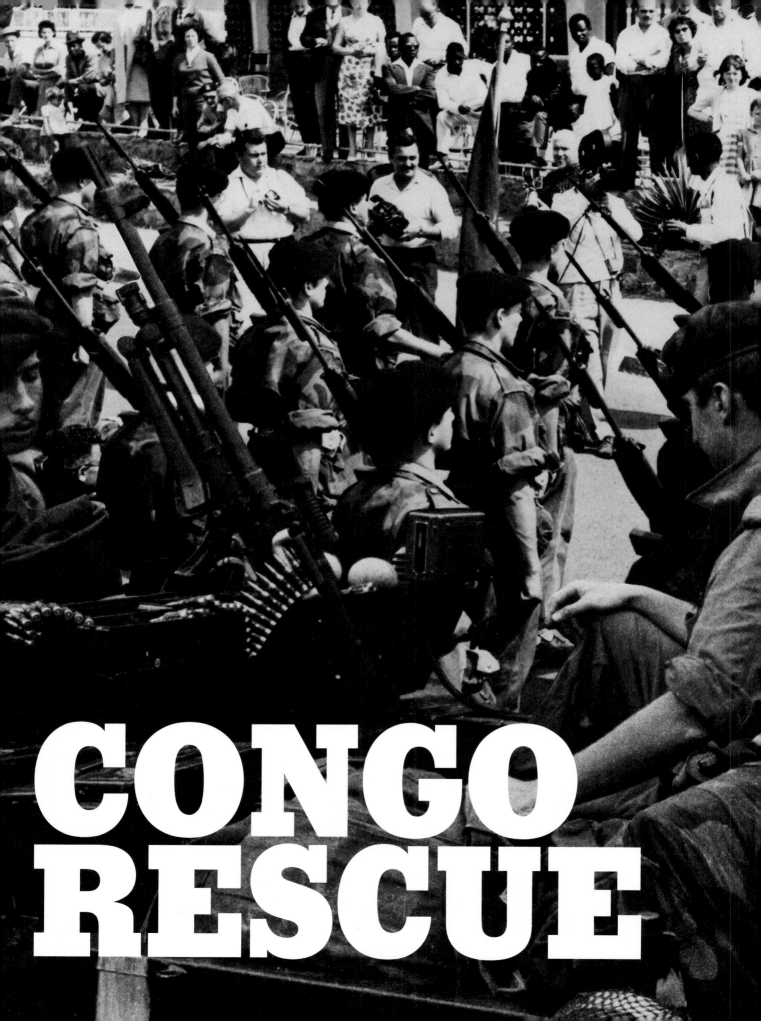

CONGO
RESCUE

When rebels threatened to massacre the Europeans in Stanleyville in 1964, the Belgian Paracommando Regiment forced a stay of execution

AT 0750 HOURS on 24 November 1964, in the Congolese city of Stanleyville (now known as Kisangani), young warriors calling themselves Simbas (lions) began firing indiscriminately upon a group of unarmed foreign civilians, mostly Belgians, who had been held hostage in the city for 111 days. During the preceding months, the Simbas had executed hundreds of defenceless civilians, and they seemed to relish the prospect of adding to their tally. But on this occasion their enjoyment was to be short-lived. Just a few minutes after the warriors began to indulge their blood-lust, troops clad in red berets, men of Belgium's Paracommando Regiment, burst onto the scene. Most of the Simbas were soon fleeing in panic from the advancing paras, who then proceeded to rescue hundreds of Belgians and other foreign nationals from Stanleyville and its environs.

The group of hostages that the paracommandos had been sent in to rescue had been unfortunate enough to have become caught up in the Simba War, a revolt characterised by a particularly high incidence of savagery and atrocity. The political leaders of this revolt – Christophe Gbenye, Thomas Kanza, Gaston Soumialot, Pierre Mulele and others, who in September 1964 formed the 'government' of the 'République Populaire du Congo' – claimed to be progressives, liberating the Congolese people from a government that had betrayed them to the West. In practice, however, the area 'liberated' by the rebel forces was subjected to a veritable reign of terror. If the central government's army, the Armée Nationale Congolaise (ANC), had become infamous for brutal and licentious behaviour, its record was soon eclipsed by the rebel 'Popular Army of Liberation', whose Simba warriors unleashed a wave of murder, rape, torture, and even cannibalism.

The Popular Army's excesses were particularly marked in Stanleyville, which had fallen to rebels commanded by 'General' Nicolas Olenga on 4/5 August 1964. After taking control of the city, the Simbas seemed set to butcher Stanleyville's white community, particularly the Americans and the Belgians, whose governments were seen as the principal backers of the Léopoldville (Kinshasa) regime. They were persuaded to postpone such a course of action, however, by Christophe Gbenye, president of the Popular Republic. Gbenye wanted to hold them as hostages, diplomatic pawns to be used in the struggle against the Congolese government. His policy was, in effect, one of blackmail: unless the Belgian and American governments restrained the ANC, he would not guarantee the hostages' safety.

When Gbenye first issued his threat, at the end of August 1964, the Belgians and Americans decided that discretion was the better part of valour. They urged Moise Tshombe, premier of the Congo, to restrict his aerial attacks against rebel-held centres and promoted diplomatic efforts to secure the release of the hostages. This cautious approach, however, seemed to lead nowhere, and as reports of rebel atrocities were received and rebel leaders made increasingly strident threats against the hostages, the US and Belgian governments began to think in terms of a rescue operation. By the end of October, a mercenary-led ANC column was advancing towards Stanleyville, thus raising the spectre of

Simba retaliation against the hostages. Accordingly, the Belgians pressed for a joint US-Belgian airborne operation, with the US supplying the aircraft and the Belgians providing the troops. The US agreed.

The difficulties involved in mounting such an operation soon became apparent. In the first place, there would be no support on the ground, for although it was militarily logical to co-ordinate the air drop with a push by ANC forces, it was politically unacceptable, since it would give the impression that the operation was designed to support the ANC campaign, rather than to rescue the hostages. Secondly, the Belgians had never jumped from US C-130s or even conducted a joint airborne operation with the Americans. And thirdly, the Belgians would be going in 'blind', since there was a dearth of intelligence on the situation in Stanleyville, such as the strength and location of the Simbas and the whereabouts of the 800 hostages they were supposed to rescue. Aerial reconnaissance was ruled out for fear that it might provoke a massacre by the rebels. On top of all this, there was the fact that the unit selected for the operation, the Belgian Paracommando Regiment, consisted for the most part of 18-20-year-old conscripts, whose training had spanned only two months in the 3rd Battalion, five and a half months in the 2nd, and 10 and a half months in the 1st; the manpower available for the operation would be restricted, therefore, to the 1st Battalion and elements of the 2nd.

Phase two would consist of a 2400-mile flight from Ascension Island to the base at Kamina in Katanga

Notwithstanding these doubts and difficulties, two governments went ahead with their planning. What emerged at the end of this process was a three-phase operation codenamed Dragon Rouge. During phase one, 12 US C-130 transport aircraft would fly from their base in France to Kleine Brogel in Belgium, where 545 officers and men of the Paracommando Regiment, plus eight armoured jeeps and 12 AS-24 motorised tricycles, would be taken on board; the aircraft would then fly some 4000 miles to the British dependency of Ascension Island, refuelling en route at a USAF base in Spain. Phase two would consist of a 2400-mile flight from Ascension Island to the base at Kamina in Katanga. During phase three, the force would fly 550 miles north to Stanleyville itself, meeting up with a flight of Congolese B-26s en route which would give them reports on weather conditions in Stanleyville and fire support for the assault. The assault itself was also to be a three-phase affair. At 0600 hours on D-day, the 1st Battalion and Regimental HQ (320 men) would parachute in from five C-130s onto the golf course next to Stanleyville airport, seizing the airport and clearing it of any obstacles. Then, 30 minutes after the departure of the first five C-130s, two more C-130s with eight armoured jeeps aboard were to fly directly to Stanleyville and land on signal. Finally, after another 30 minutes, the last five C-130s, bearing one company of the 2nd Battalion plus supplies and other logistics, were to head for Stanleyville, landing if possible, but airdropping men and material if this proved impossible. The key to success was obviously the seizure and clearing of the airfield, since only after this had been accomplished were the paras to press on the city itself in search of the hostages, using the jeeps brought in by the second wave of C-130s. Similar assault plans were attached to sup-

THE BELGIAN CONGO

The African colony of the Belgian Congo (known since 1971 as Zaire) gained its independence from Belgium on 30 June 1960. The Belgians allowed the post-colonial government to retain the services of thousands of their nationals, including the officers and NCOs who commanded the 24,000-strong 'Force Publique', and hoped that the Congo's new rulers would be able to maintain peace and stability. Law and order broke down almost immediately, however. The Force Publique, which later became the 'Armée Nationale Congolaise' (ANC), mutinied against its Belgian officers, and widespread disorder and violence erupted, sometimes caused by the army itself. The Belgians responded by sending in their own troops to help evacuate endangered Belgian nationals, while the Congolese government, finding that its writ had virtually ceased to run outside the capital city, called on the United Nations (UN) to send assistance.

The UN secured the departure of the Belgian forces, suppressed a rival regime in Stanleyville (now Kisangani) and a secessionist regime in Katanga (now Shaba), and restored a semblance of law and order before withdrawing its contingents in June 1964. By that time, however, the Congolese government had lost control over much of the eastern Congo, where rebellion had been instigated earlier in the year by the rival National Liberation Committee. By mid-August 1964 the rebels had conquered virtually all of the eastern Congo, and it was to take a determined effort by mercenary-led ANC forces to stem the tide; most areas were won back during late 1964 and early 1965, though pockets of rebels held out into 1966.

Left: Firepower of the Belgian paracommandos. Troops parade with fixed bayonets while (below) members of the 1st Battalion check their weapons after the drop on Stanleyville.

THE BELGIAN PARACOMMANDO REGIMENT

The origins of Belgium's Paracommando Regiment can be traced back to May 1942, when an independent Belgian parachute company with an initial complement of 144 men was formed in Britain. At first, this company formed part of the British 6th Airborne Division, but it was later taken under the wing of the British Special Air Service to receive training in clandestine operations. When the Allies advanced into Belgium in July 1944, the paras were actively engaged in the liberation of their own homeland.

The regiment first achieved international fame in July 1960, when some 800 paracommandos were flown out to the Congolese province of Katanga (now Shaba) at the request of the province's premier, Moïse Tshombe. The paras rescued hundreds of endangered Belgian nationals and established for themselves a reputation for courage and efficiency. Further involvement in the Congo followed in November 1964, when the Paracommando Regiment was selected to carry out rescue operations at Stanleyville (now Kisangani) and Paulis (now Isiro). Fourteen years later, they were again deployed operationally in the Congo, being used to back up French forces during the rescue of hostages in Shaba province (formerly Katanga) in May 1978.

The Paracommando Regiment has three battalions, of which the best known is the 1st, with its maroon beret and SAS cap badge. The three battalions form the Belgian Army's tactical reserve, offering a means of reinforcing Belgium's NATO commitment and providing an interventionary capability in trouble spots elsewhere.
Above: The wings of the Belgian paracommandos.

plementary operations codenamed Dragons Noir, Blanc and Vert, the rescue of foreign nationals concentrated in Paulis (now Isiro), Bunia and Watsa respectively.

By 14 November 1964 the essentials of the plan had been worked out and the two governments agreed that if their continuing diplomatic efforts to secure the release of the hostages failed, the rescue operations would be implemented. The Belgians, on their part, were already pressing for action, a not unreasonable demand considering that the ANC column was due to begin its final move towards Stanleyville on 19 November. The Americans had some reservations about 'pre-positioning', on the grounds that a time lag between phases one and two might result in security leaks, but they went along with the Belgian proposal. Thus, on 17 November, 14 aircraft of the USAF 464th Troop Carrier Wing left their base at Evreux in France for Kleine Brogel in Belgium. By 2000 hours on the 18th all the aircraft, with 545 paras aboard, had arrived at Ascension Island, whose airstrip had been made available by the British government. Phase one of Dragon Rouge was completed.

The Belgians were soon urging that phase two should be initiated. On 20 November, newspapers in London, Paris and Brussels carried reports about a 'joint Belgian-US long-range airborne training exercise', but this cover story was unconvincing and the Belgian government was forced to admit that a joint force had assembled on Ascension Island, describing the move as a precautionary measure and adding that it still hoped to obtain the release of the hostages through negotiation. However, with the secret out and with the ANC column leaving for Stanleyville as scheduled on 19 November, the Belgians saw no sense in holding back now. The US government was still cautious, but after hearing reports to the effec that the hostages would be eaten if the bombing o rebel territory did not stop, or grilled alive if rebe terms for negotiations were not accepted, the Amer icans agreed that a rapid move off to Kamina was now advisable. Having gained permission from the Con golese government, the Dragon Rouge force headed for Katanga, arriving there at 1000 hours or 22 November. Fortunately for the hostages, Gbenye and Olenga did not hear of the move, and they seem to have treated the earlier reports about landings or Ascension Island as unfounded rumour.

The Dragon Rouge force was soon on the move again. With the ANC column due to arrive at Stanleyville early on 24 November there was no time for delay, since the arrival of the ANC force might wel trigger a massacre of the hostages, or make the rebels take the hostages away to the northeast. The Belgian and American governments therefore decided that phase three should proceed as planned At 0300 hours, in perfect weather conditions – a 1200f ceiling, good visibility with broken cloud cover, and surface winds of less than six knots – the first five C-130s took off from Kamina.

By 0600 hours the C-130s, with B-26s in support were over Stanleyville golf course, and they quickly dropped 320 paras over the target. There was some resistance from rebel forces, notably around the control tower, but within half an hour the paras had seized the airport and cleared it of obstacles, thu enabling the remaining seven C-130s to land. These aircraft brought in the reinforcing company, sup plies and armoured jeeps, though unfortunately one

Main picture: A Belgian paracommando stands guard over rebels captured during the short battle for Stanleyville airport. In the background is one of the US C-130 transports which brought the rescue force and its equipment to the Congo.
Right: The commander of the paracommando operation at Stanleyville, Colonel Cheralé Laurent.

of the aircraft, bearing four of the jeeps, was an hour late after developing a fault soon after leaving Kamina.

In the meantime, Colonel Laurent, the commander of the paracommando force, had detailed part of his force to move into Stanleyville with all possible speed: at 0635, an anonymous caller had telephoned the control tower (where Laurent had established his command post) saying that hostages were being held at the Victoria Residence Hotel, a tip-off that was confirmed five minutes later by a Dutch missionary. By 0740, lead elements of the 11th Paracommando company had reached the outskirts of the city. The paras then began to advance into the city itself, brushing aside sporadic resistance from the rebels as they progressed.

The Simbas, at this juncture, decided to take their revenge upon the hostages, 250 of whom had been assembled near the Lumumba monument and forced to sit down. They began to kill the hostages with guns and spears, until three minutes later the paras arrived on the scene and quickly dispersed the perpetrators of the massacre. The paras found two young girls, five women and 15 men dead or dying, and another 40 people wounded, of whom five were later to die. This horror, however, made the paras all the more determined to press on and they continued to scour the city, street by street, linking up with elements of the ANC column at 1100. By sunset on the 25th, the paras had rescued a total of 1500 foreign nationals and 150 Congolese, for the loss of one of their own men killed and five wounded.

The Belgians and Americans now turned their attention to the supplementary operations planned

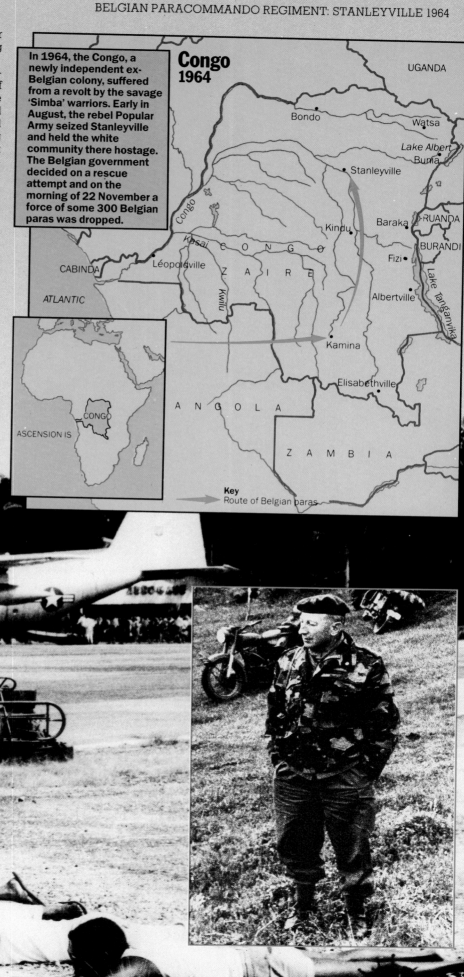

Congo 1964

In 1964, the Congo, a newly independent ex-Belgian colony, suffered from a revolt by the savage 'Simba' warriors. Early in August, the rebel Popular Army seized Stanleyville and held the white community there hostage. The Belgian government decided on a rescue attempt and on the morning of 22 November a force of some 300 Belgian paras was dropped.

UGANDA
Bondo
Watsa
Lake Albert
Buna
Stanleyville
Kindu
Baraka
RUANDA
BURANDI
Fizi
Congo
Kasai
CABINDA
Léopoldville
C O N G O
Z A I R E
Albertville
Kwilu
Lake Tanganyika
Kamina
Elisabethville
A N G O L A
Z A M B I A

Key
Route of Belgian paras

ASCENSION IS
CONGO
ATLANTIC

for Paulis, Bunia and Watsa. The two governments, however, had developed serious doubts about the wisdom of going ahead with these operations; the rebels would be on the alert, there were too few paras available to mount three assaults simultaneously, and by now the whites would probably be too scattered to make a rescue mission practicable. These considerations, plus the international outcry that had greeted Dragon Rouge, inclined the Belgian and American governments towards cancellation of the follow-up operations. But they did agree, in the event, to one more mission. Reports had come in that there was a concentration of whites at Paulis, and that they were in serious danger. Colonel Laurent therefore suggested that his paras be allowed to try just one more operation – Dragon Noir. The Belgian and US governments concurred and on 26 November Laurent received the go-ahead.

They quickly seized and cleared the airfield, allowing the follow-on aircraft to land with the armoured jeeps and supplies

The operation turned out to be a great success. The paras received a hostile welcome from the waiting Simbas, but the rebel fire was inaccurate. Of the 256 men who made the jump, 255 landed without being hit, and they quickly seized and cleared the airfield, allowing the follow-on aircraft to land with the armoured jeeps and supplies. Learning a lesson from Dragon Rouge, however, the paras did not wait for all the kit to arrive. One company, the 11th again, moved immediately into the town. Some of the hostages were already dead, but after searching the town and its environs all day and the following morning, the paras saved many hostages from certain death. By the time the force began to withdraw, at 1314 hours on 27 November, 375 foreign nationals had been freed. The last aircraft took off at 1500 hours, leaving Paulis to the Simbas. The operation had cost seven casualties, including one killed in the drop itself.

Operations Dragon Rouge and Dragon Noir were now over. By the evening of 27 November the entire Dragon force had returned to Kamina and two days later it flew on to Ascension Island and then via the Canary Islands to home base. The paras had certainly earned their laurels. They had not been able to save all the hostages in Stanleyville and Paulis, nor to do anything about scattered handfuls of Belgians in other parts of the northeast, but had succeeded in evacuating over 2000 hostages, all for the loss of only three troops killed and seven wounded. Considering the difficulties the young conscripts faced – a dearth of intelligence, a jump from unfamiliar aircraft without pathfinder teams to stake out drop zones, and no pre-assault reconnaissance – it was an outstanding achievement. The people of Belgium expressed their verdict on 1 December 1964, when the Paracommando Regiment paraded through the streets of Brussels. According to the Brussels press, not since Liberation Day in 1944 had a military unit received such a tumultuous reception.

THE AUTHOR Henry Longstreet is a journalist who specialises in African conflicts since World War II.

Originating in the Nazi homelands, the men of X-Troop, No.10 (Inter-Allied) Commando, fought a highly personal war against Hitler

IT IS NOT AS well known as it should be that a number of men who escaped from Nazi-occupied Europe during World War II became commandos – and first-rate commandos at that. The largest group were those who made up the various national Troops of No.10 (Inter-Allied) Commando, which included French, Belgians, Norwegians, and so on. The Inter-Allied Commando was a unique set-up within the British Army, a polyglot group of men whose one aim was to drive the hated Nazis out of their homelands.

Within this unusual unit was an even more extraordinary band of men. Never more than 90 strong, they were known initially as X-Troop – a designation coined by Winston Churchill – and then simply as No.3 (Miscellaneous) Troop. They came, not from countries overrun by the Nazis, but from those that had allied themselves to Hitler's cause and from Germany itself. Either political or racial refugees from National Socialism, they loathed the Nazi regime with a burning hatred that made them a potent weapon in that grey area which divides ordinary military combat from clandestine operations. At first they were led by British officers, and their Troop leader was an outstanding linguist, Captain Bryan Hilton-Jones. Later they were commanded by

officers who had risen from their own ranks. Towards the end of the war many of the original intake were commissioned, quite a number in the field, for bravery, and all reached non-commissioned rank. Many spoke perfect German and all operated under false English names.

There is no absolute proof of it now, but it is highly probable that X-Troop was originally formed as a specialist high-risk unit trained in sabotage and subterfuge, one capable of surviving behind enemy lines until its mission was accomplished. In fact, at least two such operations reached an advanced stage of planning but were never launched – the destruction of U-boat pens at Lorient and of the early V-1 launch sites in the Pas de Calais. Had they gone ahead, the chances of the men returning would have been practically nil. Instead, X-Troop was used in small groups or singly, and by the end of the war had proved indisputably its value in combat. But the price was high. A large proportion of the Troop were killed, wounded, or taken prisoner.

Early on, a few of X-Troop were seconded to Special Operations Executive (SOE) or its military wing, the Small-Scale Raiding Force (SSRF), and the Troop suffered its first casualties when five members were attached to special intelligence parties during the Dieppe raid of August 1942; only two returned and both of them had been wounded.

A proportion of the Troop was also specially trained for the three series of cross-Channel raids, codenamed Forfar, Hardtack, and Tarbrush, that

X-TROOP

Below: X-Trooper Anson in training with one of the classic weapons used by British commandos in World War II, the American-made 0.45in Thompson Model 1928A1 submachine gun. Right: The commandos of X-Troop were sent to Achnacarry in Scotland for full infantry assault training. Below right: Linguists of the Troop seek information from civilians on SS troops in the St-Aubin-sur-Mer area following the D-day landings at Ouistreham. Bottom right: No.3 (Misc) Troop, including Germans, Austrians, Hungarians and Greeks, is photographed with the troop's bulldog mascot in Wales prior to the first operation.

took place during 1943 and 1944, prior to D-day. Some were trained in handling the dories used to take the raiders to the beach, while others became radio operators for these operations. The whole Troop received parachute training, but only one member actually took part in an operational airdrop as the parachute reconnaissance raid assigned to the Troop was cancelled.

Early into action was a small group attached to units of No.2 Commando Brigade for the invasions of Sicily and Italy, and it was during the fighting in this combat zone that X-Troop members became acknowledged as experts in interrogating prisoners and interpreting captured documents, and their numbers in Italy were soon augmented. Their perfect knowledge of colloquial German was also invaluable during night patrols and for deception purposes. All these skills were put to more intensive use when the remainder of the Troop was similarly deployed among the 1st and 4th Commando Brigades taking part in the Normandy landings.

For these, the men were divided up and attached to the eight Commandos which formed the two brigades, and to both brigade headquarters. This meant that each Commando received four or five men and occasionally one was attached to each Troop, though often the commanding officer kept one or two with his own Tac HQ or attached to the unit's intelligence section.

The toll on the Troop during the early days of the fighting in Normandy was alarmingly high. Privates Franklin, Webster and Laddy all died on the beaches, or before they even reached them, and others were seriously wounded. Fuller, the sergeant in charge of the detachment with

No.47 (RM) Commando, was in no-man's land guiding American B-26 Marauders onto a troublesome German position when one of the bombs fell short and killed him. The same day Corporal Moody and Private Norton were killed by a shell while on patrol, and soon afterwards Private Lawrence, attached to No.3 Commando, was captured while attempting to take a prisoner behind enemy lines. Lawrence was a man of astonishing bravery, for he would go regularly into the enemy's lines at night, whisper 'follow me' to a bemused German sentry and lead the man back to the Commando's positions before the German realised what was happening. On the night he was captured he must have tried the trick once too often and was grabbed. He was never seen again.

Another X-Troop member, Sergeant Thompson, who was attached to No.4 Commando, was also captured during a patrol that was typical of the Troop's kind of action. Ordered to infiltrate the German lines in order to observe traffic on a certain crossroads, Thompson and an English officer managed to reach the road that marked the Germans' front lines but found it impossible to cross, even though it was dark. Instead, they lay up in a ditch and all the next day they observed the enemy from a distance of about 50yds. When night fell once more they made another attempt to cross the road but were spotted and fired on. The officer was hit but managed to escape after feigning death, but Thompson was captured. Luckily, his true identity was never discovered and he returned to England safely at the end of the war. The others in Thompson's detachment fared worse, however, and were wiped out within two weeks of landing: Howarth, the sergeant in charge of it, was wounded on the beach, as was Corporal Sayers, a Hungarian who had served in the French Army before the war, while Private Graham was killed on 13 June.

Those with No.45 (RM) Commando also suffered heavily during the first days of intense fighting. During the Commando's attack on Merville-France-

ville-Plage, Private Arlen, a prizefighter in civilian life who had sworn to win the VC, was so infuriated at being fired on while carrying a white flag during negotiations with the Germans to surrender that he charged the Germans single-handed and was killed

Top right: Commandos prime grenades en route to Normandy. Above: La Grande Ferme du Buisson, situated near Sallenelles and Merville on the Orne River, marked the front for some weeks after D-day; controlled by No.47(RM) Commando in daylight, it was visited by German patrols during the night, and was the scene of numerous ambushes and firefights. Right: Men of X-Troop, fully equipped for war, photographed in Germany in 1945; for some it was a return to their homeland after years in exile.

Political and racial refugees from Nazi-dominated Europe, the men of X-Troop were trained in the deadly arts of sabotage and were taught to survive deep behind the front line. During the liberation of France and the Low Countries, they spearheaded the Allied landings in Normandy and took part in the recapture of Walcheren, a heavily defended island fortress.

...tright. The next day another member of the detachment, Private Saunders, was wounded and captured, but the remaining two members, Sergeant Stewart and Corporal Shelley, survived a fierce German attack on the Commando's positions in Merville. It was there that the two X-Troop members distinguished themselves by driving off an attack on a farmyard in which part of the Commando was trapped. The Germans were lobbing in hand grenades and the two commandos reckoned that if the Germans could lob them in, then they could lob some back. They went round gathering everyone's grenades in a large camouflage scarf and when they saw a grenade coming in they threw one out in the same direction. This had positive results and eventually they were able to set up a Bren gun at one of the entrances to spray the surrounding area so that the others could escape. For their bravery during this incident both were awarded immediate commis-

...sions in the field.

By D+18, 24 June, the Germans attacking the Allied bridgehead at Merville were being held, and control of no-man's land on their part of the eastern flank lay indisputably with the two Commando brigades. In one part of no-man's land there were three farm buildings called La Grande Ferme du Buisson where a cat-and-mouse game was played with the Germans. During the day the commandos used it as an observation post, abandoning it at night to the Germans, who left messages for the commandos scribbled on the walls in bad English. The farm was the starting point for many of the commandos' fighting patrols and in the weeks before the Allied break-out it was to be the area in which still more members of X-Troop would die or be critically wounded. Corporal Terry, attached to No.47 (RM) Commando, was wounded near there, Private Andrews was killed by a mine while beyond the farm, and Corporal Gilbert was shot in the leg when he clashed with a German patrol within the buildings. Sergeant Villiers and Corporals Drew, Envers and Harris also became casualties, either in this period of static warfare or during the Allied break-out. In all, 27 members of X-Troop out of the original 44 who took part in the Normandy landings were either killed, wounded or made prisoners of war during the first three months of fighting in France.

'We set out at about 0300, crossed the minefield and established ourselves behind German lines'

During October 1944, reinforcements for the heavily depleted Troop began to be recruited but only a handful of these were to see action. By this time, Captain James Griffith, a German medical student who had risen to the rank of sergeant in the Troop before being commissioned, had taken over command. Hilton-Jones had been seriously wounded while on patrol in France, and he and other surviving members were returned to England with their adopted units for rest and recuperation. However, those X-Troopers with No.4 Commando Brigade were launched into yet another battle. On 1 November 1944 the brigade stormed the fortress island of Walcheren, which guarded the mouth of the Scheldt river. In the eight days of bitter fighting the handful of anti-Nazi German speakers again suffered casualties. Corporal Hamilton was killed during the landing and another X-Trooper was wounded. However, both Sergeant Gray and Corporal Latimer, who were attached to No.41(RM) Commando attacking northeast towards Domburg, landed unscathed. Once ashore, they were soon undertaking what by then had become a typical activity of X-Troop, that of infiltrating the enemy's lines to secure a prisoner for interrogation and identification. Sergeant Gray was to report:

'We set out at about 0300 hours, crossed the minefield and established ourselves behind the German lines. We picked up a few prisoners who were carrying coffee and interrogated them as to where their commanding officer was. They were very reluctant to tell us. I told them I'd shoot them and they cried. Then I suddenly saw a figure come out of a bunker and stand there in the half light demanding his coffee. I knew this was the man we wanted and was about to tackle him when out of the sky – or so it seemed – flew Latimer and landed on him. He knocked the man to the ground and that was the end of him. When we got him to

CAPTAIN BRYAN HILTON-JONES

Bryan Hilton-Jones, the son of a Caernarvon doctor, earned a First Class degree in the Modern Languages Tripos at Cambridge University and spoke perfect German. He was a brilliant rock climber, and his youthful features belied a toughness of character and physique. With a dry sense of humour, and quiet to the point of being taciturn, he was a totally dedicated officer who was known to all his men simply as 'The Skipper'.

When war broke out he joined the Royal Artillery and then volunteered for the Commandos. Serving as a lieutenant in No.4 Commando, he was picked to lead X-Troop of No. 10 (Inter-Allied) Commando. He moved to Wales with a small nucleus of volunteers and immediately took them on a 53-mile route march from Harlech to the top of Snowden and back again. In action, Hilton-Jones was equally decisive and thorough. In May 1944 he commanded a series of vital cross-Channel reconnaissance raids, and was awarded the Military Cross for bringing them to a successful conclusion. Promotion to major and second-in-command of No. 10 (Inter-Allied) Commando the same month did not keep him from the fighting in Normandy, but he was severely wounded while leading members of the French Resistance through the German lines at night. His fighting days were over, but the elan and fighting efficiency with which he had imbued his men were to carry them through some of the fiercest frontline fighting of the war.

the CO, I translated what he wanted to say to the German officer. He persuaded him to surrender and the German agreed to go round his own strongpoint to tell his men to give up.'

By January 1945 both Commando brigades were back in action, this time in northwest Europe taking part in the final drive towards Germany. By now many of the X-Troopers who had been wounded in Normandy were back with their units, only to be wounded a second time, or killed. Corporal Harris, gravely wounded on the Aller river with No. 45 (RM) Commando, was subsequently awarded the Military Medal for his courage during the fighting there; Howarth, who had risen to be the Troop's sergeant-major, was killed by a shell just after receiving his commission; Griffith was shot by a sniper during a raid on an island on the Maas river; and Sergeants Villiers and Seymour both died during the Rhine crossing when their Buffalo amphibious vehicle received a direct hit.

Despite these heavy losses, X-Troop members continued to operate with a fervour and dedication that continually evoked the admiration of the British who fought with them. One, caught with the Brigade Major and his driver in an ambush while approaching Osnabrück, grabbed the bicycle of a passing civilian and peddled off to get help. A barrage was laid down and the trapped party managed to extricate itself, but the Brigade Major then saw an astonishing sight:

'Shortly before the enemy fire ceased, I noticed Corporal Clarke, now disguised in civilian clothes, riding the bicycle down the road towards us. He gave a brief wave, shouted the information we required to know, and cycled towards the town. He told me later that he was then able to contact German civilians and ascertain what the exact positions of the enemy were. This was a very courageous act which required not only courage but initiative of the highest order.'

Clarke's actions did not go unrewarded, for he was later Mentioned in Despatches for his bravery.

When victory finally came and Germany capitulated, those members of X-Troop who had survived became vital members of Allied intelligence networks and interrogation teams, deployed in tracking down wanted Gestapo and SS men and helping with

Below: A Jeep leads a column of prisoners through the streets of Osnabrück after the successful assault by 1 Commando Brigade during the night of 3/4 April 1945. The brigade, which included German-speaking members attached to each Commando, was under the command of the 6th Airborne Division for the attack, and the photograph is a still from a newsreel produced by the Airborne Brigade Film Unit.
Bottom: Members of X-Troop in the early days of the unit – Corporal Wilmers and Lance-Corporals Howarth and Griffith. Following promotion, Griffith succeeded Hilton-Jones as leader of the Troop when that officer was severely wounded in France.

the denazification of German industry. Some found the work harrowing beyond endurance. One X Trooper had to interrogate the former commandant of Auschwitz, Rudolf Hoess, who had been found hiding in a farmhouse. 'I was drunk for a week,' he wrote later. 'I just could not live with myself. He was the man who had killed my mother.' Another member of the Troop spent some time as an inmate of a lunatic asylum because it was suspected that a wanted Gestapo officer was being sheltered there. It was grim but urgent work, for there were several groups of fanatics who had sworn to carry on the fight and they had to be run to earth.

It took as long as two years for some of the Troop to be demobilised, so valuable was their contribution to the rehabilitation of Germany. When they eventually reached civvy street, nearly all of them applied for and were granted British citizenship. A few returned to Germany, but most settled either in the United States, Canada, or Britain, where they were to become as successful in civilian life as they had been in uniform. Among their number can be found two judges, a Fellow of Balliol College, Oxford, a vice-president of American Express, a Fulbright scholar ... Truly, as remarkable a group of men as ever fought in any war anywhere.

THE AUTHOR Ian Dear served as a regular officer in the Royal Marines, 1953-56. He is now a professional writer on military and maritime subjects and is author of *Ten Commando*, a book on No. 10 (Inter-Allied) Commando, which is to be published in 198[ ] by Leo Cooper Ltd.

In April 1982, several weeks before the main landings at San Carlos, the men of M Company, 42 Commando, RM were tasked with the retaking of the island of South Georgia

Right: 'Humphrey', HMS *Antrim's* Westland Wessex HAS Mark 3, was used to rescue an SAS reconnaissance patrol stranded in a freezing blizzard on Fortuna glacier, South Georgia. Below: Marines of the 'Mighty Munch', M Company, 42 Commando, as it became known, following the recapture of the island.

OPERATION PARAQUET

SOUTH GEORGIA

On 3 April 1982, after doing its utmost to defend the island, the small but gallant garrison of Royal Marines stationed on South Georgia surrendered to an Argentinian invasion force. The British soldiers were supplanted by two detachments of Argentinian marines who based themselves in the settlements of Leith and Grytviken: the rest of the island was extremely inhospitable and no further outposts were considered feasible.

Situated over 800 nautical miles east of East Falkland, South Georgia was recognised by the British as a suitable target for a retaliatory measure against the Argentinians. Its recapture would satisfy the growing demand in Britain for action, and it was beyond the range of Argentinian aircraft. Should hostilities continue, it would make a useful refuelling and rallying point for eastbound vessels. In addition, it would provide shelter for ships caught in the frequent South Atlantic storms, and it was proposed as a base and last-minute training ground. On 7 April, Admiral John Fieldhouse received orders to organise the recapture of the island. The task of re-possessing South Georgia was given the codename Paraquet, an obscure spelling of 'parakeet'. However, the Task Group formed by Major-General Moore, Fieldhouse's land commander, immediately renamed their action Paraquat, after the powerful weedkiller. The men selected for the duty were M Company of 42 Commando, Royal Marines (whose badge is shown above), D Squadron of the 22nd Special Air Service Regiment, and 2 Section, Special Boat Squadron.

ON SATURDAY, 3 April 1982, I was recalled urgently from leave. The crisis in the Falkland Islands had broken and, as second-in-command of 42 Commando, Royal Marines, I had much to do to ready the Commando for operations. Then, on 6 April, my commanding officer, Lieutenant-Colonel Nick Vaux, told me that I was to prepare a force for a separate operation in South Georgia.

The force of Royal Marines was to comprise M Company under Captain Chris Nunn, a section of 81mm mortars under Sergeant Day, two sections of Recce Troop under Sergeant Napier, and a section of assault engineers under Corporal Bath. I was also taking two Naval Gunfire Support Forward Observation (NGSFO) officers, an NGSFO adviser from 148 Commando Forward Observation Battery, RA, and a small medical team under Surgeon Lieutenant Crispin Swinhoe.

On 9 April, the force embarked on two VC10s to join the ships of the Task Group anchored off Ascension Island. The flagship was HMS *Antrim*, commanding the frigate HMS *Plymouth* and the tanker RFA *Tidespring*, and these were later joined by the ice patrol ship HMS *Endurance*. Aboard *Tidespring*

there were two Wessex Mark 5 helicopters, ea[ch] marked for the insertion of my main force into Sout[h] Georgia. The group was to set out and rendezvous a[t] sea with 2 SBS and D Squadron, 22 SAS, who ha[d] sailed ahead of us on RFA *Fort Austin*.

My orders were to capture the towns of Grytvike[n] and Leith, to neutralise Argentinian communication[s] in the area, to capture or kill Argentinian arme[d] forces personnel, and to arrest and remove Argent[i-] nian civilians. All this had to be achieved specificall[y] with the minimum loss of life or damage to propert[y]. To achieve these objectives I knew that it would b[e] essential to carry out covert reconnaissances in th[e] critical areas of the island in order to learn th[e] strength and dispositions of the enemy. I therefor[e] allocated the reconnaissance of Grytviken and Kin[g] Edward Point to 2 SBS, and that of Hurvik, Stromnes[s] and Leith to D Squadron.

On 15 April, we received the formal order to p[ut] our planned operations for the retaking of Sou[th] Georgia into effect. All units worked up to fu[ll] readiness as we steamed towards the island, and [I] tasked Chris Nunn to prepare a quick-reaction forc[e] from M Company, now sailing in *Tidespring*, to b[e]

ready to assist the SAS and SBS reconnaissance teams in case of difficulty.

The weather as we approached the island was fast deteriorating, and eventually the wind increased to a southwesterly Force 9 gale. The first reconnaissance was to be carried out by D Squadron's Mountain Troop, commanded by Captain John Hamilton, but it was not until 0900 hours on 21 April that a helicopter lift became feasible. The two Wessex Mark 5s and the Wessex Mark 3 on *Antrim* took off at 1000 to make the 50km journey, but were forced to return after being unable to land. They tried again at 1300 and this time the troop was successfully landed on the Fortuna glacier. The helicopters returned safely through a wind which had now increased to Force 10, and were battened down in their hangars aboard the wildly pitching ships. At last light, with the wind gusting at 70 knots, 2 SBS launched their Wasp helicopters from *Endurance* into the Sörling Valley.

The silence in the ops room was electrifying as we waited for the first indication from the on-watch signaller of contact with the two patrols.

Below: Captain Chris Nunn, commander of M Company, with Surgeon Lieutenant Crispin Swinhoe, the task group's medical officer.

Above: The sorry hulk of one of the Westland Wessex HU Mark 5 helicopters that crashed onto Fortuna glacier while airlifting an SAS patrol from the ice in atrocious weather.

Above: Marines of the Mighty Munch at Wideawake airfield on Ascension Island wait to move out. Left: Men and their equipment are loaded on lighters to be transferred to their ships.

GEARING UP FOR PARAQUET

Coming at the beginning of the hostilities with Argentina, the early preparations for Operation Paraquet were extremely sensitive. So much so that when the main body of 42 Commando departed on 7 April, in order to sail to the Falklands aboard SS *Canberra*, M Company was hidden in the gymnasium at the barracks in Bickleigh, just outside Plymouth, forbidden to show themselves or telephone out. Only then did Lieutenant-Colonel Nick Vaux inform them of their impending operation.

Before leaving Britain, Major Sheridan signalled Ascension Island to request a firing-range on which his men could rezero their

weapons. On the journey down, the zero (the accurate adjustment of a weapon's sights with the point of aim) was inevitably displaced, and the SBS constructed a 30yd range for their use.

Although Major Sheridan was informed unofficially that an element of D Squadron, 22 SAS, was to participate in the operation, it was not until all their mountain and Arctic stores were being transferred from Wideawake airfield to *Antrim* that he received a handwritten note, delivered by helicopter, to confirm that the entire squadron was to be under his command. Since the Royal Marines' Mountain & Arctic Warfare Cadre could not be made available for reconnaissance on the island, that task was shared by the SAS and SBS.

Nothing was heard until 1100 hours on Thursday, 22 April, when a weak signal was received from John Hamilton on Fortuna glacier. He requested immediate extraction of his patrol and reported that casualties as a result of the hurricane-force blizzard were imminent. The men had been unable to move with their huge loads from the point at which they were dropped the day before, and their tents had been blown to shreds by the gale. The wind eased to Force 7 but the cloud base was low and snow showers remained frequent. At 1115 the Wessex Mark 3, piloted by Lieutenant Commander Ian Stanley, took off and led the two Wessex Mark 5 helicopters to Fortuna glacier. In the atrocious weather they could not locate the patrol and returned to *Antrim* to refuel. They returned to the search, and saw the patrol through a gap in the clouds; quickly descending to the glacier they snatched the patrol from their position on the ice. But then disaster struck. As the two Wessex 5s took off to follow the Mark 3 through the cloud, one crashed into the glacier. The accident was seen by the other Mark 5 which turned, landed and picked up the crew and passengers who had all miraculously survived the crash. Fairly heavily laden, the Mark 5 took off but then it too lost its horizon in the cloud and crashed. Meanwhile the Mark 3 arrived back on *Antrim* with no knowledge of what had happened to the other two aircraft. The extent of the casualties was unknown, but it was certain that if there were any survivors they wouldn't last long in the freezing blizzards.

In a remarkable and brilliant piece of flying Ian Stanley brought his helicopter back to *Antrim*

It was not until about 1500 that Ian Stanley was able to take off in his Mark 3 to look for the 13 missing men, and about half-an-hour later he radioed to say that he had found them and they were all alive. There was relief and jubilation on board. What we did not know at that moment was that he had decided to load all 13 and make one journey. To take only half would almost certainly condemn those waiting for the second flight to severe injury from the cold, or even death if he failed to relocate them in the atrocious weather. So all 13 men were bundled into the ageing Wessex, and in a remarkable and brilliant piece of flying Ian Stanley brought his helicopter and his frozen, exhausted passengers back to *Antrim*.

Anxiety had passed momentarily and it was a great relief to all that there had been no loss of life, but with my only troop-lift helicopters now lying useless on the Fortuna glacier, and with no information yet on the disposition of Argentinian forces on the island, I seemed even further away from my objective than before. There was still no news from the SBS patrol when I sat down that evening with Major Cedric Delves, commander of D Squadron, to plan our next move.

We concluded that the atrocious weather, which was blowing a Force 7 gale, had given sufficient cover to enable all the operations of the day to remain covert. His Boat Troop was aboard *Antrim*, so together we made a hasty plan to deliver the Troop silently into Stromness Bay. From there they would continue in Gemini inflatable boats to Grass Island and carry out the same task that earlier had been given to the Mountain Troop.

At 0330 hours on Friday, 23 April, *Antrim* moved slowly and silently under a starlit sky into the outer reaches of Stromness Bay. Five Geminis and their

Operation Paraquet
South Georgia, April 1982

Operation Paraquet — the retaking of South Georgia — was launched on 21 April 1982 with the insertion of an SAS reconnaissance team on the Fortuna glacier. Further SAS and SBS teams were landed soon afterwards, and at 1445 on 25 April the main invasion was set in motion when a combined force of marines and SAS troops landed near Grytviken.

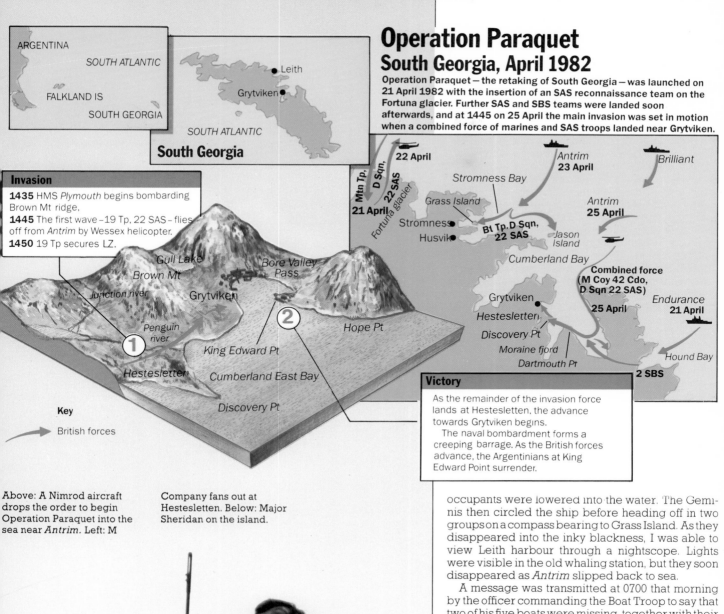

ARGENTINA
SOUTH ATLANTIC
FALKLAND IS
SOUTH GEORGIA

Leith
Grytviken
SOUTH ATLANTIC

South Georgia

Invasion

1435 HMS *Plymouth* begins bombarding Brown Mt ridge.
1445 The first wave – 19 Tp, 22 SAS – flies off from *Antrim* by Wessex helicopter.
1450 19 Tp secures LZ.

Gull Lake
Brown Mt
Junction river
Grytviken
Penguin river
Bore Valley Pass
King Edward Pt
Hope Pt
Hestesletten
Cumberland East Bay
Discovery Pt

① ②

Key
→ British forces

22 April
Mtn Tp, D Sqn, 22 SAS
21 April
Fortuna glacier
Stromness
Husvik
Grass Island
Stromness Bay
Bt Tp, D Sqn, 22 SAS
Antrim 23 April
Brilliant
Antrim 25 April
Jason Island
Cumberland Bay
Combined force (M Coy 42 Cdo, D Sqn 22 SAS) 25 April
Grytviken
Hestesletten
Discovery Pt
Moraine fjord
Dartmouth Pt
Endurance 21 April
Hound Bay
2 SBS

Victory

As the remainder of the invasion force lands at Hestesletten, the advance towards Grytviken begins.
The naval bombardment forms a creeping barrage. As the British forces advance, the Argentinians at King Edward Point surrender.

Above: A Nimrod aircraft drops the order to begin Operation Paraquet into the sea near *Antrim*. Left: M

Company fans out at Hestesletten. Below: Major Sheridan on the island.

occupants were lowered into the water. The Geminis then circled the ship before heading off in two groups on a compass bearing to Grass Island. As they disappeared into the inky blackness, I was able to view Leith harbour through a nightscope. Lights were visible in the old whaling station, but they soon disappeared as *Antrim* slipped back to sea.

A message was transmitted at 0700 that morning by the officer commanding the Boat Troop to say that two of his five boats were missing, together with their occupants. The other three were established ashore and on Grass Island and were observing Leith and Stromness. I had to assume now that the secrecy of the whole South Georgia operation had been jeopardised, as it was quite possible that the boats and the six missing men had been captured by the Argentinians. For the second time in 24 hours we were faced with a major catastrophe.

The Navy was becoming increasingly concerned at the possible presence of a submarine, but at that moment Cedric Delves and I were mainly concerned with finding the missing SAS men. The Wessex Mark 3, piloted again by Ian Stanley, took off shortly after to sweep the area of sea off Jason Island in the hope of finding the two boats. At 1030 he returned with three troopers. Their boat had been blown out to sea, and despite the men's frantic paddling it had drifted some six miles eastwards. They had been winched aboard the helicopter, the last man up piercing the inflatable Gemini to sink it. With the weather worsening, no further search was possible for the other boat.

There was still more bad news to come. Early that afternoon we received a message from 2 SBS to say that during the night a strong northwesterly gale had blown large chunks of ice from the sea into Cumberland East Bay and their inflatables had been ripped open as they tried to reach Dartmouth Point. They had managed to return to the shore and now needed more boats in order to continue with their mission. If that was not possible, then they asked to be extracted and reinserted elsewhere.

At 0300 in the morning of 24 April, the commander of *Antrim*, Captain Young, ordered his group to clear the island and rendezvous 200 miles to the northeast, where they could refuel from *Tidespring*, now joined by RFA *Brambleleaf*. The tankers were heeding the submarine warning and were remaining well out of sight. While the Navy planned how to deal with the submarine, I was put under more pressure from London to act, but I repeatedly declined until I had some firm intelligence of enemy strengths and dispositions. That evening we set course at 22 knots to return to South Georgia to do battle with the submarine, being joined on our way by HMS *Brilliant*, one of the Navy's most modern anti-submarine frigates. To my great relief I saw two Lynx helicopters on her flightdeck, and I now knew that a helicopter assault was again possible. *Tidespring*, meanwhile, carrying M Company, was to steam in and join the main group later on.

It was vital that we moved immediately to land and exploit the demoralised state of the enemy

In the early morning of 25 April the helicopters of the Task Group engaged the Argentinian submarine, *Santa Fé*, and damaged it sufficiently to force it into the relative safety of Grytviken. This was a major success, and I realised that we needed to follow it up quickly if the momentum was to be maintained and if the initiative were to remain firmly ours. I surmised that if the sailors from the submarine got ashore they would almost certainly be deployed in defence of King Edward Point, so it was vital that we moved immediately to land and exploit the demoralised state of the enemy.

I reviewed the locations of the combat units in the Task Group. *Tidespring* was 200 miles away with M Company. I had 2 SBS and a troop of SAS on *Endurance*, and another SAS troop on *Plymouth*, but *Endurance* was to the southeast hiding in Hound Bay, and *Plymouth* was unable to land either the Wessex or the Lynx helicopters on her flightdeck. This meant that my initial landing force must come from *Antrim* and subsequent deployment of troops would have to follow winching up from the other two ships. I had 65 men on *Antrim*, increased to 75 with the addition of her own Royal Marine detachment under Sergeant Kendall. This force had just over half of the estimated strength of the enemy, a ratio of two to one against. Not the most favourable situation, I thought, but I knew it was a gamble that we would have to take.

While Chris Nunn organised the 75 men into three small troops of 20 men each, and a small command element for me, I sat down in the ops room to prepare my orders. Our NGSFO adviser, Lieutenant-Colonel Keith Eve, worked out a fire-plan based on the use of the twin 4.5in guns on *Antrim* and *Plymouth*. My plan was to land the first wave, namely 19 Troop, 22 SAS, under command of Cedric Delves, by Wessex Mark 3 and two Lynx helicopters onto Hestesletten, an area of flat glacial moraine about four kilometres from Grytviken. Thereafter, the two small rifle troops under command of Chris Nunn and an SBS officer would stream ashore using the same helicopters. The Tac HQ, the medical party and I would go in the last aircraft after the 81mm mortars had deployed. My plan also included one NGSFO officer deploying with the first wave, and the other airborne in a helicopter to direct the pre-bombardment. I also wanted 2 SBS and the two SAS Troops from *Endurance* and *Plymouth* to land by helicopter in Bore Valley Pass once the slopes of Brown Mountain were secure. Their particular task would be to move to the high ground above Grytviken and King Edward Point and provide covering fire for the advance to contact from Brown Mountain through Grytviken to King Edward Point.

This plan was put before the commander of the Task Group at 1000, but he wished to debrief the captain of *Brilliant* and the helicopter pilots after the submarine action before deciding on a time for

Above: Marines of 42 Commando inspect captured Argentinian weapons following the garrison's surrender. Above right: South Georgia's Neumayer glacier, seen from a helicopter cockpit. Right: Marines wait on the jetty at Grytviken as divers discuss the extent of the damage below the waterline to the Argentinian submarine *Santa Fé*. Bottom: Argentinian prisoners marshalled at King Edward Point on Cumberland East Bay.

MAJOR GUY SHERIDAN

Guy Sheridan joined the Royal Marines in 1960, and after completing the officers' course at the Commando Training Centre at Lympstone, he was posted to serve with 45 Commando in Aden. Returning in 1962, he underwent specialised training in mountain and Arctic warfare.

Sheridan then joined 40 Commando for service in Malaya and Borneo. Apart from serving with the Royal Marines he was seconded to the Sultan of Oman's Army from 1968 to 1970, where he commanded an Arab/Beluch company on active service for a year in Dhofar province with the Muscat Regiment.

In 1972 he was given command of the Mountain & Arctic Warfare Cadre, a position he held until 1974.

After staff training at Camberley and Bracknell, he served for two and a half years in Iran with a British Military Training mission. During the Falklands crisis in 1982, Guy Sheridan was second-in-command of 42 Commando, and he commanded the landing forces that repossessed South Georgia. He subsequently rejoined his Commando for the remainder of the conflict, and he was awarded the OBE for distinguished service in the campaign. He is now a lieutenant-colonel.

Sheridan represented Britain in the World Biathlon Championships in Finland in 1971, and was a member of the squad which trained for the 1972 Winter Olympics. He has completed long ski traverses of the Zagros mountains in Iran, the western Himalayas, and the Mackenzie mountains in Yukon, Canada.

H-Hour. A period of three hours followed while this went on and I became more and more anxious that the enemy, now boosted in numbers by the crew of the submarine, might be using the time to organise proper defences at Grytviken and King Edward Point. It was not until 1330 that H-Hour was finally agreed as 1445. I gave my orders, which included a fire-plan at 1345, and radioed the orders to 2 SBS and the two SAS Troops for their Bore Valley Pass landing.

It was to be approximately a five-minute flight from *Antrim* to the planned landing site (LS) as Hestesletten, flying close to the southern shore of Cumberland East Bay and passing over Dartmouth Point and Moraine Fjord. The three helicopters were loaded one by one on *Antrim's* flightdeck, and at H−10 the first salvo of 4.5in shells was fired from *Plymouth*. Directed by one of my NGSFOs, now airborne in a Wasp helicopter from *Endurance*, this bombardment was set up to neutralise the slopes of Brown Mountain which dominated the whole of Hestesletten. At H-Hour, 1445, the three helicopters, doors off and loaded to bursting point with 19 Troop, took off in wave formation. Simultaneously, *Antrim's* 4.5in guns launched their devastating fire onto the landing site to neutralise the area, switching at H+5 onto the slopes of Brown Mountain.

The SAS Troop's mission was to secure the landing site for the first of the small Royal Marine Troops to arrive. They were then to advance and secure the steep ridge that descended to the sea from the summit of Brown Mountain. This ridge dominated Hestesletten and as 19 Troop arrived on the landing site, the navel shells were raining down upon it.

At last we were ashore, and when Ian Stanley reported an unopposed landing I knew I was half-way to achieving my task of repossessing the island. Looking northwest, a kilometre of level, stony ground, covered in places with large clumps of tussock grass, stretched away to the steep slopes leading up to the Brown Mountain ridge. I assumed that all this was in dead ground to the enemy, whom I believed were grouped in and around Grytviken and the British Antarctic Survey (BAS) base at King Edward Point. A shallow river, known as Penguin River, wound round the foot of those steep slopes to the sea, and it was about 15m wide. It was clear that there was no enemy on those slopes and, if there had been, the 4.5in bombardment had done its job. But when I arrived in the last helicopter stream, I was surprised to find the SAS Troop still on the LS. I angrily told them to get on with their task, which they did after firing two Milan missiles onto the top of the mountain and engaging a herd of elephant seals blocking the way on the banks of Penguin River.

This was the third phase of my fire-plan, and it was designed to demoralise the Argentinians

Not a shot had been fired at us and it was not long before the Troop was clambering up the very steep shale to the crest of the Brown Mountain ridge. I was hard on their heels with Corporal Stannett, my signallers and the medical team. Meanwhile, the other two Troops had fanned out and were advancing on my right and to the rear. One of my NGSFOs, Captain Chris Browne, was now positioned on Dartmouth Point and was directing naval gunfire onto the exposed and rocky ground between the ridge and King Edward Point. This was the third phase of my fire-plan, and it was designed to demoralise the

Above: The commander of the Argentinian garrison on South Georgia, Captain Alfredo Astiz, signs the formal surrender document in front of Captain David Pentreath of *Plymouth* and Captain Nicholas Barker of *Endurance*. Although Astiz had gained a dubious reputation while serving his government on the mainland, he was eventually repatriated without interrogation. Background: The Union Jack and the White Ensign of the Royal Navy are raised over South Georgia.

Argentinians, the gun line passing over the BAS bas to explode the shells on the other side of the cove the enemy. Once on the crest we observed Gry viken and King Edward Point through binoculars.

On the Point, at the end of a jetty was the sub marine, and there were numerous sailors movin about on the casing and on the jetty, I swung m binoculars further along the settlement and saw large, orderly group of personnel in blue and gree uniform lined up on the foreshore by the mai flag-pole of the BAS base. From the flag-pole flu tered the blue and white Argentinian flag, and then saw a large white flag hanging from a buildin beyond. A glance up to Shackleton House, the larg building at the end of the base, revealed anothe and there was one more near the radio shack. The across the water came the distant sound of patrioti singing, and the reality of the moment manifeste itself. 'They've surrendered,' said Cedric Delves.

'Good,' I replied and, turning to my signaller, gav the order, 'Cancel the Bore Valley Pass landing Cedric and his small command team walked roun through Grytviken and I asked for a Wasp helicopte to take me over the cove to the BAS base. I aske *Antrim* to sail into the bay and be prepared to give u support if necessary. As Chris Nunn's Troop cam over the crest, he formed his men into an arrowhea formation for the final three kilometres to Grytvike The next day the small enemy detachment in Leit under Captain Astiz, surrendered to *Plymouth* with out a shot being fired.

South Georgia was back in British hands without casualty to us. There were 137 enemy prisoner joined the next day by another 15 marines and 4 scrapmen from Leith. The only casualty that day, 2 April, was an enemy sailor who lost a leg in the initia attack on the submarine. We had achieved the tas with the minimum loss of life and damage to proper ty. I noted in my diary that evening, 'A satisfying day

THE AUTHOR Lieutenant-Colonel Guy Sheridan, whil a major and second-in-command of 42 Command RM, commanded the land forces that repossesse South Georgia. He was awarded the OBE for disting uished service during the South Atlantic campaig

RLI
SUPPORT COMMANDO

SUPPORT COMMANDO

After the break-up of the Central Africa Federation in December 1963, the Rhodesian Army's battalion support weapons and specialist platoons all operated as independent platoons under the command of a headquarters company (later designated as Base Group).

During 1964, the Rhodesian Light Infantry (RLI) was reformed as a commando battalion, and it was decided to gather the support weapons into one group. Consequently, on 1 January 1965, Support Group was officially formed under the command of Captain A.P. Stephens, with Colour Sergeant Harry Birkett as Group C Sergeant.

After a number of structural changes, the intervention of Major Pat Armstrong resulted in the Support Group eventually being reformed as Support Commando on 6 January 1976. The RLI became an airborne commando battalion the following year, and Support Commando's first two dozen men were para-trained in March 1977.

The final structure of Support Commando comprised a headquarters company and four troops: mortar, assault pioneer, reconnaissance and anti-tank.

The Commando was directly responsible for providing the battalion with supporting fire and specialist resources in both conventional war and counter-insurgency (COIN) operations.

The unit badge consisted of an eagle, gripping a telescope (symbolising the recce role) and an 81mm mortar round in its talons. A series of eagles were adopted as the unit emblem and official mascot; the longest-serving was 'Henry', an African Hawk Eagle.

In late April 1979 troopers from the Rhodesian Light Infantry Support Commando launched a lightning cross-border operation against guerrilla staging camps in Mozambique

DURING THE SPRING of 1979 the attention of the Western world was focused on events in Rhodesia. It was the time of the much-publicised April elections, a democratic contest that was to result in Bishop Abel Muzorewa becoming Rhodesia's first black premier.

According to contemporary media reports, this was a relatively peaceful time during an otherwise

turbulent period in African history. Not even the combined forces of Robert Mugabe and Joshua Nkomo's Patriotic Front (PF) could dissuade the men and women of Rhodesia from queuing at the polling booths. Yet for those of us in the bush, April was an eventful month indeed. It is a credit to the Rhodesian security forces that the election proceeded so smoothly.

We had been warned to expect an increase in terrorist activity over the voting period. Intelligence sources had indicated that a substantial number of experienced guerrillas had long been held in reserve by the PF for just such an occasion. My unit, Support Commando 1st Battalion, The Rhodesian Light Infantry was therefore deployed on Monday 2 April. A small group of commandos was detached to provide protection for some of the more vulnerable polling stations, and the remainder of the men were initially divided into two 'Fire Force' groups. My group moved straight to Grand Reef, near Umtali in eastern Rhodesia, while the other was deployed to Inyanga, 55 miles to the north.

The Commando soon became embroiled in frequent call-outs. To date, such encounters with the guerrillas had usually resulted in heavy 'terr' casualties compared to minimum losses among security force personnel; the formidable reputation of the Rhodesian Light Infantry (RLI) had invariably been sufficient to cause an adversary to break and run during a contact! However, ZANLA's latest offensive exhibited a fresh determination – within the first three days of the bush trip our unit lost one man killed

Page 139. Above: Members of Recce Troop, Support Commando, pose for a photograph before setting out on the raid into Mozambique. Below: An RLI cross-border patrol. The trooper in the front is armed with a captured Soviet RPK light machine gun.

and another wounded. A large-scale operation was therefore planned in an attempt to suppress enemy activity in our area. On 11 April elements of Support and 3 Commando (RLI), together with a detachment from the Rhodesian African Rifles (RAR), were detailed to attack a complex of five staging camps allegedly holding up to 250 guerrillas. But at the last moment, even as paratroopers circled the drop zone (DZ), it was discovered that the security forces had arrived too late. The camps were already deserted. To our great disappointment, the raid was called off. We made our way back to Grand Reef, where we were reinforced by the Inyanga detachment.

There was very little opportunity for action during the next few days and the Commando only received a couple of call-outs, both of which proved uneventful. Just as it was beginning to appear that our mere presence had once again become a sufficient deterrent to guerrilla activity, the enemy struck hard and fast. Our Commando was involved in several days of hectic fighting during which Mortar Troop lost three men killed. This reduced the unit's effective strength to only 13 personnel! The situation was considered serious enough to grant the survivors four days rest and recreation in Salisbury. Here, on 25 April, I

Left: RLI troopers man a Soviet-built Degtyarev 12.7mm HMG at a base camp during a cross-border operation. Left inset: Rhodesian troops snatch a little sleep between operations. Top and above: One of the keys to RLI operations was the speed of deployment afforded by their Huey 'Cheetah' helicopters.

witnessed crowds of chanting Africans celebrating Bishop Muzorewa's rise to power. Although the elections had passed, the war in the bush continued.

Upon their return to the RLI barracks at Cranborne, the men of the Mortar Troop were greeted by a pile of captured communist weapons and ammunition. Our suspicions were well and truly aroused when these were loaded onto the trucks that were to transport us back to the bush. At Grand Reef the next day, a number of men were issued with light machine guns and RPG-7 rocket launchers. Along with the rest of the Commando, I was told to draw as much ammunition and as many grenades as I could carry. The riflemen each drew up to 10 magazines of 7.62mm ammunition plus another 100 loose rounds, making a grand total of some 300 rounds apiece! To a man, we equipped ourselves with numerous grenades of various types. The machine-gunners stuffed their web pouches full of link ammunition and distributed extra belts among the riflemen. Similarly, those with RPGs shared out their 40mm rounds. Nobody was exempt from carrying an additional load, be it ammunition, a radio or a medical pack.

The Rhodesian Air Force would subject the target to a precision bombing raid prior to the assault

Although we had been offered no reason for this sudden flurry of activity, it came as no surprise when, on the evening of 28 April, we were flown to Buffalo Range airfield on Rhodesia's eastern border with Mozambique. That night, Intelligence officers provided us with a detailed briefing. They explained that a large military complex had been located some 50km inside the Mozambican bush. Although this important staging area had been monitored by our forces, it had deliberately left alone. As expected, the result was an influx of ZANLA guerrillas massing for an armed crossing into Rhodesia. The sudden decline of hostilities following the election was now deemed an appropriate time to hit ZANLA in its own territory. This task had fallen on the shoulders of Support Commando.

Among those gathered at the Chicualacuala staging camp, according to our sources, were at least two members of the ZANLA hierarchy, identified by their distinctive camouflage uniforms with hammer-and-sickle collar insignia. Intelligence also indicated the presence of Eastern-bloc military advisers in the vicinity. In what was a highly secret operation, our orders were to bring back any high-ranking officials we could lay our hands on. At the very least, we were expected to capture one ZANLA guerrilla who could be interrogated by Intelligence. We were also instructed to destroy any equipment that we were unable to carry away from the camp.

The Rhodesian Air Force would subject the target to a precision bombing raid immediately prior to the assault, with the ground troops arriving as the last jet aircraft unloaded its bombs. While elements of the Commando attacked the camp, a 'stop group' would lay an experimental land-mine along the camp's approach road. Details concerning the workings of this device were classified at this time, its future depending on an efficient performance during the raid. As events unfolded, it became clear that our lives had also depended on the mine functioning smoothly.

We numbered close to 50 heavily armed men, and two Huey 'Cheetah' helicopters and eight Alouette III 'G-Cars' were required to ferry us to the target

STAGING CAMPS

There were two guerrilla movements operational against the Rhodesian security forces during the late 1970s: the Zimbabwe African National Liberation Army (ZANLA), the military wing of Robert Mugabe's Zimbabwe African National Union (ZANU) party, and the Zimbabwe People's Revolutionary Army (ZIPRA), the military arm of Joshua Nkomo's Zimbabwe African People's Union (ZAPU). Although intense rivalry existed between ZANLA and ZIPRA, they were ostensibly united under the umbrella of the Patriotic Front (PF). ZANLA was equipped largely by communist China, while ZIPRA received its supplies of arms and ammunition from the Soviet Union and East Germany. The assistance and support given by neighbouring black African states enabled Nkomo to set up bases in Zambia. Mozambique provided a similarly convenient staging place for Mugabe's followers.

The guerrilla offensive began in December 1972. As the war progressed, communist military advisers arrived in Zambia and Mozambique and were active in designing and constructing fortified military complexes deep in the heart of the African bush. These camps were used as training centres and staging posts for guerrillas en route to Rhodesia. Well-sited trenches and dug-outs provided the occupants with superb defensive positions, and sandbagged emplacements protected anti-aircraft guns. Tents and other quarters were usually undetectable from the air, hidden by trees and thick bush.

The first major cross-border raids mounted by Rhodesia began in 1976, followed in November 1977 by a massive assault on Chimoio and Tembue in Mozambique. By March 1978, large-scale raids were being launched against Zambia.

The last year of the war saw several raids, including a much-publicised five-day operation in October 1979, when the Rhodesians successfully neutralised the large military complex at Chimoio in Mozambique.

area. Air cover was provided by three Alouette 'K-Cars' (command helicopter gunships) and two Cessna Lynx aircraft. A low-level flight brought us to within a few miles of our objective. However, all we could see on the horizon was a brown haze hanging in the air above the flat green landscape. As we swept in over the bush, it soon became clear that the odd-looking 'fog' was in fact an accumulation of smoke and dust flung up by the rockets and bombs of our air support. From my seat aboard one of the Cheetahs I was presented with a birds-eye view of the camp site itself. It was partially obscured beneath a mass of trees and thick bush, through which could be seen dark, billowing clouds of dense smoke. After flying straight through one of these clouds, we banked sharply around an anti-aircraft gun that was still pumping rounds into the sky. Down over a clump of trees, the chopper continued its descent. Suddenly, the Cheetah was dropping almost vertically and we were leaping out into the

tall, yellow grass that fringed the camp. Seconds later, all the choppers had disappeared.

As my ears began to recover from the punishment of a long helicopter journey, I soon realised that the apparent silence was deceptive. The ubiquitous sound of exploding smallarms ammunition provided the backdrop as flames devoured trees and bushes with an audible crackle. Every few minutes a Hunter strike aircraft would appear from nowhere, screaming out of the sky and flying low to strafe yet another target. The slow-firing AA gun continued to harass our air cover until being finally silenced by one such attack. The bush reverberated with the report of our rifles as the LZ was rapidly secured.

Our 'sticks' quickly linked up and began to edge forward cautiously. My first close glimpse of the camp was of a kitchen that had been set up in the shade of a group of trees. Several dead guerrillas were scattered around a series of huge pots in which the food was still simmering – providing evidence of the speed of our assault.

On the outskirts of the camp, the Commando shot a number of ZANLA guerrillas, most of whom were dazed and disorientated by the preliminary bombing. Indeed, there were a number of unexploded 'Golf' bombs still littering the area. We prudently gave a wide berth to these round, orange-coloured shrapnel bombs.

Since the entire area was still ablaze, it was

Below: Support Commando prepares to move into Mozambique on 29 April 1979. Left: Silhouetted against the smoke created by the detonation of a grenade, a Rhodesian trooper moves forward during the raid. Above: An RLI mortar crew in action. Below right: Members of the Recce Troop at work in the ZANLA base. Right: Laying a mine.

cessary to pause and allow the flames to die down
before we were able to penetrate into the heart of the
ZANLA base. This proved to be a neatly
organised system of bunkers,
weapon pits and tents, all very
well constructed and sited.
Equipment lay every-
where. In one area, a
large number of dis-
carded Soviet army hel-
mets were scattered ab-
out the charred earth.
Anti-aircraft guns still
pointed skywards. Behind
one of these lay a dead ZANLA
guerrilla, half-buried by the partially caved-in weapon pit. He must
have been sitting in the gunner's seat when
falling debris covered his torso from head to waist.
Leaving several men behind to dismantle the AA
guns, the rest of us advanced a little further until we
were confronted by an elaborate trench system.
There was only one way of finding out whether or
not the enemy had remained in position. We thus
embarked on a nerve-racking op-
eration, oddly out of place
in the context of mod-
ern warfare. The
trenches had
been dug in a zig-
zag pattern, with
bunkers sited
every few yards.
Each section had
to be negotiated
separately in order
to deal with the bunk-
ers one at a time. The area
resounded with the dull thud
of exploding grenades and
the occasional burst of fire as
we set about our task. In the
process of securing the
objective, we collected a
vast pile of smallarms and
miscellaneous equipment
belonging to the guerrillas. It
soon became obvious that
ZANLA had deserted the

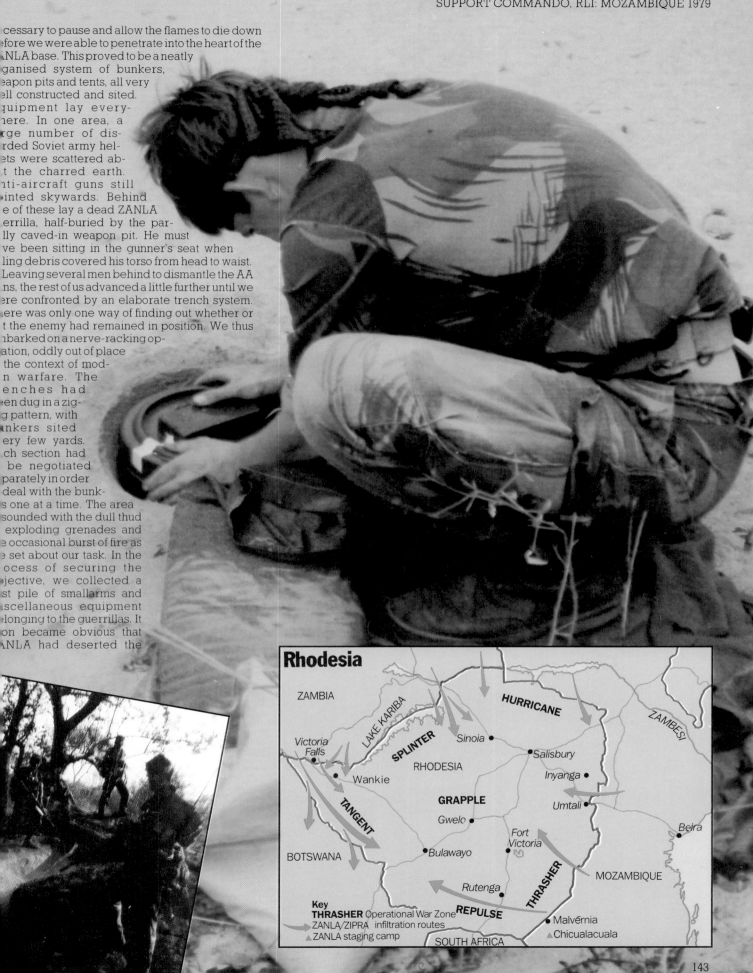

Rhodesia

ZAMBIA

LAKE KARIBA

Victoria Falls

Wankie

SPLINTER

Sinoia

HURRICANE

ZAMBESI

Salisbury

RHODESIA

Inyanga

GRAPPLE

Umtali

TANGENT

Gwelo

Fort Victoria

Beira

BOTSWANA

Bulawayo

THRASHER

MOZAMBIQUE

Rutenga

REPULSE

Malvernia

Chicualacuala

SOUTH AFRICA

Key
THRASHER Operational War Zone
ZANLA/ZIPRA infiltration routes
ZANLA staging camp

trenches long before our arrival!

We discovered numerous other weapons that must have been hastily discarded by the guerrillas during their flight. A few rifles had been abandoned, propped up in the bushes, their barrels aimed towards the attacking troops. The Cheetahs were called in and swiftly loaded up with huge quantities of AK and Simonov SKS rifles, grenades and ammunition. We also dragged one 12.7mm and three 14.5mm AA guns to the LZ. That which we could not take, we destroyed. Among the vast mound of items that perished in the subsequent fires were uniforms, personal packs and web-equipment, propaganda leaflets, and enormous quantities of tinned food.

After several hours we reached the outer limits of the camp defences where we paused for a short rest. Our commanding officer, a major, was supervising the entire operation from his K-Car, high above the camp. Shortly after he gave the order to discontinue moving forward, a small group located a leather briefcase hidden in a clump of bushes. Wary of a possible booby-trap, I carefully peeked into the case and was rewarded with the sight of a stack of type-script. We also found a few holsters containing only empty magazines. We surmised that whoever had been entrusted with the care of these items had hurriedly stashed everything before fleeing into the bush. Whoever this was, they had mistakenly deemed half a dozen pistols more valuable than the contents of the briefcase. Upon further examination, the latter revealed priceless information listing the names of hundreds of active terrorists, their bush-names, and the individual weapon types they carried, complete with manufacturer's serial numbers. There were also handwritten messages and personal letters, together with an amazing collection of photographs depicting uniformed ZANLA personnel in the company of what we presumed were East German or Soviet military instructors.

The find prompted in many of us a conviction that we were closing in on the very men we had set out to

Above: After action. Several ZANLA guerrillas lie dead in the dust after a fierce engagement with the RLI. In the background can be seen a fortified bunker, typical of the defensive positions built by ZANLA to protect their staging camps. Below: The fruits of victory. RLI troopers pose for a picture on the hull of a captured Soviet-built T55 tank.

capture. Our commanding officer, however, insisted that we abandon the search and return to the LZ.

Mine was one of the last two sticks to be airlifted out of the area late that afternoon. Unknown to us, a convoy of trucks was at that moment transporting a large number of FRELIMO troops in our direction. However, the mines laid by our stop group had worked a treat. At least one had detonated under the weight of a fully laden truck, thereby temporarily holding up the Mozambican counter-attack. We were informed of these details during the debrief back in Rhodesia. It also transpired that our commanding officer had almost delayed our airlift until the following morning due to the hazards involved in flying helicopters without the benefit of suitable night-navigation aids.

A few days after the raid we were informed by Special Branch Intelligence that our mission had been deemed a success. It was unfortunate that we had not managed to bring back a live terrorist, but the contents of the briefcase had yielded much invaluable information. Intelligence had also discovered, albeit too late, that a large force of ZANLA guerrillas had left the camp on the night prior to our attack. Nevertheless, the fact remained that four dozen men had entered an enemy stronghold, cleared the area, and remained there all day without incurring a single casualty. ZANLA, on the other hand, had lost at least 28 killed.

Ironically, many of the guerrillas that we missed during the Mozambique raid were destined to face the wrath of Support Commando two weeks later. Following a routine call-out on 14 May, in which we killed or captured 21 terrorists, ZANLA prisoners revealed that their unit included several high-ranking officials and many others who had recently arrived via Mozambique. A follow-up border operation two days later culminated in a day-long firefight with the remnants of the group. Of those guerrillas accounted for, two were found to be wearing Ethiopian camouflage. Was it merely coincidence that their uniforms, complete with hammer-and-sickle collar tabs, were identical to those we had been briefed to look out for during the camp attack on 29 April?

THE AUTHOR Frank Terrell served in the Royal Marine Commandos during the 1970s. A year after the completion of his service, he travelled to southern Africa where he signed on with the RLI.

Right inset: In late 1979 the operational effectiveness of the RLI came to an end with the arrival of the Commonwealth monitoring force. Here a group of RLI troopers watches the arrival in Rhodesia of an RAF Hercules transport. Right: An RLI corporal presents arms at the unveiling ceremony of 'The Trooper', a memorial dedicated to the RLI dead, on 1 February 1979. The 320kg statue of a trooper kitted out for operations in the bush now resides in the Republic of South Africa.

On July 19 1969, under cover of darkness, crack Israeli commandos set out to destroy the Egyptian radar station on Green Island

FROM HIS VANTAGE point behind a low sand ridge, a young Israeli naval officer, Lieutenant-Colonel Zeev Almog, peered intently through the ink-black darkness, scouring the nearby shoreline for signs of movement. Finally satisfied that all was quiet, Almog turned about and made his way back to the hollow where his team of commandos was waiting, the men huddled together against the biting chill of a desert night. Moments later, after a brief exchange of a few hushed words, Almog and his commandos padded down to the beach, launched their Zodiac inflatable assault craft into the choppy waters of the Gulf of Suez, and then set course for the Egyptian-held radar station on Green Island. After months of intensive preparations and several days of waiting for the right conditions, the raid was on.

The waterborne assault on the island, carried out during the night of 19/20 July 1969, was one of a series of reprisal raids mounted by the Israeli Defence Forces (IDF) in response to air, artillery and commando-type attacks undertaken by Egypt in the aftermath of its humiliating defeat in the Six-Day War of 1967. Between 1967 and 1970, in what became known as the War of Attrition, both sides engaged in open, but limited warfare that did nothing to ease the prevailing tension in the Middle East. At the height of these hostilities, from May 1969 until January 1970, the Israeli armed forces launched a number of cross-border hit-and-run raids aimed at undermining Egyptian military efficiency.

Having considered a variety of options during the early months of 1969, Israel's military planners decided to launch a series of limited air strikes against targets along the Egyptian side of the Suez Canal and the Gulf of Suez. But, before these plans could be put into effect, the enemy's radar installations, part of a Soviet-supplied early-warning network that could direct Egyptian MiG fighters onto interception courses and provide target data for surface-to-air

missile batteries, had to be neutralised. Green Island, lying three miles out from the port of Suez at the southern end of the Canal, was recognised as one of the cornerstones of the air defences in the area. If it was destroyed, then the Israeli Air Force would be able to hit the Egyptian naval base at Ras Adabia, a few miles southwest of the island, and deal with a number of troublesome artillery batteries that had been shelling Israeli ships in the gulf and IDF positions in Sinai. The island had been earmarked for destruction before and yet had remained operational, despite the attentions of several heavy Israeli bombardments.

When informed of the planned operation, Almog soon realised that the station was going to be a tough nut to crack. Reports compiled from intelligence sources, fleshed out by aerial photo-reconnaissance missions, indicated that the installation was heavily fortified and defended by more than 100 Egyptians, including members of a highly trained commando force. The island fort, built by the British during World War II to protect the southern entrance to the Canal from air and sea attack by Axis forces, was some 150yds long and, in places, 80yds wide. Built with reinforced concrete on an underwater rock, it consisted of a central courtyard, containing the garrison's living quarters, surrounded by an eight-foot high perimeter wall. The radar installation had been sited on the northern

Below: Heading for shore. A team of Israeli naval commandos carry out a training exercise, one of several which would have preceded the daring raid on Green Island. Each stage was planned down to the last detail, for in their underwater equipment and carried by the relatively slow Zodiacs, the commandos would be sitting ducks if the Egyptian garrison became aware of their presence on the way in. Below right: A commando brandishes his AK-47: for the raid on Green Island this weapon was dropped in favour of the more flexible Uzi sub-machine gun which could be fired one-handed – a valuable asset for the outnumbered raiders.

RAID ON GREEN ISLAND

of the island, on a detached emplacement that
[coul]d only be reached from the fort by crossing a
[nar]row walkway supported by 10 concrete pillars.
[K]nowing that the radar would be high on the
[Isra]elis' list of strike priorities, the Egyptians had
[turn]ed the island into a veritable fortress. Air recon-
[nais]sance showed that the garrison had charge of six
[emp]lacements mounting 37mm and 85mm anti-air-
[craf]t guns and, in case of surface attack, some 14
[well]-sited heavy machine guns and an unknown
[num]ber of 20mm cannon. To accomplish their mis-
[sion] successfully, the commandos would have to deal
[with] the enemy quickly and efficiently, before they
[had] a chance to man their heavy weapons.

[T]he prospect of taking on heavy machine guns and
[can]non with only Uzi sub-machine guns and gre-
[nad]es dogged Almog's thoughts as he went over the
[assa]ult plan during the run in to the target. If all went
[wel]l, his commandos would separate into three
[pre]-designated assault teams before reaching the
[isla]nd; two would attack the fort and radar station,
[whi]le the third took up position on a rock some
[yar]ds to the south to provide covering fire. Sudden-
[ly a] gentle tap on his shoulder brought Almog out of
[his m]using. Something was wrong.

[Mo]tioning to his team, he lined up on [th]e pair of sentries with his Uzi and then opened fire

[Alth]ough the sea was calm and the wind, blowing
[at a]n even five knots, was nothing to worry about, the
[cont]rary currents created by the Canal were
[ham]pering the boats' advance. It was vital that the
[men]s keep on schedule, so Almog ordered his men

into the water. After swimming underwater for 15
minutes, he then surfaced to check his bearings only
to learn that the covering party was already in
position, while his party was still 650yds short of their
objective. Rapidly changing course, and summon-
ing up their remaining reserves of energy, the
commandos struck out for the northern side of the
island and the foot of the emplacement that held the
radar equipment.

Once in position, Almog ordered the six-man
assault team carrying the demolition charges to
maintain strict silence, while the other team set about
the task of cutting a path through the razor-sharp
barbed wire coiled around the concrete pillar.
Chest-deep in icy water, trying to keep their balance
on slime-covered rocks, the men struggled with
their wire cutters to gain entry. Above, on the narrow
walkway, two Egyptian sentries argued noisily, unaware of the presence of the commandos a few feet
below. Alarmed by the delay the wire was causing,
Almog gazed aloft, searching for an easier way
through the wire. In the subdued light coming from
the radar shack he could just make out a gap in the
defences. Motioning to his team, he lined up on the
pair of sentries with his Uzi and then opened fire.

The silence was shattered, but before they could
react, the Egyptians were riddled by bullets fired at

COMMANDO SABOTAGE

Ranged against the Arab
states during the War of
Independence, Israel faced
a severe threat from the sea
and, lacking an established
navy, sought to counter this
by sabotage, using teams of
recently formed naval
commandos.
On 21 October, on their first
mission, a team of
commandos, using Italian
fast boats carrying
explosives, sank the
Egyptian flagship – the *Emir
Farouk*. This notable
success was followed by
several more acts of
sabotage, including the
demolition of the Syrian
supply ship *Lino*.
After the war, the naval
commandos were
reconstituted, training along
the lines of the British SBS.
Volunteers from within the
IDF were subjected to a
rigorous selection process,
and only the cream were
admitted into the naval
commandos. Modern
equipment was issued and
gradually the commandos
emerged as the top
specialist force in the IDF.
During the War of Attrition
the commandos performed
a number of daring
operations, including the
raid on Green Island. Two
months later, on 7
September 1969, they
attacked the Egyptian navy
base at Ras Sadat, and sank
two motor patrol boats.
With the outbreak of the
Yom Kippur War in October
1973, the expertise of the
naval commandos was again
called upon. Several
missions were undertaken,
and among these was a
successful attack on Port
Said harbour, when a well
drilled commando unit used
high explosives to sink two
Egyptian Landing Craft
Assault ships.
More recently, the
commandos have seen
action along the Lebanese
coast, harassing PLO
positions and forming the
vanguard during the
invasion of June 1982.
Above: The insignia of the
Israeli naval commandos.

147

Green Island
19/20 July 1969

In July 1969, at the height of the War of Attrition between Israel and her Arab neighbours, a small team of Israeli naval commandos was sent in to blow up the Egyptian radar installations and defences on Green Island in the Gulf of Suez. The heavily defended island, a tiny fortress some three miles from the Israeli held east shore, was a vital keystone in the Egyptian radar network defending Egyptian bases such as the naval base at Ras Adabia. The commandos landed unobserved, overcame the garrison in a fierce firefight, and blew up the installation before withdrawing.

Gulf of Suez

Suez Canal
Great Bitter Lake
Ras Adabia • Suez
Green Island
Ras Sadat
Ras Abu Daraj
Ras Zafarana
Ras Asran
SINAI (Israeli occupied)
Ras Abu Baqer
Gulf of Suez
Ras Gharib
EGYPT   Hurdaqa

Assault on Green Island

19/20 July Under cover of darkness, Israeli naval commandos move out in inflatable assault boats from the Israeli-held eastern shore of the Gulf of Suez and set course for Green Island, some three miles away. Covering the last part of the journey underwater, two assault teams silently land on the island while a covering force establishes itself further south.

Key
Israeli naval commandos

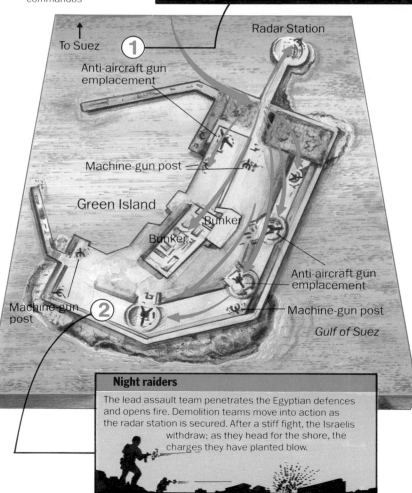

To Suez

Radar Station

(1)

Anti-aircraft gun emplacement

Machine-gun post

Green Island

Bunker

Bunker

Anti-aircraft gun emplacement

Machine-gun post

Machine-gun post

(2)

Gulf of Suez

Night raiders

The lead assault team penetrates the Egyptian defences and opens fire. Demolition teams move into action as the radar station is secured. After a stiff fight, the Israelis withdraw; as they head for the shore, the charges they have planted blow.

close range. One dropped like a stone to the crete floor while the other toppled into the waters of the gulf. Capitalising on the eleme surprise, two other commandos loosed off s cutting bursts against the shack. On cue, the sup party opened up from the south. The enemy caught totally unprepared and, with little ide where the Israelis were, blazed away indisc nately into the darkness. Only a few seconds dealing with the sentries, Almog's men were on way up. Once on top, the team paused to g bearings and then began its deadly work. Gren were lobbed left and right while automatic fire sprayed into the shack.

The Egyptians soon began to respond in for the Israeli assault team's fire. In the process of se ing the roof of the radar station, one commando c face to face with an Egyptian who was able to th hand grenade in his direction. Caught by a frag

f concrete blown off by the explosion, the Israeli
ppled off the roof, but fortunately landed in the
ms of his fellow commandos stationed below.
ndaunted, he returned to the fray, giving the Egyp-
an a taste of his own medicine. Two other enemy
oldiers, manning a roof-top machine-gun position,
ere also dealt with.

The radar emplacement secure, Almog then cal-
d in the demolition squad whose job was to blow
e fort apart. Straining under the load of their
narges, the explosive experts were helped up by
e members of the initial assault team. Now it was
ne to move into the fort itself, where the bulk of the
arrison was stationed.

While the demolition squad set about laying their
narges around the radar, other commandos clam-
ered onto the bridge and raced for their secondary
ojectives. Splitting into two groups, they began to
ear the perimeter wall and deal with the gun

emplacements in the main complex. Speed was vital.
The Egyptians had overcome their initial shock and
were busy organising for a determined counter-
attack. The night sky was lit up by streams of tracer
fire, reaching out in all directions for a target. There
was no need for any detailed orders, every Israeli
knew the routine by heart. Each man had to keep on
the move, making use of any available cover, and fire
short bursts if the enemy put in an appearance.

The commandos began to take casualties. One
officer, leading his men against a machine-gun position, was hit in the neck and killed. A captain leapt
forward to carry on the job, but stopped momentarily
to get his bearings before pushing on against three
other Egyptian positions. He was knocked down by
tracer fire from hidden gun-pits in the courtyard.
Another team member took over, leading the depleted squad against the enemy. Taking care of one
Egyptian who was unwise enough to poke his head

After the Six-Day War of
1967, Egypt embarked on a
protracted attritional war
against Israeli forces
occupying the east bank of
the Suez Canal and Sinai.
The first stage of the
campaign opened in
September 1967 and heavy
artillery duels took place
over the Canal. In October,
in retaliation for the sinking
of the Israeli destroyer *Eilat*,
the Israeli Air Force
launched a bombing raid
against Egyptian oil
refineries (below). In

elow: Commandos demonstrate their prowess during
n anti-terrorist exercise. Each man carries out his
ssigned task in silence after the unit has landed on the
each. As the commandos prepare to advance towards
nemy' positions, one of them lies ready to provide
vering fire.

September 1968 Egypt went
over to a phase of 'offensive
defence' and mounted
further bombardments
against Israeli positions.
Raids were launched by
both sides across the Canal.
May 1969 saw the opening
of a third phase, and a
serious escalation in the
fighting. In January 1970,
Israel carried out a series of
long-range bombing
missions into central Egypt.
Egypt then turned to the
Soviet Union for help, and
Soviet pilots became
involved in defensive
combat missions over
Egypt. But on 30 July they
took part in a major air
battle, which prompted the
US and the Soviet Union to
exert pressure on Egypt and
Israel to de-escalate the
confrontation. The 30 July
battle was the last major
engagement of the War of
Attrition.

out of a hatchway, he then picked off another man preparing to fling a grenade in the direction of the oncoming commandos.

A second assault group charged along the perimeter wall to root out the Egyptians manning the gun emplacements along the southern side of the fort. The commandos then descended to the floor of the yard. One man was killed, caught in the open by a sniper, but his comrades pushed on, attacking the barrack blocks around the central area of the fort. Once these buildings had been cleared, members of the demolition team placed their explosive charges and set delayed-action fuzes. Although the fort was now almost entirely in Israeli hands, a few Egyptians were still holding out and two commandos died trying to take out a machine-gun post.

As the fighting slowed, Almog glanced at the luminous dial on his watch. The commandos had been in action for nearly 30 minutes and it was vital now that they withdraw before the Egyptian forces on the western edge of the gulf responded to their incursion. If all went according to plan, the various assault groups would be picked up by the Zodiac inflatables near the radar station. Shouting above the din of the remaining smallarms fire, Almog ordered his men to the rendevous point; the last few charges were placed as the men made their withdrawal.

The Egyptians unleashed a heavy barrage from the shore but the commandos made their escape

Despite the adverse currents, the Zodiac crews were ready in position to evacuate the commandos. Enemy resistance had ceased, and Almog was able to hold a hurried roll-call: six men had been killed in the firefight and ten others had been wounded. None of the casualties were left behind. Enemy losses were unknown, but were probably much greater given the ferocity of the Israeli onslaught.

Satisfied that his men were all present and that the charges had been correctly laid, Almog gave the departure signal. The engines of the assault craft roared into life and the coxswains set course for Israeli territory. Seconds later, the Egyptians unleashed a heavy barrage from the shore, but the commandos were able to make their escape, aided by the welcome blanket of night, and suffered no casualties from the often wild enemy fire. Glancing back over their shoulders, the weary men had a grandstand view of the results of the night's work. The charges they had placed with great precision detonated, and huge blocks of concrete were flung into the air, wrecking the fort beyond easy repair.

The loss of the radar station on Green Island was soon felt by the Egyptians: during the following weeks, Israeli aircraft struck deep inside Egypt, destroying a variety of military targets.

THE AUTHOR William Franklin is a military historian who has contributed to a number of military books and publications. His particular interest is in specialist fighting units.

Above and below: Two view of the island fortress of Gree Island. The radar station is linked to the garrison by a causeway (see top of aerial photograph), and the damag caused by the raid can be clearly seen.

Left: The men who cleared the beaches. Royal Navy Commandos are photographed in front of a Landing Craft Mechanised (LCM) which sailed on Operation Overlord. Below: Second Lieutenant J. Taylor (left) and Lieutenant H. Hargreaves, two of the first men ashore in their sector. Bottom: The Allied tide rises against Hitler on 6 June 1944. Without the efforts of the RN Commandos, many more would have died in the chaos of the beaches.

Among the first to storm ashore on D-day, the RN Commandos were asked to destroy Germany's complex lines of defence on the Normandy beaches

FIRST WAVE

A HUGE PALL of smoke and dust spread over the Normandy coastline as D-day, 6 June 1944, dawned. Announcing Operation Overlord, the pounding of heavy naval guns loosing off salvo after salvo made a deafening roar; the Allied invasion of German-occupied Normandy had begun. Along the shoreline, shell bursts sent up giant plumes of smoke accompanied by brilliant flashes of light, and overhead an unbroken stream of heavy bombers headed home after saturating the German coastal defences. The heavy seas of the previous day had abated, but there was still a swell strong enough to be noticeable aboard the myriad of tiny craft that were already beginning their run-in to the beaches.

From Lieutenant-Commander W.F.N. Gregory-Smith's assault landing craft (LCA), looking astern, the Allied invasion fleet was visible as a solid mass of shipping packing the English Channel back as far as the eye could see – infantry assault craft, tank landing vessels, landing ships, escort destroyers and gunboats, and the bombarding force of cruisers and battleships. Stunned by the noise, but with their resolution undaunted by the massive columns of water thrown up around them, as shells from the German battery at Mont Fleury exploded, Gregory-Smith and his fellow naval commandos prepared themselves for the ordeal ahead. The commandos, and the assault infantry from the British 69th Brigade, 50th Infantry Division, that were to accompany them onto King Beach, near La Rivière in the British 'Gold' sector, waited for touchdown and the fight that would inevitably follow.

H-hour on the Gold beaches was timed for 0725. As the first waves drew near to the shore, the heavy bombers overhead were replaced by light bom-

151

SPEARHEADING THE INVASION

The Royal Navy's experience of large-scale amphibious operations in North Africa, and during the Italian campaign, had brought home a number of important lessons. One of the most crucial was that a major landing on a heavily defended coast can become dangerously chaotic within a very short time, unless strong, highly trained naval beach parties are landed during the first waves of the assault. The RN Commandos, specialising in this role, had been forming since the spring of 1942; by 1944, 22 brigade-front Commandos were in existence, and many of the individual commandos had seen hazardous service in several regions of the world. Operation Overlord – far and away the largest amphibious landing to date – was no exception to the rule. Involving some 7000 vessels and assault craft, landing armoured vehicles, men and huge quantities of stores, it would present unprecedented problems of beach organisation once the assault was under way. As a result, Overlord saw the largest ever effort by the RN Commandos. A total of eight Commando units, each under the command of a Principal Beachmaster (PBM), were assigned to the Gold, Juno and Sword sectors – one Commando to each infantry brigade landing beach – under the overall charge of the Chief PBM, Captain Colin Maud.
Above: Lieutenant-Commander W.F.N. Gregory-Smith, one of the Principal Beachmasters who landed in Gold sector.

bers and fighter-bombers tasked to take out particular targets. At 0720 the naval bombardment on the shoreline lifted. As the assault craft neared the shore, the men came under smallarms and artillery fire. Lieutenant-Commander John Mitchell, commander of T Commando, senior Beachmaster for King Beach and deputy to Principal Beachmaster Gregory-Smith, later recalled the last moments before landing:

'As we approached the beach the whistle of bullets could be heard above the crash of the surf. The furrows of the sea from the rise and fall of the waves were not deep enough to afford us even intermittent cover from the shore batteries, which by now had been well aroused and were giving us all they could.'

Shortly after 0730, Mitchell and Gregory-Smith reached King Beach. Among the dunes, the fight was well under way: several hundred first-wave assault troops were clawing their way up the beach, under heavy smallarms fire from German strongpoints. Out to sea, the flood tide, driven higher than expected by the storms of the previous day, already held its grim flotsam: stores and equipment, the bodies of dead and wounded assault troops, and the shattered hulls of landing craft damaged by offshore traps and mines. Ignoring the danger from smallarms, the two Beachmasters sprang into action, Mitchell running west and his superior turning east towards the German-held strongpoint of La Rivière. The ordeal of D-day had begun in earnest.

The invasion of Normandy had started hours earlier with an airborne assault on the flanks of the planned landing area by three airborne divisions. But the main operation was to consist of an amphibious assault by two Allied armies, under the overall command of General Bernard Montgomery. Supported by two naval task forces, 'Eastern' and 'Western', these armies would land on five pre-arranged sectors of the Normandy coast between Le Havre in the east and the Cotentin peninsula in the west. The Western (US) Task Force was responsible for landing the US First Army on the beaches of the 'Utah' and 'Omaha' sectors. To the east, in the Gold, 'Juno' and 'Sword' sectors, the British Second Army provided the assaulting troops, while the Eastern (British) Task Force, consisting of three bombarding and three assault forces under Rear-Admiral Sir Philip Vian, made up the naval component. In the British sectors the arduous task of securing and organising the beachheads fell to the RN Commandos. The assault forces, S, J and G – assigned respectively to the Sword, Juno and Gold sectors – were each tasked to land the assaulting and follow-up units of one infantry division, plus ancillary armoured, engineer and support units.

The British landing plan called for the assault force landing ships to anchor at the lowering position some seven miles offshore, lower landing craft and embark troops and equipment. Destroyer escorts were to accompany the assault force, neutralising coastal defences. On each brigade-front beach, four tank landing craft (LCTs), each carrying four 'Duplex drive' (DD) amphibious tanks, were to land at H minus five minutes and engage enemy strongpoints, followed at H-hour by a further wave of four LCTs bearing specialised armour – minesweeping flail tanks and crocodile flamethrowers –

Above: Germans wheel a steel 'hedgehog' beach obstacle into position. Each was armed with a Tellermine anti-tank charge, and 2500 were found on a three-mile stretch of Gold sector alone

Above: Rear Admiral Sir Philip Vian was commander of the naval task force supporting the British Second Army's landings on the Gold, Juno and Sword sectors of the Normandy beaches. Below: Vian's RN Commandos obliterate 'hedgehogs' on the waterline.

Principal Beachmaster, RN Commandos, D-day 1944

Although he is clad in khaki battledress, items of this lieutenant-commander's apparel proclaim that he is serving with the Royal Navy. He has a navy-blue officer's peaked cap and shoulder slides, and his white-on-black RN Commando flash is worn with the flash of Combined Operations. He carries a pistol in '37 web equipment and is equipped with the binoculars and map case of a Principal Beachmaster.

together with teams of sappers. As the sappers and flail tanks worked furiously to clear mines and obstacles – including ramps, concrete blocks, and 'hedgehogs' composed of six-inch angle irons bolted together with explosives attached – two companies of assault infantry, embarked in eight LCAs, would hit the beach at H plus seven minutes.

Accompanying the first wave of the infantry assault on each beach would be the RN Commando's Assistant Beachmaster (ABM) and his bodyguard. Armed with Thompson sub-machine guns and equipped with signal torches, they would move onto the beach and conduct a lightning reconnaissance before deciding whether the next wave of the assault could safely land at the same place. The decision would have to be rapid: at H plus 20, just 13 minutes later, a further eight LCAs carrying the next two companies of the assaulting brigade would arrive at the beachhead, followed only five minutes later by the remainder of the beach group embarked in two more LCAs. With the Commando ashore, there would be no time to lose: during the next hour several more waves would hit the beach, bearing bulldozers, tanks, self-propelled guns, stores, ammunition and more infantry.

The naval commandos, particularly those that landed with the first wave of assault infantry, could expect – and in the event they received – very high casualties. Even on the Sword beaches, where the landing went surprisingly well and losses were much lower than expected, three out of the four advance guards lost one member of the party almost immediately on hitting the beach. The bulk of the naval commandos landed on their beaches in all sectors while the battle for the shoreline was at its height. With the beaches raked by smallarms and mortar fire, the commandos went about their tasks – and in more than one instance they became involved in the fighting to secure the beachhead.

Sword sector, running from the Orne estuary at Ouistreham to the village of Luc, lay on the extreme eastern flank of the Allied invasion. The assault there was spearheaded by the 8th Infantry Brigade reinforced by army and Royal Marine Commandos. Royal Navy F and R Commandos were assigned as the beach parties. The first waves hit the beaches on schedule under comparatively light shelling from enemy batteries, and much of the armour was landed successfully. Queen Beach, in the centre of the sector, proved the most accessible: an exit was quickly cleared and columns of armour and infantry were soon moving inland towards Ouistreham and Hermanville. To the right, on Peter Beach, offshore sandbars proved a major problem and elements of R Commando were forced to move leftwards, to join their comrades in the assault on Queen Beach. Mortar and smallarms fire continued to be a problem, as did a number of German coastal strongpoints. One, at La Brèche, held out for three hours during which time it was able to rake the Sword beaches with damaging fire, inflicting casualties on troops in the water as they landed, and on the beaches. On Queen Beach, a lone French girl struggled under fire in the shallows to haul the wounded out of the water, and the naval commandos, striving to create order out of the beachhead chaos, repeatedly had to dive into their slit trenches for cover.

A few miles to the west, L and P Commandos were supporting the Canadian 3rd Infantry Division's assault on Juno sector. L Commando landed on the

One of the disadvantages of the section of coastline chosen for Operation Overlord was that the invasion area lacked deepwater harbours. The Allies could not count on a harbour capable of accommodating large merchantmen until the capture of Cherbourg. Given the vast quantities of stores and equipment that the Allied armies would need to keep them in the fight for Normandy, the Overlord planners adopted Commodore Hughes Hallett's proposal for constructing giant artificial caissons and towing them over to Normandy in prefabricated sections.

The proposal was codenamed 'Mulberry'. Two harbours were planned, one near Arromanches in the British sector, and one on Omaha beach in the American sector.

On D-day a fleet of tugs began towing the sections across the Channel. A total of some 60 old ships were sunk end-to-end to provide each harbour with a breakwater; prefabricated pierheads were moved into position and long pontoons linking them to the shore were constructed. By D+13 most of the work was complete and coasters had begun unloading within the harbour areas. On 19 June, however, a bad storm blew up, wrecking the Mulberry on Omaha beach and causing serious damage to the British Mulberry.

The harbour at Arromanches, where men from the RN Commandos were involved in the construction work, was quickly repaired and gave good results, easing the task of moving supplies to the front lines and contributing to the vital battle of the build-up that preceded the Allied breakout from the invasion area.

Nan Beaches, between St Aubin and Courseulles on the left flank of the sector, and began to take casualties very early. German opposition was tough: it took three hours for the Canadian infantry to capture St Aubin, while fighting continued after that in the streets of Courseulles. The assaulting company, landing near the village of Bernières, lost half its strength in advancing just 100yds. When the Germans launched a counter-attack, L Commando was sent off to the slit trenches to help repulse it. By 1000 the beaches themselves had largely been cleared. Most of P Commando had landed on the Mike Beaches, on the right flank of Juno. After experiencing heavy fire on the way in, the Commando dug in and took control of the beach.

Petty Officer Bob McKinlay was one member of P Commando who did not manage to get ashore with his unit. Included in one of the early waves of LCTs, McKinlay's craft was hit on the run-in by a German 88mm shell which wrecked the ramp at the front and made landing impossible. The craft drifted out of control, towards the western edge of Sword sector some seven miles to the east. McKinlay was eventually able to land in another vessel. He reached Sword some time after noon, and joined a mixed party of naval ratings and soldiers attempting to cross the German-held ground between Sword and Juno to rejoin their units.

He managed to lob three grenades at the strongpoint before charging it headlong and taking the only survivor prisoner

McKinlay's group became pinned down by a combination of smallarms and mortar fire, and 88mm shelling from a German position some 50yds away. Borrowing grenades for the purpose, McKinlay set off to cover the distance to the enemy position. He managed to lob three grenades at the strongpoint before charging it headlong and taking the only survivor prisoner. The party continued their journey towards Juno sector, harassed by enemy fire much of the way. Crossing an open stretch of sand further along the beach, under fire from enemy snipers, McKinlay rescued a wounded man, bringing him safely to cover. By evening, the party had reached Juno. McKinlay was eventually awarded a Conspicuous Gallantry Medal for his actions.

To the west, on the British far right flank, lay Gold sector where Lieutenant-Commanders Gregory-Smith and Mitchell had landed shortly after H-hour, in the company of assaulting forces of the British 50th Division. Naval beach parties in Gold sector were provided by J, Q and T Commandos, with T Commando landing on King Beach to the far left, J Commando on Jig Beach near Asnelles, and Q Commando on Item Beach near the tough German positions around Le Hamel.

German resistance on King Beach was concentrated around La Rivière. As the German defenders brought their mortar and 88mm fire to bear, chaos mounted in the shallow waters offshore. Nevertheless, both here and on Jig Beach – where the naval commandos were pinned down for half-an-hour before assisting the army to clear the beach with sub-machine gun fire – beach organisations were built up, exits were cleared, and movement inland began.

On Item Beach, the assaulting 231st Brigade, 50th Division, had the most difficult task in Gold sector: the capture of Le Hamel. The fortified positions of Le Hamel had remained intact throughout the preliminary bombardment, and when the first waves of assault troops hit the beach, they came under fierce attack. Mortar and smallarms fire raked the beaches and an unexpectedly high number of underwater obstacles added to the confusion. One particular 88mm gun emplacement in Le Hamel was causing havoc amongst the assault troops. Petty Officer Williams and Hodgetts of Q Commando stormed up the beach and silenced the gun by hurling grenades through slits in the emplacement. Naval commandos also assisted in the 1st Hampshires' assault on Le Hamel itself, launching a grenade attack on the town's defences. By mid-afternoon, Le Hamel was in British hands and further landings could take place unopposed.

With D-day drawing to a close, the assault phase had been successfully completed. However, while the British Second Army was established ashore, the naval commandos' work was far from over. The battle of the build-up had yet to be fought: no sizeable harbours had fallen into Allied hands, and unless the beaches could be organised effectively, the Allied advance would be starved of men and materials. Shelling continued on some of the beaches, yet many of the commandos worked for three or four days after D-day without sleep. Tasks included directing landing craft, salvaging sunken vessels, removing obstacles and helping with the construction of temporary piers and the British 'Mulberry' harbour. Most of the commandos remained in Normandy, working on the shoreline, until mid-July; the last unit stayed until November. Nor was that the end of RN Commando operations in northwest Europe: naval commandos worked with the army and Royal Marines in numerous operations, including the crossing of the Rhine, until the end of the war in Europe in May 1945.

THE AUTHOR Barry Smith has taught politics at Exeter and Brunel Universities. He is a contributor to the journal *History of Political Thought* and has written a number of articles on military subjects.

Above left and right: For the inner breakwaters of the vast artificial Mulberry harbours created on the Normandy coast, great concrete caissons were constructed and then towed into position and sunk. It took eight months to make ready 146 caissons.

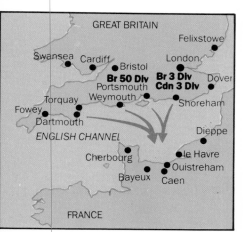

Overlord
6 June 1944

The greatest amphibious assault in history, the Allied invasion of German-occupied Normandy, was launched on the morning of 6 June 1944. With an assault on such a large scale the potential for confusion and disaster in the early stages of the assault, and for failure to build up men and material once the beaches had been secured, was immense. In the British Gold, Juno and Sword sectors on the Allied left flank the dangerous task of staking out the assault beaches fell to the Royal Navy Commandos.

Juno
6 June 0745 The assaulting Canadian 3rd Infantry Division, delayed by adverse tidal conditions, hits the beaches and begins to take heavy casualties. L and P Commandos form the naval element.
1000 The beaches are largely secured. Naval commandos are involved in repulsing German counter-attacks later in the day.

Gold
6 June 0725 The beaches of Gold sector are assaulted by lead elements of the 50th Infantry Division. Naval beach parties are provided by J, Q and T Commandos. Assaulting forces meet tough resistance at le Hamel where naval commandos storm German positions.

Sword
6 June 0725 The British 3rd Infantry Division provides the assaulting forces on the beaches between the Orne estuary at Ouistreham and the village of Luc. The naval contingent consists of F and R Commandos. Despite resistance from enemy positions, including la Brèche, the assault is successful.

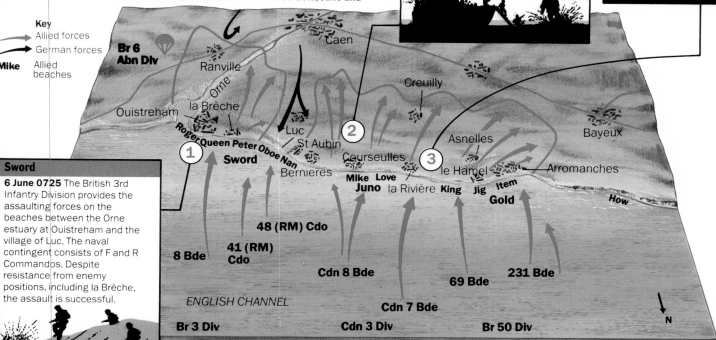

Key
→ Allied forces
→ German forces
Mike Allied beaches

155

CAPTAIN CHARLES TRIPP

The First Commando Fiji Guerrillas was led from its inception by a New Zealander of exceptional qualities. A farmer in civilian life, Charles Tripp (above) was born at Timaru on 22 February 1902 and educated at Cambridge University, where he excelled at rowing. In April 1942, while still a lieutenant, he was given command of Southern Commando in Fiji. His qualities of leadership and determination were soon recognised both by his superior officers and his men, and by July 1943 he had risen rapidly to the rank of major. He had a theory, which proved correct, that if he placed absolute confidence in the men under his command, they would do their utmost to live up to it. The coolness and courage of this tall, raw-boned man became legendary. During the heat of one jungle firefight, some untried American troops panicked and began to run away. A few of the commandos fighting alongside them panicked too, but were stopped in their tracks when Tripp leapt to his feet and yelled above the din of battle, 'Get back to your bloody foxholes and stay there.' Such was the force of this command that not only did his men immediately obey, but the Americans did too.

Later, Tripp's American corps commander wrote of his 'outstanding services, characterised by devotion to duty and gallantry'. He was subsequently awarded the DSO and the American Silver Star.

Employing their exceptional skills in tracking and bushcraft, the New Zealander-led First Commando Fiji Guerillas saved many American lives by obtaining vital intelligence of Japanese defensive positions in the Solomon Islands

OF ALL THE Allied and Axis commando units that were formed during World War II, none was more unusual in its make-up and battle role than the First Commando Fiji Guerrillas. This small group of men – consisting of Fijians, Solomon Islanders, and Tongans – was led into action by two English officers and 44 New Zealand officers and NCOs. The dangers faced by the officers and NCOs of this force can best be appreciated when it is known that 40 per cent of the officers and 30 per cent of the sergeants were killed in action behind Japanese lines, while the unit itself was eventually so seriously depleted by casualties and malaria that in May 1944 it had to be disbanded.

Within months of the Japanese strike on Pearl Harbor in December 1941, the Japanese advanced across the Pacific as far south as Guadalcanal in the Solomon Islands, also establishing bases in the Gilbert group of islands, less than eight hours' flying-time from Fiji. The threat of a Japanese attack on Fiji, which consists of some 250 islands and was then a British crown colony, was very real, for Fiji's geographical position put it astride sea and air routes used in the transport of vital sup-

WAR IN THE ISLANDS

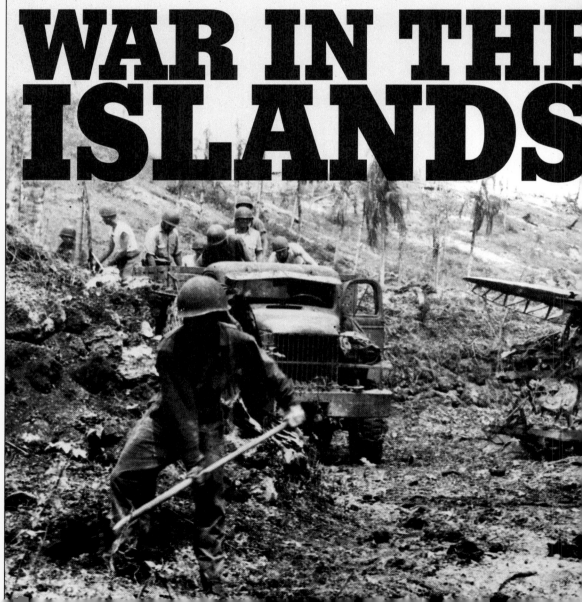

Below: The airfield of Munda on the southwest tip of the Solomon Island of New Georgia was perhaps the most important American objective on the island. Japanese aircraft had operated from there to bomb the American forces on Guadalcanal, and possession of it would give a springboard to Rabaul, lying to the northwest. Munda was heavily defended, however, and was taken only after 35 days of intense and costly fighting.

plies from the United States to Australasia.

Every New Zealand soldier that could be spared was therefore sent to Fiji, with the forces being concentrated on the main island, Viti Levu. Large areas of dense bush in the centre of the island remained unpatrolled, however, and in April 1942 it was decided to form three commando units capable of carrying on a harassing guerrilla role from the centre if the enemy invaded. The Western Commando, composed almost entirely of New Zealanders, patrolled its area on horseback, but the Eastern and Southern Commandos, which drew on Fijian volunteers who were trained and led by New Zealanders, worked entirely on foot.

The Commandos were soon ready for battle, but they did not see any action until after the Battle of the Coral Sea of May 1942 had finally stopped the Japanese advance in the Pacific. This success relieved pressure on Fiji and allowed the Americans to launch a campaign to start driving the Japanese back, a campaign which they began with landings in the Solomon Islands.

At the beginning of December 1942, 30 men selected from the Southern and Eastern Commandos, under the command of a New Zealander, Captain David Williams, were sent to join the Americans then fighting to clear Guadalcanal. This Special Party, as it was called, soon proved its usefulness by undertaking a series of reconnaissance patrols that pierced the enemy's lines and brought back vital information on Japanese dispositions.

The Special Party's success on Guadalcanal led the American corps commander to request more commandos and it was then that Captain Charles Tripp, the leader of the Southern Commando, was given orders to form the First Commando Fiji Guerrillas from Eastern and Southern Commando volunteers. This unit totalled 39 New

Zealand officers and NCOs and 135 Fijians, who were later joined by 27 Tongans led by a Tongan officer, Lieutenant Henry Taliai. The Fijians were divided into an HQ company and two rifle companies, and initially each company, consisting of 75 men under a lieutenant, was sub-divided into three platoons, each led by a sergeant. Later, however, it was found that a more efficient organisation could be created by splitting the rifle companies up into independent patrols of 15 men, each led by a New Zealand officer or NCO.

After additional intensive training, the unit embarked on 15 April 1943 for Guadalcanal, where they were joined by the Special Party. The Commando now totalled 44 New Zealanders, two Englishmen, 156 Fijians, 28 Tongans, and 200 Solomon Islanders who had been trained by the Special Party. The unit became acclimatised to jungle warfare by being used, first to comb Guadalcanal for any Japanese who might still be hiding there, and then by carrying out the same task on other islands recaptured by the Americans. Late in June 1943, Tripp was ordered to prepare for participation in an American attack on New Georgia, situated in the centre of the Solomon Islands group.

The main American objective on New Georgia was Munda airfield, situated on the southwest tip of the island, and the initial attacking force consisted of two regiments of the US 43rd Infantry Division. An island off the coast, called Roviana, was used as a springboard for the invasion and the Commando's first task was to clear some small islands near to it before the main force crossed Roviana Lagoon to land at Zanana, some seven miles from their objective. It had been planned that these seven miles could be covered in 10 days, but the tenacity of the 5000-strong defending force which ringed the airfield, and the almost impenetrable jungle that lay before it, extended this time to 35 days.

The attack began on 4 July 1943 when the leading American battalion, accompanied by the Tongans, advanced to the Bariki River and set up a defensive perimeter on the eastern bank. From this base the Tongans reconnoitred ahead and they soon became involved in several clashes with the enemy at close

Although officially called the First Commando Fiji Guerrillas, this unique fighting unit was known to the Americans, with whom it fought, as the South Pacific Scouts. In fact, this was a much more accurate title, for the unit's expertise in reconnaissance was of far greater consequence than either the commando or guerrilla tactics it employed fighting the Japanese. And, although Fijians made up the greater part of the unit, it also contained New Zealanders, Englishmen, Tongans and Solomon Islanders.

The Fijians had exceptional hearing and eyesight, and they must be among the world's greatest bushmen. Their powerful physique, coupled with a perfect ability to stalk and shoot their prey, made them ideal scouts. But they were uneducated men who were sometimes unable to control their emotions and superstitious fears. Well led, they were magnificent soldiers, but they did not provide their own leadership. The Tongans, on the other hand, being similar to the Maoris, had outstanding fighting temperaments, but they were unequal to the Fijians when it came to bushcraft. The Solomon Islanders, though willing, did not easily absorb Western military discipline. Most rendered valuable service away from the battlefield but only a few proved capable of handling the tension of jungle warfare.

Whatever their individual deficiencies as jungle fighters, all three groups of islanders worked well with the New Zealanders who were their officers and NCOs, and their collective talents were an invaluable addition to Allied resources in the Pacific.

quarters. In one incident, a Tongan and a Japanese dived for cover behind the same tree. The Japanese asked whether the Tongan was friend or foe and soon knew the answer when the Tongan despatched him with a single rifle shot.

In order to establish better communications on New Georgia, a patrol of 30 commandos, led by Lieutenant Ben Masefield, was sent up the Munda Trail to set up a radio transmitter on high ground. This patrol, too, soon clashed with a Japanese unit and a three-hour firefight ensued, during which one Fijian was wounded, but the enemy was pushed back two miles before darkness terminated the encounter. The next day Masefield led another patrol into enemy territory, this time behind Munda airfield. No Japanese were encountered and the commandos set up a bivouac overlooking the Bairoko-Munda Trail, from where they were able to send back information which proved vital to the forward planning of the American attack.

It was the kind of close-combat bush fighting for which the commandos had been well trained

A regular front was not possible in the thick bush, and confused fighting ensued between the Americans and the Japanese, with both sides penetrating the other's perimeter. However, the commandos continued to send out patrols, scouting ahead of the main American force and probing to find out where the Japanese were hidden.

By 8 July two more American battalions had arrived to reinforce the attack and the Japanese began to be pushed back until the Americans were astride the Munda Trail. Tripp's HQ was relocated forward to a regimental command post near the trail and two commando patrols were despatched to locate the enemy's new positions. The campaign was now a week old, but although the Japanese around the airfield were being pounded by both artillery and naval bombardments, they refused to surrender. Instead, they were driven back into the bush around the airfield and there they put up fanatical resistance against the advancing American infantry. It was the kind of close-combat bush fighting for which the

commandos had been well trained, and psycholog[ically] they were better prepared for the strain im[posed] on them than were the Americans. They di[d] suffer from lack of sleep, however, for every night th[e] Japanese launched attacks against the America[n] perimeter, but while the toll of battle-fatigue casual[-] ties rose alarmingly in the American ranks, not on[e] commando was sent to the rear for psychological aid[.]

Nevertheless, they did begin to take fatal battl[e] casualties, their first loss coming when a Fijian wa[s] killed during a Japanese night attack. A more sever[e] blow to the unit came when Masefield, who ha[d] already been recommended for the American Silve[r] Star for bravery, was killed while on patrol. Thoug[h] the weight of the American attack pushed th[e] Japanese back, the fighting was bitter and every inc[h] of the ground was contested. For a time the pressur[e] on the Americans was relieved when a small patrol [of] Tongans, led by a New Zealander, Sergeant Enso[r,] penetrated the enemy's lines and found a suitabl[e] landing place on Laiana Point for a second America[n] attack. This was intended to put the attacking force[s] a good deal nearer their objective, but while leadin[g] a platoon of the 172nd Regiment towards the beach[-] head, Tripp and 28 of his men were cut off an[d] became engaged in a desperate struggle for surviv[-] al. To avoid known enemy positions, they had struc[k] the Lambeti Trail that led to Laiana south of i[ts] junction with the Munda, but had then run into a[n] ambush. The American platoon managed to extri[-] cate itself, but Tripp and his men, who were workin[g] about 100yds ahead, found themselves surrounde[d.]

After some fierce fighting, during which Lieute[-] nant Taliai, a New Zealand sergeant and a Fijia[n] commando were killed, the patrol split up into sma[ll] groups to try and infiltrate back to the America[n] lines. Most of them eventually reached safety, an[d] some had remarkable escapes. For example, on[e] Tongan commando was knocked unconscious, an[d]

Far left: Lieutenant Henry Taliai, commander of the Tongan element of the First Commando Fiji Guerrillas, was killed in the battle for New Georgia. Left: A Fijian member of the Commando is photographed with an Owen sub-machine gun. Although the Commando was originally issued with Thompsons, the Owen was soon found to be a superior weapon in the bush. It was simple to use and highly reliable, even in the wet, muddy conditions of the Solomons. Bottom left: New Zealand troops join the Americans in the campaign to take the Solomons. Bottom: A New Zealander and US troops keep silent watch in their hidden observation post.

when he came round he found he had been stripped naked and was surrounded by inquisitive Japanese, one of whom fired at him as he lay on the ground. By some miracle the bullet missed and the Tongan dived into the jungle, eventually returning to the American lines dressed only in a few leaves.

Tripp, too, had a narrow escape from the ambush. A machine gun opened up at short range, and when Tripp attempted to engage it with his American carbine the weapon jammed. Tripp threw it at the gunner and then flung himself into the bush. As the Japanese closed in, he shot one with his pistol before managing to evade the enemy and return to his patrol, whom he immediately ordered to scatter.

At dusk the Japanese, who had a rough idea where the commandos were, began mortaring to force them out of their hiding places, and Tripp and some Tongans soon found themselves in the middle of a Japanese bivouac. One Japanese jumped out of his foxhole and grabbed Tripp while a second took a bead on him at point-blank range. Tripp shot the first man just as the second was shooting at him, but the Japanese bullet was deflected by Tripp's cigarette lighter and Tripp was then able to shoot him too. By

Fiji Commandos July-August 1943

As a part of the general strategic plan to neutralise the important Japanese base at Rabaul, American and other Allied forces launched a series of attacks in June 1943 designed to seize the enemy-held New Georgia group of islands. The First Commando Fiji Guerrillas was assigned to the New Georgia Occupation Force which would conduct the operations. The main landing on New Georgia took place on the night of 2/3 July 1943, after preliminary operations on other islands in the group.

Solomon Islands Theatre 1943

GILBERT IS.
NAURU
BISMARCK ARCHI-PELAGO
PACIFIC OCEAN
NEW GUINEA
New Georgia
ELLICE IS.
SOLOMON IS.
CORAL SEA
NEW HEBRIDES
FIJI
AUSTRALIA
NEW CALEDONIA

Key
Limits of Japanese Empire, 1942-43

New Georgia Operations
June-July 1943

KOLOMBANGARA
4/5 July
Vila
ARUNDEL
NEW GEORGIA SOUND
GIZO
WANA WANA
23 Aug
NEW
Munda
Roviana
2/3 July
GEORGIA
Laiana Point
RENDOVA
30 June
Segi Point
VANGUNU
Kaeruka
TETIPARI
21 June
21 June
30 June
Vura
GATUKAI

Key
Allied landings, June-July 1943

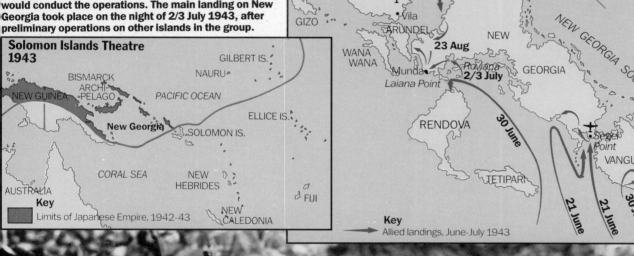

now the Tongans had scattered and Tripp lay doggo while the other Japanese hunted for him. Eventually they must have decided that he had escaped, for they began to walk without caution around the bivouac area.

Tripp now decided that the only way he could escape was to act as though he were Japanese. Incredibly, this worked and he was able to walk boldly through the area, inspect some of the defensive positions, and cut some telephone wires before heading north through a swamp. Eventually, he made his way back to the American perimeter, and his knowledge of the Japanese positions enabled the Americans to push through to the coast, allowing the landing at Laiana to proceed.

In the following days the fighting continued to be confused and inconclusive. The Japanese cut the American supply lines from the Zanana beach-head, and for a time the Laiana beach-head became a no-man's land – though one which the commandos frequently infiltrated. On 16 July reinforcements for the Commando's killed, wounded, and sick arrived: they consisted of 14 New Zealanders, 11 Tongans, 40

Below: New Zealanders take advantage of a boat abandoned by the Japanese for a patrol in Vella Lavella Island. Without craft, Allied patrols could entail wading neck deep between outcrops of firm land, a harrowing experience in territory with Japanese troops still at large. Bottom: Members of the First Commando Fiji Guerrillas are photographed in Vella Lavella. By this time, however, losses from battle casualties and malaria had reduced the Commando to 11 New Zealanders, 28 Fijians and six Tongans, and in May 1944 the Commando was finally disbanded.

Fijians and 23 Solomon Islanders. They were given their baptism of fire almost immediately, when they were thrown into the defensive perimeter of 43 Divisional HQ at Zanana after the Japanese launched a surprise attack. The assault was eventually driven back, but the situation remained desperate as Japanese reinforcements continued to infiltrate the American perimeter. The commando patrols were in such demand that Tripp had to cut each one down to four Fijians and one New Zealander to ensure that there were enough to go round the numerous American units struggling towards the airfield.

On 23 July the US 37th Division was thrown into the battle to aid the depleted US 43rd Division, and the commandos were attached to the fresh division. These reinforcements, and a third division that was committed at the end of the month, slowly turned the tide of battle, and the outskirts of the airfield were reached by Corporal Skilling and his Fijians on 27 July. The airfield finally fell on 5 August, and these last days were marked by ruthless fighting.

No fewer than 35 members of the First Commando Fiji Guerrillas were decorated for gallantry during the fighting for Munda airfield, several of the men receiving American medals for bravery in action. One, Sergeant MacKenzie, was awarded the Legion of Merit for his patrol work while attached to the 169th Regiment. It was a record that any unit could be proud of, and the First Commando Fiji Guerrillas are credited with performing some of the most hazardous work carried out by a small unit in the Pacific Theatre during World War II.

THE AUTHOR Ian Dear served as a regular officer in the Royal Marines, 1953-56. He is now a professional writer on military and maritime subjects and is author of *Ten Commando*, a book on No. 10 (Inter-Allied) Commando which is to be published in 1987 by Leo Cooper Ltd.

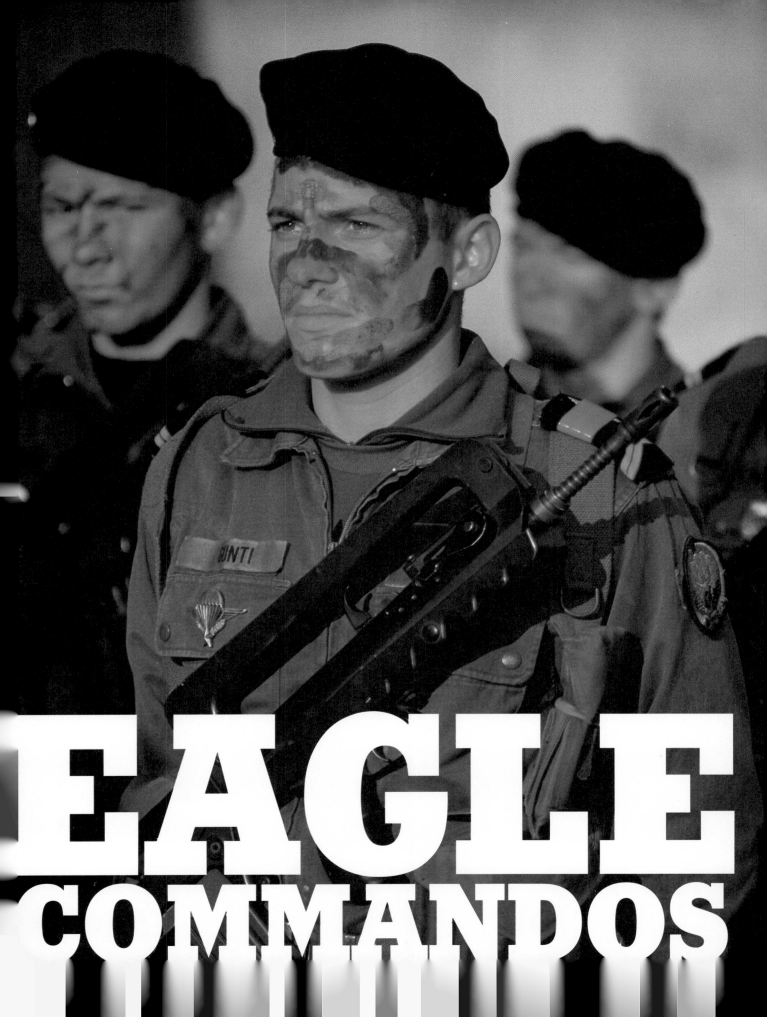

EAGLE
COMMANDOS

AIRBASE SECURITY

Airbase protection is the primary responsibility of the Groupement Fusiliers Commandos de l'Air. France's Armée de l'Air (Air Force) is divided into eight military commands: FAS and FANTAC (the strategic and tactical nuclear commands); CAFDA (interception); COTAM (transport); School; Communications; Engineering; and the Air Commandos. The first three commands are the 'fighting' arms, the fourth is the air transport command, equipped mainly with C-160 transport aircraft, and the final four are support commands. The Air Commandos are tasked with the ground security of the other seven commands. Of the Air Commandos' total strength of 9000 men, about 75 per cent are conscripts serving for one year, but an increasing number are now enlisting for five years in order to secure better pay, improved service conditions and the opportunity to serve abroad. The Air Commandos, nearly all of whom are trained paratroops, are responsible for manning the air defence systems, mainly 20mm cannon or surface-to-air missiles, and for mounting vehicle-mounted rapid-response units. These latter are equipped with 4x4 VAB/ VIB armoured personnel carriers and jeeps for their airfield reinforcement and perimeter security duties. In a recent airbase security exercise mounted in Corsica, the Air Commandos were set against the French Foreign Legion's elite parachute battalion, 2 REP. Nine four-man patrols were sent in under cover of darkness to penetrate the Air Commandos' defences. Only three succeeded in reaching their targets, and all the 2 REP personnel were captured before they could make their escape. Above: The beret badge of the French Air Commandos.

Every nation with highly developed aircraft and missile systems is rightly obsessed with airbase security. In France, this important responsibility rests in the capable hands of the elite Air Commandos

AT FIRST LIGHT the three six-man Zodiac inflatables moved silently with the current through La Baume gorge in southern France. On reaching the point where the steep cliffs came down to the water, the commandos in the first two craft swung their small vessels into the bank, while the remaining boat moved on to beach a further 100m down river.

With swift movements born of continual practice, the first group moved up to the cliff and one of their number aimed a strange-looking device at a rocky ledge 20m above. Moments later, the grapnel-launcher had placed a 9mm climbing rope in position and within two and a half minutes the 12 men of the first group had reached the top of the cliff and were ready for the second part of their operation.

Meanwhile the second group had landed and its members had taken up positions, in pairs, at 30m intervals along the shoreline. As they settled down to wait, the first group divided into a six-man assault group, a four-man fire-support group and a two-man cut-off group before setting off to their respective startpoints for the attack phase of the mission. The target, a group of four dilapidated buildings which had previously been an hotel, had been partly destroyed by an air strike the evening before. The buildings were known to house members of a terror-ist organisation, and it was the commandos' mission to take out any terrorists who might have survived.

At a pre-arranged signal, five smoke-grenades were thrown into and around the buildings. While the fire-support group put down short, aimed bursts to cover the assault group, the six men moved forward under cover of the smoke from the gre-nades. Working in pairs, the assault team moved steadily forward through the buildings, using their anti-personnel grenades and FA-MAS assault rifles to engage and neutralise any targets they encoun-tered. After completing the house clearance, the assault team adopted an all-round defensive position while the fire group moved to support their advance down to the second group on the shore. While the attack on the ruined hotel had been taking place, the second group had cleared the area of the beach head, engaging and neutralising two targets lying between themselves and the buildings.

France was one of the first countries to realise the need for airborne troops

The entire area was now completely secure, and the mission a success. After checking their equipment, the two groups boarded their Zodiacs and began to paddle the three kilometres downstream to their exfiltration point, leaving only the directing staff on the bank to check and clear away the targets. Another counter-terrorist exercise had just been completed by the Escadron de Protection et d'In-tervention (EPI) – an elite quick-reaction force within France's Groupement Fusiliers Commandos de l'Air (GFCA).

The Commandos de l'Air, or Air Commandos, were France's first paratroop unit. Formed in 1936 by an air force captain named Geille who had been trained in the USSR, the Air Commandos began with

Previous page: An Air Commando trooper, the French para wings on his right breast. The Air Commandos (right) are able to make far more parachute jumps per year than their counterparts in the French Army. Below: Six Air Commandos paddle their Zodiac inflatable assault boat down La Baume gorge in southern France.

a total strength of 150 men. France was one of the first countries to realise the need for airborne troops, and the unit continued to grow until the French defeat in 1940, when the Commandos de l'Air were disbanded. This was not the end, however. A number of commandos left France for service in Algeria and still more made their way to England to continue their fight against the Third Reich. It was the men who joined the Allies in England who became the founder members of two French SAS regiments which fought throughout the war alongside their British and Belgian colleagues. Then, in 1945, the Air Commandos were re-formed as part of the French Air Force, taking on many ex-French SAS members with operational experience. When France became involved in colonial conflicts after World War II, the knowledge of these men stood the Air Commandos in very good stead. However, during the war in Algeria they were disbanded. Officially for 'political reasons', it was because, as one senior French officer put it, 'they were on the wrong side.'

Nevertheless, this situation did not last for long. In 1965 the Fusiliers Commandos de l'Air were once again re-formed as part of the air force, and in 1976 the unit finally achieved proper recognition by becoming a command in its own right. This was an important step for the commandos, for it made them one of the air force's eight military departments, along with the two nuclear strike commands (tactical and strategic) and the interception command. The Commandos de l'Air had at last become 'high-fliers'.

On its formation, the GFCA established its base at Nîmes in southern France. Close to Athos Naval Air Base, the GFCA is ideally placed to carry out the basic training of both conscripts and regulars, with the La Baume training area a short drive away to the north and the huge Larzac training area less than one

hour's flying time away. Like almost all formations in the French armed forces, the Air Commandos consist of approximately 75 per cent conscripts and 25 per cent professional servicemen and officers. All conscripts, many of whom have volunteered to serve with the Commandos (such is their reputation), pass through Nîmes for their 16 weeks of basic training. This includes instruction in basic military skills, fieldcraft, weapon handling and an introductory parachute jump. This unusual feature of their basic training is designed to encourage conscripts to volunteer for the parachute course proper – and over 95 per cent do so. Apart from the active encouragement they receive from their colleagues, there is also the inducement of parachute pay, which effectively doubles the income of a conscript.

In a recent basic training cadre of 30 recruits, 15 initially volunteered for parachute training, followed by a further 13 over the next month, leaving only two who declined the offer. Considering that some of the conscripts who join the Air Commandos do not do so out of choice, and therefore do not realise what the job entails, the fact that such a high proportion of them end up volunteering for parachute training says much for the unit's high esprit de corps.

The base at Nîmes is not only responsible for training conscripts. All the regular Air Commandos undergo their initial military training there, and various skill-at-arms and trade courses are taught by the GFCA, as well as command courses for the sous-officiers (NCOs) and junior officers. Nîmes is very much the home of the GFCA and the Commandos de l'Air as a whole; it is also the headquarters of the Escadron de Protection et d'Intervention.

Almost unknown outside the French Air Force, the battalion-sized EPI is entirely composed of professional servicemen or short-service volunteers. The short-service volunteers are often men who joined the Air Commandos as conscripts but decided to extend their service in order to get into the EPI. The professional element contains some of the most experienced NCOs within the Air Commandos and the EPI is the spearhead of the Fusiliers Commandos de l'Air.

Those men chosen to join the EPI must pass a rigorous selection course before going into one of

Below left: Tasked with the defence of French airbases worldwide against many different types of infiltration and sabotage missions, the Air Commandos, and the Escadron de Protection et d'Intervention (EPI) in particular, must be ready and equipped to deal with any form of attack. Climbing techniques are taught, as abseiling is often the quickest form of inserting a security force into a trouble spot of limited access.

Below: Two six-man Zodiac teams head towards a limestone shore. Although the Zodiac may be fitted with an outboard motor, all the advantages of surprise would be lost by its use on operations. Below right: The combined muscle-power of six trained oarsmen is more than sufficient for rapid insertion missions. The design of their 5.56mm FA-MAS assault rifles allows the men to paddle unencumbered while being fully armed.

the EPI's three fighting companies. This selection course tests and assesses the mental and physical qualities of the volunteer while he is under stress and carrying out various tasks, either as an individual or at group level. A series of forced marches and battle runs weeds out those not physically equipped, and the specially designed commando course at Nîmes, which is one of the toughest in France, is an excellent test of a man's confidence and physical courage. All these tests are timed events and those who do not make it within the time are taken off the course and posted to other Air Commando units specialising in airfield defence. Only those with ability and motivation succeed in getting through the selection. On passing out, the volunteer goes on to the continuation training phase, which concentrates on military skills and small-unit tactics. The latter are of particular importance. The EPI, like the army's Compagnies de Reconnaissance et d'Action en Profondeur, is expected to operate in small teams, often behind enemy lines.

Unarmed combat, a mixture of various martial arts, is another important aspect of EPI training, and one in which its men become very proficient. This fact was borne out in 1986 when one of them was attacked by three knife-wielding Arabs in Nîmes old town. Although alone and unarmed, he was not exactly defenceless, as he proved when he disarmed one of the men and despatched him, much to the surprise of the other two, who quickly departed. Although this did not do much for relations between the two communities, it did prove the high standard of the EPI unarmed combat training.

Small EPI teams are capable of bringing in ground-attack aircraft to engage enemy targets

Training in various skills is continuous, even when the man has been accepted by one of the companies. Communications is one skill vital to the success of small-unit operations and is either taught at Nîmes or, at a higher level, at the French Air Force communications school. Apart from signalling, which is an individual skill, all junior NCOs are trained in Forward Air Control (FAC) and small EPI teams are thus capable of bringing in ground-attack aircraft to engage enemy targets. By being part of the air force, which they are, despite their dark-blue berets and parachute brevets, the EPI paratroops benefit by having direct access to aircraft. Whereas the paratroops of the army's 11th Parachute Division have to rely on what is for them another branch of the armed forces (the air force) for air support, the Air Commandos can usually obtain the aircraft they need – even at short notice. This can be seen in the number of parachute jumps the EPI manage to get in each year – usually over 80 per man – as opposed to the army parachutists, whose annual average is around 15 jumps. In spite of this there is a good deal of co-operation between the Air Commandos and the army, and both open up a number of their specialist courses to each other. This close relationship can be seen at the French Parachute School at Pau in southern France. Many Air Commandos attend advanced courses there (especially freefall and heavy drop), at this army-run school, and at present two of the basic parachute course instructors are Air Commandos themselves.

The role of the EPI differs greatly from that of army paratroops. The term EPI stands for 'protection and intervention squadron' and goes some way in de-

scribing the unit's primary role. Since its formation, the EPI has trained to provide close support for airfield defence units. Capable of rapid deployment, elements of the EPI are on constant standby, ready to reinforce airfields either in mainland France or overseas. Lightly equipped, the EPI is an ideal unit for rapid deployment in defence of French interests abroad, and men of the squadron have taken part in every French overseas operation since 1965, including the French peacekeeping mission at Beirut in 1982-84 and Operation Manta in Chad, which took place in 1983.

The EPI is well equipped to carry out its tasks. The personal weapon of most of the EPI's paratroopers is the 5.56mm FA-MAS assault rifle. This highly effective weapon is capable of accurate semi- or fully automatic fire over ranges in excess of 300m, as well as being able to launch either anti-armour or anti-personnel grenades up to a range of 320m. Some marksmen are equipped with FRF 1 or FRF 2 snipers' rifles. This type of semi-automatic weapon is an ideal complement to the FA-MAS, being capable of accurately engaging targets up to a range of 1000m with 7.5mm ammunition. The FSA 49 Model 56 machine gun also fires the same round and is used in the close-support role by the EPI. At present the FSA 49/56 is all but replaced by the more recent AA 52 machine gun, which also fires 7.5mm ammunition. Because the latter uses 50-round link belts as opposed to the Model 56's 10-round magazine, it is a better weapon in the sustained-fire role.

The EPI is equipped with Hotchkiss and Peugeot jeeps, both of which can be parachuted

Although it is essentially an airmobile and paratroop formation, the EPI is equipped with Hotchkiss and Peugeot jeeps, both of which can be parachuted into an operational area to provide the EPI with extra mobility. These would be crucial to a rapid deployment mission, especially one in support of one of France's former overseas territories. The Hotchkiss is essentially the same as the Willys jeep that has been in service with the French armed forces since 1945. Although small, it is capable of carrying four men and their equipment over rough terrain, and is a proven and reliable vehicle. The newer Peugeot jeep is a cross-country vehicle similar to the Steyr Puch/Mercedes but fitted with a Peugeot engine. Currently undergoing trials with the French armed forces, the Peugeot is a larger vehicle, capable of carrying six men and their equipment, and will almost certainly eventually replace the Hotchkiss.

The EPI relies primarily on the Air Transport Command for its mobility. In its rapid reinforcement role the EPI uses either the C-160 Transall or, less often, air force Puma or Super Puma helicopters. The C-160 is capable of transporting up to 60 fully-equipped paratroops, and the newer C-160NG is fitted with extra fuel tanks and an in-flight refuelling system that considerably increases its range, making it an ideal carrier for out-of-area (OOA) operations. For shorter distances, helicopters are used. But the type of operation for which the EPI trains, that

Above right and far right: The skills of unarmed combat are highly valued by the Air Commandos. Within the Escadron de Protection et d'Intervention, all NCOs are qualified unarmed-combat instructors who have reached black-belt standard in one or more of the martial arts. Right: An Air Commando deploys his FA-MAS assault rifle in the static defence role.

THE FA-MAS
ASSAULT RIFLE

The 5.56mm FA-MAS rifle, or more correctly, the 'Fusil d'Assaut MAS Modele F', is the current personal weapon of the French armed forces. This highly effective assault rifle was designed and built by the Manufacture d'Armes, St Etienne – MAS – and replaces all the rifles and sub-machine guns of the French armed forces.

The weapon is of 'bullpup' design with the action well to the rear and the magazine sited below the firer's cheek when the rifle is drawn into the shoulder. This design reduces the weapon's length to 0.76m, making it suitable as a personal weapon for the crews of such armoured vehicles as the Air Commandos' VAB series.

The FA-MAS is fitted with a 25-round magazine, although usually only 20 rounds are loaded to ease the pressure on the magazine's spring and ensure trouble-free feeding. Air Commandos equipped with the weapon carry two pouches, each containing three magazines of 20 rounds, giving them a minimum of 140 rounds for immediate use. A quick-release sling keeps the weapon positioned diagonally across the commando's chest or, if freedom of movement is required, in the centre of his back.

The FA-MAS can be modified to fire three-round bursts. Also, by switching the case extractor and ejection port from the right-hand side of the weapon to the left, it can be adapted for the use of left-handed troops.

Reliable and advanced in design, the FA-MAS, already in use with a number of former French territories, including Gabon and Djibouti, promises to see service well into the next century.

of airborne support and assault, involves the use of the parachute as a method of entry. It is in this role that the EPI differs from the other Air Commandos.

Parachuting is taken most seriously by France's paratroops in general, but it is of particular importance to the Air Commandos – France's original paratroops. The most recent innovation in military parachuting in France has been the introduction of the EPI 682-12 main static-line parachute. Named after the squadron, this particular 'chute replaces the TAP 661-12 and allows the paratroopers to jump from 150m, a height which would be almost too low to deploy the TAP-503 reserve parachute in the case of a main 'chute's malfunction. Operationally, the introduction of the EPI 682-12 parachute has greatly increased the squadron's ability to put men down quickly in a limited area – an important consideration when bearing in mind the EPI's mission to reinforce units defending airfields which are already under attack.

Apart from the EPI's commitment to parachuting as a method of entry into a combat zone, it is also more than capable of conducting amphibious assaults and reinforcements. Trained in the handling of small boats, the EPI paratroops are equipped with six- and 10-man Zodiac 'marine commando' inflatables. These French-manufactured craft can be inflated by a carbon dioxide gas cylinder, and can be fitted with an outboard motor. They offer the EPI an alternative method of transportation to the target area, and are an important asset, considering that many airfields are either close to the coast or have rivers or lakes in their immediate vicinity.

The performance of the EPI, especially in OOA operations, relies on the unit possessing a great deal of flexibility, and this is reflected in its organisation. Each of the squadron's three fighting companies is divided into four sections, each of which is roughly equivalent in size to a standard infantry platoon. Each section comprises the section staff (a lieutenant, a sous-officier and a radio operator), and three fighting groups of between 10 and 12 men each. The latter comprise a sous-officier

(either a sergent or a sergent-chef), a sniper (armed with an FRF 1 or 2), and either two fire teams and one 'choc' (assault) team, or one fire team and two choc teams. The fire team consists of two men; one armed with an AA 52 machine gun, and the other with an FA-MAS. A choc team, on the other hand, comprises four men, each armed with an FA-MAS assault rifle. In certain circumstances, when the mission requires an anti-armour capability, a section will be equipped with LRAC-89 anti-tank missiles. This French-manufactured light support weapon has an effective range of 1000m, and comprises a throw-away, pre-loaded, fibre glass tube that is clipped to a firing system.

All EPI NCOs must be qualified unarmed-combat instructors, having reached black-belt standard

Despite the array of weapons that the EPI has at its fingertips, it is the training and experience of its personnel that make the unit so effective. Although the men are carefully selected and trained, the high standards achieved by the EPI are due to the quality of the unit's NCOs. The sergents and sergent-chefs are among the most experienced commandos in the French armed forces. Throughout their careers these sous-officiers attend a wide and varied range of skill-at-arms and trade courses, both within and outside the air force. All EPI NCOs must be qualified unarmed-combat instructors, having reached black-belt standard in one or more of the martial arts. Each is a freefall parachutist and trained medic, as well as being a qualified instructor in a specialist skill such as demolitions or anti-armour warfare. These skills are then passed on to the men in the EPI or the Air Commandos stationed with air defence units at home and abroad. Because the EPI is a relatively small formation within the Air Commandos, the NCOs tend to spend a tour with them before going off to an airfield defence unit, where they will do a tour as a group commander. Many then return to instructing posts at the Air Commando Training School in Nîmes, before a second or third tour with the EPI. In this way their skills and experience are passed on to men throughout the Commandos de l'Air.

The mission of the EPI, that of rapidly reinforcing other Air Commando units defending French air bases, is the one for which they constantly practise. This role makes them ideally suited for testing the defences of France's airfields. The only British unit which has a similar role is No. 2 Squadron, The RAF Regiment, a fully parachute-trained formation with which the EPI shares certain tasks.

France's Escadron de Protection et d'Intervention is a vital element in the defence of French territory. In keeping with the Air Commandos' proud tradition, which dates back to their involvement with the SAS during the last war, the EPI is a highly trained and motivated unit. Since their re-formation in 1945, men of the Air Commandos have served in every French colonial war, including the bloody conflict in Algeria, with the loss of only 80 men. That figure includes three officers killed during 'peacekeeping' duties in the Lebanon since 1978. Those losses give some indication of both the unit's active service and its professionalism. Capable of responding swiftly to a variety of threats, the EPI lives up to its group's motto 'Sicut Aquila' – Like An Eagle.

Left: Air Commandos pause during an exercise as a smokescreen is laid over their insertion area. Far left: The techniques of fighting in built-up areas are essential to the role of the Air Commandos, who may well become involved in combat within the perimeters of airbase installations in the future. Top left: An Air Commando trooper practises methods of entering an enemy-held building. Above left: Keeping watch with the FA-MAS at the ready.

THE AUTHOR Peter Macdonald is a freelance defence photo-journalist and served with the British Army and Rhodesian Security Forces between 1974-80.

SOLDIERS
OF FORTUNE

The mercenaries of Mike Hoare's 5 Commando made their reputation with stunning victories in the chaos and confusion of the Congo

Elite forces take many forms and the men of Mike Hoare's 5 Commando proved themselves the best soldiers in the war-torn Congo, but mercenaries, selling their guns to the highest bidder, have never been renowned for their military ethics. Looting was an accepted, and organised, practice, while the killing of civilians by trigger-happy soldiers led Hoare to order that only those carrying weapons were to be treated as the enemy. (He later found one mercenary jeep, however, stuffed with spears to issue to dead 'rebels' posthumously.) Hoare was determined to change the image of the mercenary as a pillaging thug. To this end he circulated the following 'rules for battle':

1. Pray God daily
2. Make a fetish of personal cleanliness; take pride in your appearance, even in the midst of battle; shave every day without fail
3. Clean and protect your weapons always. They must be bright, clean and slightly oiled. Examine your ammunition frequently. Check and clean your magazine springs and clips
4. Soldiers in pairs; look after each other; be faithful to your mate. Be loyal to your leaders
5. Tell no lies in battle. All information must be accurate or your unit will suffer. Exaggerate to your girl friends later, but NEVER, NEVER in battle
6. Be ready to move at a moment's notice. Mark all your equipment. Keep it handy at all times. Develop a routine for finding it
7. Look after your vehicle. Fill it with petrol before resting. Clean it. Do not overload unnecessarily
8. Take no unnecessary risks
9. Stand-to dawn and dusk. Have confidence in your sentries; post as few as the situation demands
10. Be aggressive in action – chivalrous in victory – stubborn in defence.

MIKE HOARE flew into Leopoldville, the capital of the Congo, in July 1964. His job was to raise a mercenary force of white soldiers of fortune that could engage and defeat the Simba rebellion raging over the eastern half of that vast country. He succeeded beyond the wildest dreams of either himself or his employers, winning the nickname of 'Mad Mike' and a reputation as the most successful mercenary leader of modern times. The unit that he recruited, shaped, trained and led was that elite mercenary force known as 5 Commando. The extraordinary thing about 5 Commando, victor over literally thousands of armed Simba rebels, was that it never at any time consisted of more than three hundred mercenaries.

To Moise Tshombe, restored to power as prime

The Belgian Congo (renamed Zaire in 1971) was made independent on 30 June 1960, after a hopelessly inadequate preparatory period of five months. Central government collapsed almost immediately. President Joseph Kasavubu and Prime Minister Patrice Lumumba were unable to control the many tribes of the huge state, and Moise Tshombe, president of the wealthy southern mining province of Katanga, declared his region an independent state. Kasavubu and Lumumba appealed to the UN for assistance.

A UN force arrived to reassert stability, but was prevented from tackling Katanga by a large Belgian military presence and a small but powerful army of white mercenaries which included Major Mike Hoare. Lumumba, frustrated by the deadlock, launched an unsuccessful attack with Soviet-armed troops. For this he was dismissed by Kasavubu. Then Colonel Joseph Mobutu, chief of staff of the Congolese Army (ANC), arrested Lumumba and had him transferred to Katanga, where he was shot by Tshombe's men.

Lumumba's successor as leader of the communist-backed forces set up an alternative government at Stanleyville in Oriental Province. In August 1961 central government, now under premier Cyrille Adoula, succeeded in stabilising the Congo except for Katanga, and this increased pressure on Tshombe and the white mercenary army he had recruited to defend Katanga against the UN forces. On 21 January 1963 Tshombe capitulated and fled.

However, in July 1964 Kasavubu recalled Tshombe to take control in Leopoldville and counter new rebellions in the east and southwest. Former supporters of Lumumba, including Pierre Mulele, leading a fanatical young army, the Simbas (Lions), had seized Stanleyville and Albertville and founded the 'People's Republic of the Congo', taking many hostages. The rebel capital of Stanleyville fell in November after a combined assault by Tshombe's mercenary commandos, the ANC and Belgian paratroopers, but there were many atrocities and thousands were killed.

Tshombe and Kasavubu failed to achieve complete control, however, and the unrest continued. Then, in November 1965, General Mobutu seized power. His authoritarian military government has since ruled the Congo.

Below left: Mercenaries of 5 Commando cautiously enter a house in the town of Kindu, a rebel stronghold until the mercenaries captured it on 5 November 1964 in a typical example of their audacious tactics – Hoare's men simply drove down the main street with all guns blazing. This put the main rebel force to flight, and mopping up could then begin. Jeremy Spencer, one of Hoare's most important subordinates, was killed in Kindu during a rebel counter-attack mounted from Stanleyville later in November. Far left: Mike Hoare, leader of 5 Commando from July 1964 until November 1965. In common with his men, he made use of a personal choice from British, American and European clothes and equipment, rather than the complete uniform of any single armed force. The cap badges and insignia of 5 Commando, however, were entirely original.

minister of the Congo in July 1964, the choice of a mercenary force to suppress the Simba army was an obvious one. As president of the province of Katanga he had employed French mercenaries under Colonel Roger Faulques and his lieutenant Bob Denard to keep the forces of the United Nations out of his territory. Clearly a mercenary force could act as the spearhead of the Belgian-trained Armée Nationale Congolaise (ANC) now at his disposal. Tshombe sent for Hoare, then living in Durban, who had been among his mercenaries in Katanga.

Hoare was very much the officer and the gentleman. Small, dapper and well-mannered, he had served, as a young officer in World War II, first with the London Irish and then on Earl Mountbatten's staff during the Burma campaign, ending the war as a major. He had emigrated to South Africa but retained both his Irish nationality and his romantic attachment to the name of the most famous mercenaries of all time, the 'Wild Geese', those Irish gentlemen of fortune who had hired their swords all over Europe in the 18th century. Hoare's second-in-command in 5 Commando, Alastair Wicks, was an Old Harrovian who lent – in the words of one Western journalist – 'a touch of elegance to often bloody proceedings.' Hoare's two favourite lieutenants were Jeremy Spencer, an Old Etonian who had done his national service in the Coldstream Guards, and Gary Wilson, a South African who had served in the Household Cavalry. However, the first men Hoare recruited in South Africa, Southwest Africa and Rhodesia were very different to those experienced soldiers. Most of them were young Afrikaners who replied to newspaper advertisements offering jobs to 'fit young men' and who signed a contract for six months at a wage of £140 a month. This very raw material had to be licked into shape and that job fell to Hoare's regimental sergeant-major, RSM Jack Carton-Barber. With his enormous bulk and his moustaches, Carton-Barber was almost a caricature of the traditional sergeant-major, but his training programme, implemented at Kamina Base in Katanga, was based entirely on British Army principles.

The very first batch of mercenaries to reach Kamina Base had to be thrown into action immediately. There were only 38 of them, mainly Germans from Southwest Africa (which had been a German colony until World War I), and nine of them left immediately. Hoare explained to the remaining 29 the desperate urgency of rescuing the many hostages who were now in the hands of the Simba rebels. He put Siegfried Mueller, a Prussian, in command of them and launched a lake-borne attack on rebel-held Albertville. The assault ended in ignominy, however, and led to the first deaths, those of two mercenaries under Mueller's command, Nestler and Kohlert. The Simbas had themselves photographed, a jeering, triumphant group jabbing with their bows and arrows at the bodies of the white men dying at their feet.

Mueller, Hoare's first field officer, wore the Iron Cross which he had won fighting at the Russian front with the Wehrmacht. He was even rumoured to wear it on his pyjamas. Despite his reputation, Mueller was more of a showman than a soldier, and eventually he lost his command. But in the early days of the conflict, as 5 Commando pulled itself together, Mueller was

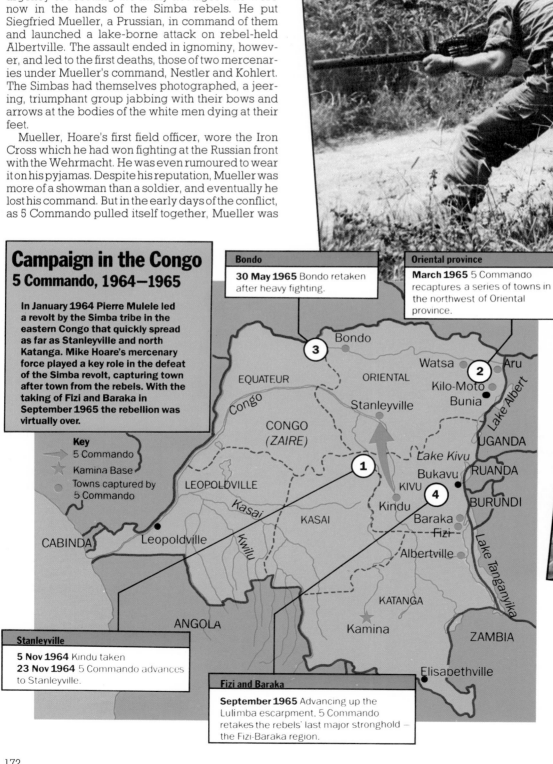

Campaign in the Congo
5 Commando, 1964—1965

In January 1964 Pierre Mulele led a revolt by the Simba tribe in the eastern Congo that quickly spread as far as Stanleyville and north Katanga. Mike Hoare's mercenary force played a key role in the defeat of the Simba revolt, capturing town after town from the rebels. With the taking of Fizi and Baraka in September 1965 the rebellion was virtually over.

Key
- 5 Commando
- ★ Kamina Base
- ● Towns captured by 5 Commando

Bondo

30 May 1965 Bondo retaken after heavy fighting.

Oriental province

March 1965 5 Commando recaptures a series of towns in the northwest of Oriental province.

Stanleyville

5 Nov 1964 Kindu taken
23 Nov 1964 5 Commando advances to Stanleyville.

Fizi and Baraka

September 1965 Advancing up the Lulimba escarpment, 5 Commando retakes the rebels' last major stronghold — the Fizi-Baraka region.

Top: Mercenaries move into the town of Boende, armed with Belgian FN FAL rifles and a 0.3in machine gun. The machine gun was the most important part of 5 Commando's firepower, and a barrage of such weapons mounted on jeeps frequently put larger forces of rebels to flight.

put in command of one of the sub-units that consisted of 30 men and two officers and which were known as 51 Commando, 52 Commando, and so on. The sub-units tended to operate separately, in jeeps, lorries and, when available, light armoured cars such as Ferrets and Dingos. Speed and mobility were to become the force's most valuable weapons.

When 5 Commando next set out, 51 Commando under Lieutenant Gary Wilson was the most immediately successful. They avenged the initial disaster by recapturing Albertville. That was an important victory in itself – Albertville was a sizeable town and whoever held it could threaten either Katanga province to the south, as the Simbas had been doing, or Oriental province to the north, as 5 Commando now prepared to do. But above all the victory boosted 5 Commando's morale: they had proved themselves superior to the Simbas and laid the foundation of their reputation as the 'white giants', the name by which they eventually came to be known throughout the north.

The tactics developed by 5 Commando were unconventional to say the least. They relied on speed and firepower alone. Not for 5 Commando the laborious approach by 'bounds' or an infantry sweep in extended line through the bush. They simply drove at full speed into an enemy position or village and

Above: Mercenaries on the move. Note the French Foreign Legion cap badge of the driver of the jeep. While 5 Commando found recruits from all over the world, the majority came from South Africa.

opened up with every weapon they had. There was never any warning of an attack by 5 Commando, such as a preliminary artillery bombardment or air strike, since they had no artillery or air support. They relied entirely on surprise, speed and noise to throw the enemy into confusion. It has to be said that they were fighting an unsophisticated enemy, but on the other hand the Simbas were fanatical fighters, often armed

with automatic weapons, and there were hordes of them, heavily drugged with marijuana and *dawa*, a preparation that they believed would protect them against bullets. Even when sawn almost in two by mercenary machine guns firing at point-blank range, they would charge forward waving guns or spears, disregarding their mortal wounds. Coping with such a foe, the mercenaries suffered many casualties.

'Terrific bombardment and nobody knows what the hell was going on. Lots of tracer flying about...'

Lieutenant Jeremy Spencer led his unit, 56 Commando, north in late October. On 4 November they encountered:

'a rebel armoured car coming towards us which opened fire with a .50 Browning at the leading Ferret armoured car. Terrific bombardment and nobody knows what the hell was going on. Lots of tracer flying about which luckily did no damage, and then eventually we managed to kill the chap on the rebel armoured car and all was peace.'

Next day, Guy Fawkes Day, they arrived at the rebel-held town of Kindu where:

'we had a terrific shooting match at nothing in particular, everyone blazing away as we drove through the centre of the town. We then drove down to the ferry where Volunteer Patience [the mercenaries were officially described as 'volunteers'] killed General Olenga. We also managed to sink a barge with about 50 rebels on board!'

On Friday 13 November Spencer continued his diary: 'A nervous early morning for superstitious people like myself. Having heard nine trucks had left Stanleyville three days ago to attack us I was fully expecting some sort of attack, but as usual nothing materialised.' However, the entry for 14 November was written in a different hand: 'This morning at 0700 hours Lieutenant Spencer killed by enemy fire which opened up on us at 0535 hours. Jeremy was hit in the head and died without regaining consciousness; sadly missed, a good officer and friend.' Hoare, in Leopoldville at the time, heard of this first death among his officers with great distress. His wife Phyllis had just given birth to a son in Natal, and he cabled her to call the new-born child Jeremy. Spencer was given a funeral in Kindu Cathedral, with a High Mass celebrated by the bishop himself, a demonstration of the fact that Hoare, however unorthodox he was in tactics, was very much a traditionalist as far as discipline and behaviour were concerned. Indeed, every Sunday he held church parades for 5 Commando, and in the sweltering heat of the Congo his mercenaries were set to playing football on Sunday afternoons.

The Simbas were threatening to massacre their hostages and speed was essential

With Kindu secured, 5 Commando was able to launch its major assault against the rebel capital of Stanleyville in the northern Congo, situated on the banks of the mighty river that gave the country its name. Shortly before dusk on 23 November, 5 Commando moved out of Kindu at full speed, heading north as the vanguard of Lima One, a column that combined all the government's forces. Hoare had made it a rule never to move by night, but the Simbas were threatening to massacre their white hostages and speed was essential. Alastair Wicks described that night as the most nerve-racking experience he had ever had. Time after time the column was ambushed. Lieutenant Hans von Lieres was wounded twice and several 'volunteers' were killed. Lima One reached Stanleyville on the following day, only to find the city in the hands of 600 Belgian paratroopers who had been specially flown in to rescue the hostages. The Simbas' president had been making public threats that they were about to make fetishes out of the hearts of their Belgian and American captives, and clothing out of their skins. In the event, the rebels shot 29 hostages and then fled from the city.

The commandos dashed between rebel strongpoints, liberating towns and rescuing hostages

Five Commando garrisoned the city, 'liberated' a few banks and then indulged themselves in other rather less pleasant activities. One mercenary not only raped a black girl but then took her down to the river's edge and shot her. In spite of Hoare's attempts to control his men, they did not consider looting and rape as particularly serious offences, and in the end the discipline of a mercenary unit depends on general consent and not on the rule book. However,

Below: A member of 5 Commando blasts away with his jeep-mounted machine gun during the advance on Stanleyville in 1964. 5 Commando's great successes, from the summer of 1964 to October 1965, were all gained under the command of Mike Hoare. He was dismissed in November 1965, however, when a new ruler, General Mobutu, took over in the Congo, and control of the elite mercenary force passed to John Peters, formerly an NCO in the British Army. Under Peters, 5 Commando was associated with some unsavoury episodes, including the massacre of 3000 surrendered Katangese soldiers in July 1966. Peters left the Congo in February 1967, and 5 Commando was disbanded in May of that year – by then, the Congolese government regarded white-run mercenary forces as a threat to its stability.

cold-blooded murder is another matter. A drum head court-martial was held. The man was foun[d] guilty. Despite urging from the men, Hoare fe[lt] unable to execute him. So as the man was a profe[s]sional footballer, Hoare personally shot off his bi[g] toes, an act later described by a British officer a[s] 'orthopaedically unjustifiable'!

By January 1965 the mercenaries' six-month con[t]racts had expired, and almost all the original mem[b]ers of 5 Commando had left. In those six months the[y] had suppressed the Simba menace that ha[d] threatened to overwhelm the whole country, an[d] recaptured the Simba capital. It was an extra[ordinary achievement.

Hoare recruited 150 new mercenaries, mainly i[n] Johannesburg. Over the next six months he and th[e] commandos he had based all over the northeaster[n] provinces dashed between rebel strongpoint[s,] liberating towns and villages and rescuing whit[e] hostages, in particular nuns and missionaries, fro[m] the clutches of the vengeful Simbas. Meanwhile, th[e] Egyptians and the Algerians were supplying th[e] Simbas with more modern arms and weapons, main[ly via the Sudan, and there were even rumours o[f] Chinese 'advisers' leading the rebel forces. Th[e] tactics of the Simbas certainly improved, but Wats[a] in Kivu province was liberated in March and wit[h] Watsa the rebels lost their main source of wealth, th[e] fabled gold-mines of Kilo-Moto.

At one stage Hoare even considered 'borrowing' regular South African troops in disguise

One rebel redoubt remained — the wild Fizi-Barak[a] region in the south of Kivu province, inhabite[d] mainly by the Bahembi tribe. The second set o[f] six-month contracts had drawn to an end befor[e] Hoare could get ready to crack this very tough nu[t.] Fizi-Baraka was a mountainous plateau, and the onl[y] road approach led up the Lulimba escarpmen[t,] giving the rebels an absolutely impregnable posi[tion. At last, after some difficulty, the Commando'[s] ranks were refilled (at one stage Hoare even cons[i]dered 'borrowing' regular South African troops i[n] disguise). On 27 September 1965 a 'combined opera[tion' of land and water-borne attacks, with air sup[port, was launched. Wicks led 100 men to assault th[e] mountain fortress of Lulimba, diverting attentio[n] from a larger force that landed at Baraka on Lak[e] Tanganyika. After prolonged fighting with heav[y] casualties the town was taken and the force rapidl[y] advanced inland to take Fizi and join Wicks in [a] pincer attack on Lulimba. After that, only sma[ll] strongholds on the lake shore remained, and b[y] October 1965 the Simba revolt was virtually over. [A] month later on 25 November, General Mobut[u] seized power in the Congo and the very next da[y] Hoare and Wicks were dismissed – men dangerous[ly loyal to the old regime. In any case they ha[d] successfully and magnificently completed their task[.] In 18 months, with only a handful of mercenaries a[t] their disposal, they had suppressed the most exten[sive rebellion ever seen in Africa's largest blac[k] country and had earned 5 Commando a place in th[e] annals of modern military history.

THE AUTHOR Anthony Mockler is a journalist an[d] author who has specialised in the history of moder[n] Africa and of mercenary forces. His books includ[e] *The Mercenaries* and the widely acclaimed *Hail[e Selassie's War*.

FIRING POSITIONS

One of the most basic, but very crucial, combat skills of the individual soldier is the effective use of the rifle. As a rifleman, you are at the core of infantry operations, and whether you spend days patrolling desert or jungle on foot, or swooping into combat in a helicopter, your ability to hold your own in a firefight with a rifle can mean the difference between victory and defeat.

Every operation is different; sometimes there will be a lot of available cover, sometimes you will be out in the open. There are four standard firing positions for the rifleman which can be adapted to fit most fighting situations, and these are designed to achieve maximum effectiveness against your

Above left: A British soldier demonstrates the kneeling position for firing the SLR rifle. This position provides a fair degree of stability for the weapon, but only for a short period of time. Bottom: Firing the new SA 80 in the standing position. When shooting in this position it is often useful to lean your shoulder and forearm against something solid, such as a wall or a tree, since this will stabilise your left arm and provide a steadier firing platform.

COMBAT SKILLS OF THE ELITE

enemy in both static and mobile combat.

The most common, and most effective, is the prone position. Not only does this position give you the most stable platform to fire from, but it also reduces your silhouette to a minimum and allows you to use very low cover for protection. Lie face down on the ground so that your spine and your right leg are directly in line, and your left leg is spread out to the side. Support the weight of your upper body on your elbows and pull the rifle stock well into your shoulder with your right hand. Your left hand should support the front handguard firmly, and your left elbow should be kept directly under the receiver. Make sure that both elbows are stable and comfortable before you commence firing, and that your body is well behind the stock to absorb the recoil.

In a rapid assault, however, or in a firefight where the ground is strewn with obstacles, the prone position is not always the most practical. In these circumstances, it is often more effective to fire from the kneeling position, especially if you are using low walls, vehicles or trees for cover. Dashing from point

Kneeling position

to point to keep up the momentum of an attack, you can drop to one knee, loose off a few fairly accurate rounds and move on. In the kneeling position, your left knee should be raised to support your left elbow, while your right elbow is pushed outwards, parallel with the rifle. The weight of your body should rest on your right foot. While the kneeling position allows you to fire fairly accurately for a short period of time, your muscles will soon begin to ache and your shooting will suffer.

Standing position

Sitting position

Similar to the kneeling position is the sitting position but, again, this is not a position that is comfortable to fire from for any length of time. In the sitting position your body should be turned 45 degrees to the right of the line of fire, your knees raised, and your feet spread. Your left elbow should rest on your left shin, just below the knee, with your forearm extended to support the rifle. This is the standard sitting position, but there are several different ways to place your feet. Some riflemen prefer to shoot with their legs crossed, for example, while others will cross only their ankles. All are equally satisfactory.

A rifle can also be fired when you are standing up. In the standing, or 'offhand', position your weapon will have very little support and your fire will be restricted to a few rounds before your stance becomes unstable. You do, however, have the advantage of much greater mobility when you are on your feet, and you will be able to engage more targets at greater speed than when in the other three positions. The secret of good shooting when standing up is to make your body as stable a platform as possible.

COMBAT SKILLS OF THE ELITE

Left: Firing the M16 assault rifle in the standing position. This technique provides a very wide field of fire for the infantryman, but with the left arm unsupported it is difficult to keep the rifle steady for more than a few rounds.
Bottom: French Foreign Legion troops practise firing the MAS Automatic Rifle in the prone position on a range. The prone position provides the greatest accuracy over extended periods of combat and has the added advantage of keeping the rifleman's silhouette to a minimum. The French MAS is provided with a bipod, further increasing the weapon's stability, but when firing weapons without such added luxuries, a fallen branch or piece of rubble will serve equally well to support the rifle.

Your left foot should be placed forward of the right, and your body weight should be supported by the left leg. Bend your left knee slightly. The rifle should be borne by your left hand and forearm, and your right elbow should jut out horizontally.

Since World War II, most modern armies have equipped with automatic assault rifles such as the M16, AK-47 and G3, weapons capable of firing in bursts and designed to accommodate 20 or 30-round magazines. This relatively recent development in the rifle has resulted in the adoption of less orthodox firing techniques which are better suited to the quick-reaction firepower now at the rifleman's disposal, especially in the assault.

The basic principle underlying these techniques is automatic response. You should regard your weapon as a physical and mental extension of your body, so that when you see a target your rifle swings to engage it in an immediate reflex action. This is achieved by pivoting on the balls of your feet, your torso and hips twisting into line with the target as you push your weapon slightly forward and loose off a burst of fire.

Quick reaction is particularly important if you are ambushed, and one of the most effective firing techniques in this situation is the drop to a squat. Bringing your feet parallel, you should drop down on your haunches while releasing a short burst of fire. As your thighs hit your calves, fire a second burst and then, as you bounce back upwards, fire again.

In a final, all-out assault you may need to fire your rifle on the move. The stock should be pulled in against your side, just above the hip bone, as you charge forward, loosing off bursts at the enemy in your line of advance.

Infantry manuals the world over describe in great detail the various positions for firing a rifle, but no matter how good you are on the range, the real test comes when you have to adopt them in combat. The key to successful shooting on the battlefield lies in your personal flexibility and your ability to assess a combat situation. Firing positions are like the tools of any trade and they must be selected to meet the needs of the moment.

Prone position